Buddha Śākyamuni

Guru Padmasambhava

Longchen Rabjam Drimé Özer

༄༅། །ངལ་གསོ་སྐོར་གསུམ་ལས་སྒྱུ་མ་ངལ་གསོའི་
རྩ་བ་དང་འགྲེལ་པ་ཤིང་རྟ་བཟང་པོ་
ཞེས་བྱ་བ་བཞུགས་སོ། །

པདྨ་ཀཱ་རའི་སྒྲ་བསྒྱུར་མཐུན་ཚོགས་ནས་
སྒྲ་བསྒྱུར་ཞུས།

The Padmakara Translation Group gratefully acknowledges the generous support of the Tsadra Foundation in sponsoring the translation and preparation of this book.

Finding Rest in Illusion

The Trilogy of Rest, Volume 3

Longchenpa

TRANSLATED BY

The Padmakara Translation Group

SHAMBHALA

Shambhala Publications, Inc.
4720 Walnut Street
Boulder, Colorado 80301
www.shambhala.com

Paperback edition published 2020

Front cover art: Detail of thangka of Milarepa, Tibet, 19. Jh.; inv. no. IId 13769, Essen collection.
Photographer: Omar Lemke © Museum der Kulturen Basel, Switzerland; All rights reserved.
Back cover art: Thangka of Longchenpa. Image courtesy of Matthieu Ricard.

9 8 7 6 5 4 3 2 1

First paperback edition
Printed in the United States of America

♾ This edition is printed on acid-free paper that meets the American National Standards Institute z39.48 Standard.
♻ Shambhala makes every effort to print on recycled paper.
For more information please visit www.shambhala.com.
Shambhala Publications is distributed worldwide by Penguin Random House, Inc., and its subsidiaries.

THE LIBRARY OF CONGRESS CATALOGUES THE PREVIOUS EDITION OF THIS BOOK AS FOLLOWS:

Names: Klong-chen-pa Dri-med-'od-zer, 1308–1363, author. |
Klong-chen-pa Dri-med-'od-zer, 1308–1363. Sems nyid ngal gso. English. |
Klong-chen-pa Dri-med-'od-zer, 1308–1363.
Bsam gtan ngal gso. English. | Klong-chen-pa Dri-med-'od-zer, 1308–1363.
Sgyu ma ngal gso. English. | Comité de traduction Padmakara, translator.
Title: Trilogy of rest / Longchen Rabjam; translated by the Padmakara Translation Group.
Description: First edition. | Boulder: Shambhala, 2017– |
Includes bibliographical references and index.
Identifiers: LCCN 2017009896 | ISBN 9781611805161 (hardback: v. 1) / ISBN 9781611807523 (pbk.: alk. paper: v. 1) | ISBN 9781611805529 (hardback: v. 2) / ISBN 9781611807530 (pbk.: alk. paper: v. 2) | ISBN 9781611805925 (hardback: v. 3) / 9781611807547 (pbk.: alk. paper: v. 3)
Subjects: LCSH: Rdzogs-chen—Early works to 1800. | BISAC: RELIGION / Buddhism / Tibetan. | RELIGION / Buddhism / Sacred Writings. | RELIGION / Buddhism / Rituals & Practice.
Classification: LCC BQ7662.4 .K5465 2017 | DDC 294.3/420423—dc23
LC record available at https://LCCN.LOC.GOV/2017009896

Contents

Foreword

Alak Zenkar Rinpoche

Supreme among the vast array of pith instructions,
Bringing into one epitome
The crucial points without exception of the Tripitaka
And the four classes of Tantra,
These volumes are the summit of a myriad treatises
That heal and that protect,
A perfect chariot of teaching clear and unsurpassed,
The supreme means whereby
The minds of those who wander in the triple world,
Find rest in freedom.

Priceless in this universe,
This scripture is the image of the speech of Longchen,
Dharma king from Samyé, who in times to come
Will have the name of the Victorious Merudipa.
It is a beauteous mirror formed of flawless crystal
That reveals the sense of the essential lore
Of the three yogas and nine stages of the Mahayana,
Passed down by word of mouth and in the precious treasures,
Rich patrimony of the line of knowledge-holders
Of the Ancient Translations.

Your aspiration first arose
Upon the shoulders of the eastern hills
And now your translation in a foreign tongue

Shines like the day-creating sun
Assisted by the light of publication's wizardry.
I celebrate its coming,
The sweet friend of the lotus of the Buddha's doctrine.

From the smiling blossom of delight and happiness
There falls such honeyed nectar of rejoicing
That, not waiting for the songs of the applauding bees,
I cannot help but pour out my congratulation.

I who have grown old beneath this canopy of joy,
This great refulgence of the sunlight
Of the doctrine of the powerful Sage,
Cannot but speak my praises of your wish
To be of service to his teaching.

Therefore may this lucid textual explanation,
Indeed a health-sustaining herb
For teachings of the Ancient Translation School
And source of glorious sustenance for many beings,
Increase a hundred, thousand, millionfold
And be widely spread and propagated.

With excellent aspiration and activity for the Buddha's doctrine in general and especially for the orally transmitted and treasure teachings of the Ancient Tradition of the Great Secret, the Padmakara translators have rendered into English the root texts of the Trilogy of Rest, which are now published together with their autocommentaries, the spotlessly clear exposition of the mighty Conqueror Longchen Rabjam. With joy and admiration, I, Thubten Nyima, join my hands at my heart and offer flowers of rejoicing. Written in the fragrant city of Chengdu on the twelfth day of the seventh month, in the year 2017.

Translators' Introduction

Finding Rest in Illusion and *The Chariot of Excellence* form the concluding part of Longchen Rabjam's celebrated *Trilogy of Rest*. Their purpose, as the author himself declares, is to gather the entire teaching of Mahāyāna Buddhism into an essential point: the "yoga of the two aspects of illusion" defined and illustrated in terms of eight well-known examples taken from the Prajñāpāramitā scriptures.

The root text and its commentary are brief and pithy and their extraordinary profundity emerges only with slow, attentive, and repeated reading. They are replete with references to a wide range of scriptural sources, and the reader will soon discover that beneath their poetic surface lies an entire submerged continent of doctrine with which they may not be familiar. In the hope of being of some assistance, we have endeavoured to supply references to other texts where additional information may be found, notably Jigme Lingpa's *Treasury of Precious Qualities* and its indispensable commentary by Kyabje Kangyur Rinpoche.[1]

Identified by its author as a teaching of the Great Perfection, *Finding Rest in Illusion* touches on deep matters of great subtlety, and there is no question of providing, in a brief translators' introduction, an adequate account of Longchenpa's thought. However, in an attempt to bring the text into focus and to provide a few bearings useful to the general reader, we offer, with all due reticence, the following summary.

In introducing *Finding Rest in Illusion*, it is important to discuss, among other things, the concept of illusion itself, and to consider the way it is understood in terms not only of the madhyamaka doctrine of the two truths, but also of the teachings of the Great Perfection, where the character of illusion is applied to the entire phenomenal field of both saṃsāra and nirvāṇa—and even to the primordial ground from which these two states emerge.

In a brief explanatory teaching on *Finding Rest in Illusion*,[2] Nyoshul Khen Rinpoche once indicated its close thematic relationship with the tenth and eleventh chapters of *Finding Rest in the Nature of the Mind*, the first part of Longchenpa's trilogy. The eleventh chapter in particular expounds in general terms the path of the Great Perfection according to three levels of practitioner. Those of highest capacity are individuals—in the nature of the case, extremely rare—who achieve full realization in the very moment of being introduced to the nature of their minds. They traverse the path in a single instant, and their enlightenment is immediate. "For those who from the outset stay within this state of suchness," Longchenpa says, "There's no deviation, there's no place where they might deviate. . . . They are perfect buddhas in that very instant."[3]

For the vast majority of practitioners, on the other hand, progress on the path is gradual. They need to receive detailed instruction and to strive in meditation until, as Longchenpa says, "their ego-clinging sinks into the ultimate expanse."[4] This second category of beings is again divided into two groups: those of moderate, and those of basic, capacity. Practitioners of moderate capacity are fully trained in the preliminaries. They have a mastery of meditative concentration, have received the necessary introduction and pointing-out instructions, and are able to implement the practices of calm abiding (*śamatha*) and deep insight (*vipaśyana*) simultaneously. They have recognized the nature of their minds, "luminous and empty like the limpid sky," and, like undistracted archers, rest without hope of success or fear of failure in the uncontrived state of primordial wisdom, "like those who know they have achieved their goal."

While admitting that the nature of the mind is itself utterly ineffable, Longchenpa nevertheless continues for several extraordinary pages to describe the actual experience of yogic accomplishment.

And although he does not attempt to describe the indescribable, he nevertheless gives us a glimpse of what the realization of the nature of the mind might actually be like. He speaks with simple, awe-inspiring authority and the kind of disconcerting precision that comes only from direct personal experience. These "moderate" practitioners, he concludes, accomplish the result of freedom in this very life.

Happily for the rest of us, more than half of the eleventh chapter is devoted to those who are beginners on the path, practitioners of basic capacity. For them, Longchenpa says, it is important to train in calm abiding and deep insight separately. Calm abiding comes first, and this consists not only in techniques of concentration and mind control but also in the training and transformation of the mind through the precepts of the great vehicle: first the four unbounded attitudes of love, compassion, sympathetic joy, and impartiality, and then the practice of relative and ultimate bodhichitta. Correctly oriented in this way, the mind is then strenuously trained by concentration on a "wholesome object" (a text, an image of a deity, and so on) so that, by the end of this process, it becomes stable, undistracted, and pliable—serviceable for the higher practice of meditating directly on the view of the Great Perfection. It is at this point in the eleventh chapter of *Finding Rest in the Nature of the Mind* that Longchenpa first introduces the eight examples of illusion:

> Training in deep insight follows.
> All things appearing outwardly in both saṃsāra and
>   nirvāṇa
> Are like illusions and the stuff of dreams;
> They're like reflections, apparitions,
> Echoes, cities in the clouds,
> Tricks of sight, mirages: all without reality.
> Appearing, they are empty by their nature.

> Everything resembles space, without intrinsic being.
> Thus practitioners should stay in meditative equipoise,
> Free from all conception, in the unborn nature.
> They will understand that outer things are without self
> And that the object that is there appearing
> And the object apprehended in the mind
> Are both without existence.[5]

The Nature of Illusion

The idea of illusion is intrinsic to the doctrine of the two truths. To say that phenomena—outer objects, mental states, and the situations of everyday experience—lack intrinsic being and do not exist in the way that they appear is to ascribe to them an illusory character. Although the doctrine of two truths occurs at all levels of Buddhist tenets, it assumes a particular importance and subtlety in Madhyamaka. Here, instead of contrasting the illusory appearance of phenomena on the relative level with something considered to be more fundamental and ultimately real (the particles of the Abhidharmika schools, or the self-cognizing mind of the Cittamātra), Nāgārjuna identifies the emptiness of phenomena with the fact that they arise dependently on causes and conditions. In other words, emptiness is built into the very constitution of phenomena. The apparently discrete, autonomous existence that things and situations possess on the relative level is intrinsically illusory.

As a means of introducing the idea that phenomena are not what they seem, the Buddha referred to a variety of common experiences, the illusory nature of which is universally acknowledged. For example, we all know what it is to dream and to be completely convinced of the reality of what we are dreaming about, only to find on waking that it had no existence whatever. Likewise, mirages of water on a hot road in summer are quite convincing from a distance but disappear as one approaches them. Dreams and mirages therefore are cases of illusion and belong to the list of eight or occasionally twelve examples frequently cited in the Prajñāpāramitā literature. Following this list and with constant reference to such scriptures as the *Middle-Length Prajñāpāramitā* and the *Samādhirāja-sūtra*, Longchenpa structures his *Finding Rest in Illusion* as a series of eight "vajra points." The essential meaning of these points remains the same—the unreal, illusory nature of the ground, path, and result—but each one is presented slightly differently in order to bring out a particular aspect of phenomenal appearance.

Let us briefly review these eight examples of illusion. In the first vajra point, the phenomena of common experience are compared to dream visions, which seem completely real in the moment of their appearing but in fact have no reality at all. Here, as with the rest of the eight examples, it is important to remember that when phenomena are said to be illusory, reference is being made not to phenomena as they actually are—the transient interplay of dependent causes and conditions—but to the apparently permanent, discrete, autonomous entities that seem to populate our daily experience but turn out to be utterly fictitious when subjected to analysis. And the purpose of the first vajra point is to show that just as the things we dream about have no place in the causal sequences of waking life, neither do the permanent, independent, and intrinsically real things that we think we encounter. They too are purely imaginary. In the complex network of dependent arising that characterizes phenomenal appearance, they can have no place; they do not arise. They have no origin; they are "unborn."

Nevertheless, although phenomena have no intrinsic reality, they appear seamlessly and unceasingly for as long as the causes for their manifestation persist. As long as we are ignorant of the illusory nature of phenomena, and are under the power of the habitual tendency to apprehend them as truly existing, we are—the second vajra point explains—like bystanders taken in by the illusions conjured up by a magician. The entire phenomenal field and even the basis of such a field, namely, awareness itself, are an uninterrupted, unceasing illusory display.

The third vajra point compares phenomena to tricks of sight. Just as the objects we think we see in an optical illusion simply appear through the chance meeting of extraneous factors and are not actual things that come from somewhere else, arriving on the scene when these factors coincide, the same is true of apparently permanent, discrete, autonomous entities. They simply appear; they have not come from anywhere.

Conversely, the fourth vajra point declares, when such apparently solid and permanent phenomena are closely examined, they do not withstand analysis. Their existence—which seemed so real as long as it was not investigated—simply melts away. They are like the water that from a distance seems to lie on a hot road in the summer. As one approaches the mirage, it is not as if the "water" drains away or goes somewhere else. It just vanishes. One finds that it is not there and never was there. The supposedly truly existent things of ordinary, unexamined experience are just the same. When phenomena are examined, the intrinsic, real, permanent status habitually ascribed to them simply disintegrates. And just as "truly existent things" come from nowhere, "nowhere do they go."

Even though phenomena can thus be shown to have no intrinsic being, the fifth vajra point explains that their appearance, nevertheless, is in no way compromised. Phenomena are not nothing. Their appearance endures. They are like the reflection of the moon appearing on the mirrorlike surface of a still lake. On the visual plane (that is, until one reaches out and tries to touch it), the reflected moon seems in all respects the perfect equivalent of the moon in the sky. To the eye, the replica is so flawless that one would be at a loss to find any criterion for choosing one as true and rejecting the other as false. The same applies to phenomena generally. They look and behave as though they were utterly real.

Nevertheless, the sixth vajra point tells us, in the very moment of their being perceived, phenomena are empty of any kind of permanent, enduring existence. They are simply not present, like the voice one seems to hear in an echo.

This union of appearance and emptiness applies to the whole range of experience, and in this sense, all things—the fires of hell, the celestial pavilions of the gods—are on a level. They are all hallucinations, the seventh vajra point says, as ephemeral and ungraspable as cities of the gandharvas or castles in the clouds. There is nothing ultimately real in any of them—the three worlds, the six realms, even the wisdoms and kāyas of the enlightened state—that might, ontologically speaking, justify acceptance or rejection.

Even so, the eighth vajra point concludes, the phenomena are far from being a single, undifferentiated mass. Like the things emanated by highly accomplished yogis who have complete power over their minds, the appearances of the relative truth arise through the fructification of ingrained habitual tendencies stored within the mind. The experience of a phenomenal world is as rich and various—albeit equally illusory—as the karmic constitution of a given individual being. Neither inside nor outside the mind, the phenomenal world is simply "the clear appearance of what does not exist."

In short, the eight examples of illusion show that phenomena have no origin and yet are unceasing. They come from nowhere and go nowhere. They are not nothing, and yet they are not permanent entities. They are not different in character, and yet they are not identical or the same. It is obvious that the eight examples of illusion, as Longchenpa explicitly declares,[6] reproduce in a slightly different order the eight characteristics of dependently arising phenomena listed in the prologue to Nāgārjuna's *Root Stanzas of the Middle Way*:

> To him who taught that things arise dependently,
> Not ceasing, not arising,
> Not annihilated nor yet permanent,
> Not coming, not departing,
> Not different, not the same:
> The stilling of all thought, and perfect peace—
> To him, the best of teachers, perfect Buddha,
> I bow down.[7]

In a text that is a self-proclaimed "teaching of the Great Perfection" and that alludes to this tradition constantly, if unsystematically, this reference to Madhyamaka is both interesting and significant. And given the controversies that have marked the history of Madhyamaka in Tibet, Longchenpa's approach to this tenet system, and especially the way he related it to the teachings of the Great Perfection, is a matter of some importance.

Longchenpa and Madhyamaka

Longchenpa's statements about Madhyamaka are found principally in the *Precious Treasury of Tenets*,[8] the *Precious Treasury of Wish-Fulfilling Jewels*,[9] and the *Precious Treasury of the Supreme Vehicle*.[10] All these expositions are rather schematic and in some respects maddeningly brief, and it is unfortunate that two independent texts listed in Longchenpa's own bibliography—one on the yogācāra-madhyamaka synthesis of Śāntarakṣita, Kamalaśīla, and Jñānagarbha (known together as the "three Svātantrikas from the East"), and the other on the essential position of the Prāsaṅgikas—have both been lost.[11]

For our present purposes, however, it is not necessary to have a detailed understanding of Longchenpa's position, interesting though it is. It is sufficient to be aware of two important points. The first is that by the time Longchenpa studied the texts of Madhyamaka at Sangphu, two centuries had already passed since the translation of Candrakīrti's works into Tibetan had sparked the important controversy between the upholders of Svātantrika Madhyamaka, championed by Chapa Chökyi Senge, the abbot of Sangphu, and the proponents of Prāsaṅgika Madhyamaka gathered around Candrakīrti's translator, Patsap Nyima Drak. With the passage of time, the various interactions and crosscurrents between these two subschools had the effect of softening their contours until, by the early thirteenth century (almost a hundred years before Longchenpa's day), Sakya Paṇḍita is said to have adopted the view of Prāsaṅgika Madhyamaka—albeit with certain important modifications redolent of the svātantrika position—as the official view of the Sakya school. And such are the ironies of history that, since Sangphu (the former stronghold of Svātantrika Madhyamaka) had—by the fourteenth century—fallen largely under the influence of Sakya, it is not surprising to find that Longchenpa also acknowledged the supremacy of Prāsaṅgika and that his approach to Madhyamaka resembled the Sakya position in all important respects. Indeed, by that time, the Sakya, Nyingma, and Kagyu schools were practically united in their interpretation of Madhyamaka, so much so that they presented a united front in opposition to the mature position of Tsongkhapa and the Geluk school, which was to forcefully emerge toward the beginning of the fifteenth century, about forty years after Longchenpa's death.

The second point to bear in mind is that for Longchenpa, the aim of madhyamaka dialectic is to bring the mind into the direct realization of the ultimate truth of transcendent wisdom, understood as a state beyond discursive thought, completely free from the conceptual elaborations of the ordinary mind.[12] And the superiority of the prāsaṅgika approach consists in the fact that, in refusing to be detained by explanations of the relative truth (characteristic of the more gradual svātantrika approach), it seeks, through the simultaneous refutation of the four ontological extremes, to place the mind directly on the threshold of the state beyond conceptual construction, the ultimate truth itself. The goal of the prāsaṅgika method is to arrest the movement of the discursive intellect, to lay bare the mind's true nature, and to reveal the ultimate truth of emptiness on the path of seeing. In this respect, it is said to resemble the manner in which a master of the Great Perfection introduces a disciple to the direct experience of the nature of the mind. Commenting on this similarity, Mipham Rinpoche says in his commentary to the *Madhyamakālaṃkāra*,

> According to the view of Candrakīrti, phenomenal appearances are directly purified as they stand. All false illusory configurations of conventional phenomena

> dissolve into the ultimate expanse. This profound view resembles the manner in which primordial purity is established in the texts of the Great Perfection. For this reason, in our tradition of the vidyādhara lineage, this [prāsaṅgika] view is considered supreme.[13]

Longchenpa juxtaposes Prāsaṅgika Madhyamaka and the Great Perfection in the same way but with the following difference. Whereas in Madhyamaka, emphasis is placed on the emptiness aspect of phenomena (the object), in the Great Perfection, luminous awareness (the subject) is paramount. This is clearly stated in Longchenpa's *Treasury of Teachings*, the autocommentary to the *Precious Treasury of the Dharmadhātu*.[14]

> The manner in which freedom from extremes is assessed in the tradition of the Natural Great Perfection is for the most part similar to the method of the Prāsaṅgikas. But whereas space-like emptiness is considered fundamental in Madhyamaka, in the present context of the Great Perfection, it is simply *rigpa*—primordially pure, naked, simple, pure awareness, devoid of real existence and yet unceasing—that is considered fundamental. Subsequently, both awareness and the phenomena that arise from awareness are judged to be like space, beyond all extremes.[15]

The Great Perfection and the Turnings of the Dharma Wheel

The Great Perfection, Atiyoga, is the highest of the inner tantras and thus the summit of the nine-vehicle classification of teachings traditionally used in the Nyingma school. The particular character of the Great Perfection has been touched upon on earlier occasions, and there is no need to describe it again here except to reiterate the uniqueness of its view, which consists not so much in the intellectual understanding of a doctrinal position but in the direct vision of the nature of the mind itself. This extraordinary feature of the Great Perfection, grounded as it is in meditative practice and the direct experience of the enlightened state, does not, of course, preclude a doctrinal system, which in this case is a profound and extremely subtle description of the nature of awareness as the fundamental ground from which all phenomenal appearances unfold—appearances that may be either of nirvāṇa or saṃsāra depending on the recognition or nonrecognition, respectively, of the nature of these same appearances. The reader will discover frequent references to this doctrine in *Finding Rest in Illusion* and its autocommentary.

As one reflects on the teachings of the Great Perfection, it is natural to wonder how, granted their unique features, they relate to the other doctrinal systems of Mahāyāna Buddhism. It is well known that within the Mahāyāna itself, the teachings are generally classified into three groups known figuratively as the three turnings of the wheel of Dharma. The first turning refers to teachings held in common by all Buddhist denominations, both Śrāvakayāna and Mahāyāna: the four noble truths, the twelve links of dependent arising, the aggregates, the sense fields, and so on. The second and third turnings, on the other hand, refer exclusively to the Mahāyāna. Traditionally associated with the bodhisattva Mañjuśrī and the madhyamaka system of the second-century master Nāgārjuna, the teachings of the second turning focus on emptiness as the ultimate condition of phenomena. By contrast, the teachings of the third turning of the Dharma wheel, associated with the bodhisattva Maitreya and the yogācāra system of the fourth-century master Asaṅga, principally expound the doctrine of the sugatagarbha, the buddha nature.

These two great streams of Mahāyāna doctrine, often referred to as the paths of "profound wisdom" and "vast activities" respectively, both claim to expound, in their different ways, the essence of the Prajñāpāramitā sūtras. Nevertheless, in their general appraisal, it has usually been the difference of their approach, rather than the commonality of their source, that has received most emphasis. This was already the case in India. The Yogācāra tradition of Asaṅga—frequently, though problematically, referred to as Cittamātra (mind only) or Vijñānavāda (proponents of consciousness)—came to be seen as a more easily accessible interpretation of the Prajñāpāramitā teachings that, couched in positive terms, softened the impact of the austere madhyamaka refutations expounded by Nāgārjuna two hundred years previously. This in turn provoked resistance from the upholders of the Madhyamaka tradition, who rejected the claims of the yogācāra position particularly as this had been systematized by the sixth-century master Dharmapāla. At the conclusion of his *Introduction to the Middle Way* (*Madhyamakāvatāra*), the seventh-century master Candrakīrti speaks disparagingly of those who, "startled by the deep hue of the great and teeming waters of the mind of Nāgārjuna, have shunned and kept their distance from this great [Madhyamaka] tradition."[16] And the writings of later Mādhyamikas—Candrakīrti himself and also Śāntideva—contain explicit refutations of the Cittamātra tenet system.

This tension between the approaches of the second and third turnings of the Dharma wheel was transmitted to Tibet, particularly after the translation of the works of Candrakīrti in the early twelfth century and the eventual acceptance of the supremacy of his "prāsaṅgika" approach. Moreover, preferences for the teachings of the second or third turning of the Dharma wheel came to be identified along sectarian lines; and the conflict was intensified by the disagreement over the doctrines of "emptiness of self" and "emptiness of other."[17] In the enduring debate, the scriptures associated with the second and third turnings of the Dharma wheel are classified as definitive or provisional according to whichever position finds favor. For example, many thinkers of the Sakya and Geluk schools regard the view of Madhyamaka as paramount. They therefore classify the scriptures of the second turning as definitive and consider those of the third turning to be provisional. The reverse is generally held by the Jonangpas and many Kagyupas, who, prizing above all the doctrine of the buddha nature, take the scriptures of the third turning to be definitive and say that those of the second turning require interpretation.

In contrast with this situation, the readers of the present text will discover that, perhaps rather confusingly, Longchenpa seems at different times to adopt positions typical of both the second and the third turnings of the Dharma wheel. It is therefore important to understand that the disjunctive assessment of the teachings of the two traditions seems to have arisen principally in the course of the second diffusion of Buddhism in Tibet and is a feature mainly of the Sarma or New Translation schools, which tend to stress the differences between the teachings of the second and third turnings. The characteristic approach of the Nyingma school is quite different. Here the emphasis is placed on the complementarity of the teachings of the two charioteers (Nāgārjuna and Asaṅga) as being equally the exponents of the Prajñāpāramitā sūtras and of the Mahāyāna generally. Therefore, instead of being placed in opposition, each of the two positions is understood and evaluated in light of the other. The tradition of vast activities is clarified and refined by the doctrine of the profound view, which cuts away any possibility of reifying the buddha nature as an absolute, truly existing entity. Reciprocally, the teachings of the third turning, with their elaborate exposition of the grounds and paths and their insistence on the qualities, the kāyas and wisdoms, of the enlightened state, prevent the emptiness doctrine of Madhyamaka from becoming exclusively a system of philosophical negation with nihilistic overtones. The "official" position of the Nyingma school is therefore to say that when the teachings of the second and third turnings of the Dharma wheel are held in balance and unified, they are both definitive. When they are divided and their differences emphasized, they are both provisional.

This is not the place to investigate the origins of this liberal approach to the teachings of the second and third turnings, which perhaps owes something to the yogācāra-madhyamaka synthesis of Śāntarakṣita, one of the founding fathers of the Nyingma school. On the other hand, it seems important to advert to the fact that the complementarity of the two streams of Mahāyāna doctrine as upheld in the Nyingma tradition provides a broad and comprehensive preparation for the teachings of the Great Perfection.

We have seen how Longchenpa aligns the Great Perfection with the teaching of the second turning of the Dharma wheel, specifically the introduction to the state of freedom from conceptual elaboration produced by the simultaneous refutation of the four ontological extremes as explained by Nāgārjuna and emphasized in the prāsaṅgika school. At the same time, Longchenpa's frequent use of ideas and terms redolent of the yogācāra scriptures is very striking. In *Finding Rest in Illusion*, he repeatedly refers to the sugatagarbha, the buddha-element, defined as self-cognizing awareness, as the sole source of both saṃsāra and nirvāṇa.[18] On the other hand, whenever he refers to the nature of the mind or awareness as the fundamental ground of the phenomenal display, he never fails to repeat that such a mind is devoid of intrinsic being. In brief, we might say that in *Finding Rest in Illusion*, Longchenpa freely adopts the concepts and language of the second and third turnings of the Dharma wheel, highlighting the fact that their complementary positions may be regarded as steps leading to the view of the Great Perfection, which transcends them both.

Finding Rest in Illusion

The essential message of the Great Perfection is that the character of the phenomenal field, whether of saṃsāra or nirvāṇa, depends upon the recognition or nonrecognition of their common ground, the nature of the mind. As it is said in the *Aspiration of Samantabhadra*,

> All phenomenal existence, saṃsāra and nirvāṇa,
> Have but a single ground, and yet there are two paths and
> two results.
> These are the display of knowledge or of ignorance. . . .

> The recognition of that very ground is buddhahood.
> But beings fail to recognize it and they wander therefore in saṃsāra.

We have seen that all phenomena of both saṃsāra and nirvāṇa are by definition illusions. For whether imprisoned in saṃsāra or free in the enlightened state, the mind retains a kind of phenomenalizing activity, which, Longchenpa says, is its "self-experience."[19] The phenomena of saṃsāra are the mind's deluded perception of the three worlds and the six realms, all marked by impermanence, endless repetition, and pain. By contrast, the phenomena of nirvāṇa are the kāyas and wisdoms and the compassionate unfolding of enlightened activity, the qualities of self-cognizing awareness. In that they are phenomena, the six realms of saṃsāra and the kāyas and wisdoms of nirvāṇa are all illusory. They appear but are not truly existent; they have no intrinsic being. Longchenpa therefore speaks of two kinds of illusion: illusions of mistaken perception and illusions of perfect purity, or rather illusions that are perfectly pure.[20] Thus far, the account is fairly straightforward. When pursued further, however, the notion of illusion becomes more difficult to grasp. Given that the states of both saṃsāra and nirvāṇa are illusory, one may be tempted to suppose that the ground, the foundational level of the mind upon which such illusions arise, must in some sense be real—the basis in relation to which the illusions arise. But this Longchenpa strenuously denies. As in the madhyamaka dialectic in which nothing, not even emptiness itself, is able to withstand analysis, likewise in the Great Perfection, everything, even self-cognizing awareness, the fundamental ground of all illusory appearance, is itself devoid of intrinsic being and therefore an illusion. Were it otherwise, if the nature of the mind were ultimately real and not illusory, it would necessarily be a self-existent transcendent entity, something completely excluded by the Buddhist view. Like the truly existent mind propounded in the Cittamātra tenet system, it would be (to use Candrakīrti's expression) no more than the ātman in disguise.

What then does it mean to find rest in illusion? Since the qualities of enlightenment have been described as illusory, it might be argued that, since enlightenment is preferable to the unenlightened state, the answer is simply to abandon the illusion of saṃsāra and to opt for the illusions of nirvāṇa. Figuratively, it may be possible to speak in such terms. And yet a more profound understanding is called for. In *An Ocean of Elegant Explanations*,[21] the general presentation of the *Trilogy of Rest*, Longchenpa justifies his choice of title for *Finding Rest in Illusion* with the following explanation:

> Although the illusions of saṃsāra are without any intrinsic being, they appear unceasingly. They are like a traveler, and just as one might give rest to exhausted travelers as they go on their way, illusory appearances (that is, whatever the mind perceives) must be brought to rest in the utterly pure expanse of dharmatā. This is because one must go beyond and free oneself from samsaric suffering in relation to these appearances. Furthermore, by *knowing* that saṃsāra is an illusion, and by *experiencing* all that appears as being devoid of intrinsic being, one comes to freedom in the expanse of the illusion of utter purity. It is said in the *Laṅkāvatāra-sūtra*, "The three worlds of existence are illusions; they are dreams and mirages. When they are seen to be illusions, they are arrested."
>
> Alternatively, we may say that the title *Finding Rest in Illusion* is also acceptable because the utterly pure illusion is an extraordinary ground that is like a resting place for the illusion of mistaken perception. The nature of the mind, pure and luminous, is itself intrinsically an illusion of utter purity. Within this nature of the mind, which is free from the conceptual elaborations of self and other, all the illusions of mistaken perception—all hallucinatory appearances and thoughts—find rest in being groundless and unsupported.[22]

To attain liberation from saṃsāra, therefore, is not simply a matter of exchanging one set of illusions for another. On the contrary, freedom from the hallucinatory and deceptive power of an illusion is achieved primarily by knowing that it *is* an illusion, that it lacks intrinsic being. Consequently, once the illusory nature of phenomenal appearance is ascertained—once its constitution and the reason for its appearing are understood—one is no longer deluded even if illusory phenomena continue to manifest. As Nāgārjuna pointed out, saṃsāra and nirvāṇa are not two separate things. Instead, they are two ways of perceiving the same phenomenal field. Longchenpa reiterates this point clearly in the eighth vajra point:

> Saṃsāra in itself is just deluded thought.
> And when the nature of the mind is seen,
> It is nirvāṇa—there from the beginning.
> It is primal wisdom, free of all fixation,
> That, in self-knowing, knows its object.
> Nothing that appears is real;
> There is no apprehending it as this or that.
> The mind finds comfort in a state
> Where mind and what appears
> Are seen as emanated apparitions.

The root text is then completed with the following comment:

> Saṃsāra consists of discursive thoughts. When it is understood that these have no existence even though they appear—in other words, when their empty nature is realized—nirvāṇa, the state beyond sorrow, automatically manifests. So it is that thoughts and appearances sink back into emptiness without leaving any trace.

The Paths of Yogis and Paṇḍitas

We have already seen how the eleventh chapter of *Finding Rest in the Nature of the Mind* specifies that the calming and focusing of the mind through techniques of meditative absorption—grounded as this must be in the practice of pure ethics, the cultivation of the four boundless thoughts, and bodhichitta—must be completed by the understanding and eventual realization of the view: transcendent wisdom, understood in terms of the Great Perfection.

It is sometimes said that for the realization of this view, there are two approaches: the way of scholarship and the way of yogic practice. However different in their methods, these two paths are focused on the same object and are interconnected in the sense that, with greater or lesser emphasis, they may both be pursued in the life of any given practitioner.

The way of the scholars, most obviously exemplified in the madhyamaka tradition, involves the strenuous use of reason and intelligence as means to investigate and lay bare the nature of the phenomenal world, marked as it is by inescapable sorrow. Not simply a matter of intellectual curiosity, this investigation is intended to lead to wisdom, the perfect realization of the nature of phenomena, and to the state beyond suffering that such a realization is said to produce. Given the requisite aptitude and conditions, a thirst for understanding, and a humble willingness to be guided by the tradition, the student may, after long and arduous effort, succeed in grasping without any doubt the essential points of the madhyamaka view, thereby arriving at a state of complete and irreversible certainty as to their truth. This is not easy. As one comes to grips with the intricate arguments laid out in the madhyamaka texts, it is impossible not to be struck by the subtleties involved and the intellectual energy required in such an enterprise. For it is necessary not simply to accept on trust what Nāgārjuna and his followers have written, but to examine, grasp, and put to the test the arguments that they rehearse. It is thus that, on the basis of one's own hard work, one constructs for oneself a conviction in the truth of these arguments that can come only from seeing their validity for oneself—a conviction, as Mipham Rinpoche says, that is unshakable and far stronger than the sense of assurance that may derive from faith alone.

Step by step, one follows Nāgārjuna's systematic refutation of the four ontological extremes—the four possible ways in which the existence of phenomena might be conceived. After long and successive meditation on these four refutations, there comes a point, so it is said, when all four ontological extremes come to be refuted simultaneously at a single stroke, at which point the mind is propelled beyond its ordinary condition and, passing into a state of wisdom that is free from any kind of conceptual proliferation, tastes directly the ultimate truth of emptiness on the path of seeing. Amazing as such an accomplishment may seem, we are assured that, given the right conditions, it is possible to arrive at this realization simply on the basis of persistent intellectual endeavor. The way of scholars is, however, a long and arduous process. As Mipham Rinpoche remarks,

> A state of freedom from conceptual constructs . . . may indeed be induced in the mind by virtue of no more than the certainty arising from analytical investigation. This, however, is a very lengthy process and takes birth in connection with, and thanks to, an extraordinary accumulation (of wisdom and of merit).[23]

On the other hand, skillful methods exist whereby this same freedom from conceptual construction may be achieved more quickly and with comparative ease.

> It can be realized swiftly and without much difficulty in dependence on the profound methods of Mantra, and especially through the power of the pith instructions that introduce one directly to the nature of the mind.

> It is thus that the experience of the fundamental mode of being occurs.[24]

Mipham is here referring to the way of the yogis, which, in contrast with the years of study and intellectual endeavor of the way of the scholars, is pursued within the context of a teacher-disciple relationship. It depends upon the meeting of a fully qualified master with a disciple endowed with sincere devotion and, again, great merit. It is important to understand these two crucial terms, the meaning of which is easily lost in translation. Far from being a state of mere piety or unctuous obsequiousness, devotion is the state of total commitment that comes from the completely open and unshakable confidence in the wisdom and power of a qualified teacher to bring the disciple to the ultimate state of freedom and accomplishment. As for merit, this admittedly inadequate but often-used term refers to the reserves of karmic fortune—consisting of interest, intelligence, aptitude, opportunity, and so on—deriving from the virtuous actions accumulated in the course of perhaps many lives, whereby a disciple is able first to encounter a truly accomplished teacher and then to profit from the reception and implementation of his or her instructions. These same pith instructions are tools thanks to which the genuine disciples of genuine masters are able to progress on the path comparatively swiftly and without the need for much study.

Be that as it may, one should not jump to the conclusion that the way of the yogi is somehow a lighter option compared with the path of the scholar—even if (given the right conditions) its fruits may be accomplished in a shorter time. If anything, the reverse is true. For whereas a qualified master can impart profound teachings and dispel doubts rapidly, the implementation of the master's instructions implies considerable effort on the part of the disciple and may well require years of meditative practice in solitude, sometimes in situations of considerable privation. Tibetan hagiography is filled with stories of the hardships endured by great practitioners—Yeshe Tsogyal, Milarepa, or indeed Longchenpa himself—in order to follow and obtain the results of their teachers' instructions. It is a well-known saying in the Great Perfection tradition that it is easier to prostrate one's way from Kham to Lhasa than it is to watch the nature of the mind without distraction for a single day.

In *Finding Rest in Illusion*, Longchenpa does not, like the great madhyamaka authors, lay out his teachings in the form of dry, closely reasoned arguments demanding hard intellectual effort on the part of the reader. In explaining the meaning of the teachings, he aims not to demonstrate but rather to describe. He speaks from the depth of his own realization using examples and imagery, making full use of his superlative poetic gifts. And in order to inspire his disciples and to reassure them that their confidence in him is well founded, he does not shrink from explicit declarations of his own realization and level of accomplishment.

It is thus that the practitioners of the yogic path depend not so much on their own understanding but on the enlightenment of their teacher—thanks to which their progress may well be swift. Once again, a path of this kind requires great faith, diligence, and an unflinching devotion and confidence in the authenticity and capacity of the teacher—assuming that such a teacher can be found. Conversely, it is with students of this kind that an authentic master is able to work most effectively in bringing them to realization and accomplishment.

The careful reader will have already discovered in the wide-ranging presentation of the path in *Finding Rest in the Nature of the Mind* and in the instructions for practice in *Finding Rest in Meditation* that Longchenpa constantly combines the scholastic expository style with essential instructions useful for practitioners. The same is true for *Finding Rest in Illusion*, although here, despite the proliferation of quotations from the scriptures, it is surely the pith-instruction style that receives the greater emphasis.

> Here I have distilled the sappy essence
> Of the sūtras, tantras, pith instructions.
> Listen! I shall set it forth as I myself experience it.

As a bestower of pith instructions, moreover, it is fair to say that Longchenpa seems less confident than Mipham in the ability of analytical investigation to place the mind of the disciple in the state beyond conceptual elaboration. It is true, of course, that when Mipham speaks of "analytical investigation," he is certainly not referring to private investigations independent of the tradition of the kind one might find in the modern academy, unaided by the disciplines of the path and the authentic lineages of interpretation. Be that as it may, Longchenpa's position seems to be that even if the madhyamaka dialectic is able to bring the ordinary mind to the limits of its cognitive range and reduce it to silence, it is nevertheless the prompting of an authentic master that provides the impetus for the next crucial step of actually entering the state beyond mental elaboration. As he says in the eighth vajra point:

> The intellectual evaluation of emptiness will by no means lead to the realization of emptiness, the nature of the mind—the ultimate truth that is the fundamental nature of all things. This nature utterly transcends all names and definitions. It is beyond all conception. Intellectual evaluation, by contrast, leads only to broad, rough estimates of objects hitherto unknown. It is like a blind person who comes to an idea of various objects only by means of a good explanation. . . .
>
> But when the blessings of a teacher
> Penetrate your heart,
> It's like the sun that rises in a cloudless sky. . . .
> Such realization manifests
> To none but those whose hearts
> Are touched by blessings
> Of a master of a thousand skillful means.[25]

Speaking of the transmission of wisdom that occurs in the introduction to the nature of the mind, the importance of which he would certainly in no way deny, Mipham nevertheless adds the following important point:

> When this [the introduction to the nature of the mind] happens, if the person concerned is someone who has already acquired—through an examination based on study and reflection—a strong conviction of the inseparability of emptiness and dependent arising, he or she will be in a position to compare the experience that occurred in the course of analysis with the experience occurring now, which does not derive from analysis but from resting in the natural state of mind free from all apprehension and clinging. On both occasions, there is no difference whatever in what is taken as the object, namely, the fundamental nature in which emptiness and dependent arising are indivisible. However, when you are analyzing it, it is like having your eyes closed and thinking about something in front of you, whereas when you are in the state that is free of clinging, it is like having your eyes open and seeing the thing directly. That is the difference. And once you have experienced this, then no matter how much other people may denigrate your practice that is free from all apprehension, and no matter how much they may explain to others the flavor of the treacle that you yourself have actually tasted, you will never have any doubt.[26]

It is important to understand, however, that when the nature of the mind is introduced and successfully recognized by the disciple, this is no more than the beginning of profound insight and the actual practice of the Great Perfection. In the months and years that remain, the yogi must continue to meditate with diligence so that the first insight at the moment of introduction is prolonged and stabilized until it becomes effortless and constant. In this connection, we may conclude these rambling reflections with the following anecdote supplied by Nyoshul Khen Rinpoche.

As recounted in the introduction to *Finding Rest in the Nature of the Mind*, Nyoshul Lungtok first realized the nature of his mind thanks to the introduction given to him by his root teacher Patrul Rinpoche while they were both lying, at nightfall, on the hill above Dzogchen Monastery. It was also mentioned that Longchenpa's writings have often been credited as being themselves vehicles of great blessings, similar to those conferred by realized masters on their receptive disciples.[27] So it was that the direct experience of the ultimate state came once again to Nyoshul Lungtok as he was studying and meditating on *Finding Rest in Illusion*—a fact he is said often to have recalled when he later expounded it himself. His realization burst forth, his belief in the true existence of appearances completely collapsed, and the entire phenomenal field of both saṃsāra and nirvāṇa arose as a vast illusory display.[28]

Acknowledgments

The translation of *Finding Rest in Illusion*, as of the other volumes of the *Trilogy of Rest*, could not have been brought to conclusion without the help of Khenchen Pema Sherab of Namdroling Monastery, Mysore, India. To him we owe a profound debt of gratitude. Likewise we wish to thank our teachers Pema Wangyal Rinpoche and Jigme Khyentse Rinpoche for their unfailing support and inspiration. By contrast, we acknowledge as our own all the inaccuracies and mistakes that may have occurred in the rendering of this difficult text.

Finding Rest in Illusion was translated by Helena Blankleder and Wulstan Fletcher of the Padmakara Translation Group.

Anniversary of Gyalwa Longchenpa
Dordogne
February 3, 2018

PART ONE

Finding Rest in Illusion

A Teaching of the Great Perfection

In Sanskrit

Mahāsandhimāyāviśrāntanāma

In Tibetan

rDzogs pa chen po sgyu ma ngal gso zhes bya ba

Prologue

Homage to glorious Vajrasattva!

All things emerging from the state of evenness unborn
Are but the great display of primal wisdom
Nondual and illusory.
Through never being parted from this unborn state,
I bow down to the nature of my mind,
The King who from the first is self-arisen.

That you may understand
The perfect teaching of the Conqueror
That all things are by nature the two aspects of illusion,
Here I have distilled the sappy essence
Of the sūtras, tantras, pith instructions.
Listen! I shall set it forth as I myself experience it.

1. The Chapter That Is Like a Dream

1. The ground's expanse beyond all change,
The vast sky of the nature of the mind,
Is empty, luminous, and free from mind's elaboration.
Therein like the sun, the moon, and all the stars,
The pure, unstained phenomena of buddhahood
Are present of themselves:
The threefold kāya never sundered
From the five primordial wisdoms,
And all the qualities of luminosity naturally complete.
This primal, fundamental, natural state
Is said to be the entirely pure illusion of the ground.

2. Within this ground,
Through coemergent ignorance
(Like sleep that brings forth dreams,
Which are like clouds of momentary illusion)
And through conceptual ignorance
(The mind impaired by apprehension
Of duality where there is no duality),
There appear the various false appearances of
The six migrations similar to dreams.

3. Though nonexistent, yet appearing still,
Beings feel different pains and pleasures—
Habits gained through long protracted time.

Places, bodies, property, and more
Are but their mind's experience.
Joys and pains, the wages of both good and evil deeds,
Resemble drawings traced in varying forms.
And from one delusion many more are spawned.
Apprehended thus in multiplicity,
These false appearances arise in seamless continuity.
Éma! Existence is, by nature, like a dream.

4. Within the single nature of the self-arisen mind,
Through ignorance's sleep,
A dualistic, subject-object apprehension
Of false appearances occurs.
These dream visions manifold and various
Are nothing other than the mind itself—
Illusions that arise through false perception.
This the Conqueror himself has said.

5. To those intoxicated by datura
Various things appear—
Hallucinations one and all.
Through the intoxication likewise
Of the sleep of ignorance,
The six migrations manifest
To the deluded mind.
Now therefore you should understand:
They are not truly there.

6. From deluded thought
Derives perception equally deluded,
And thence delusory appearances.
Not true, not false, not both,
Beyond the ordinary mind,
They should in truth be named
"Awareness, self-arisen, self-cognizing."

They are without identity, without existence,
A vast expanse where all extremes subside.
Know them to be similar to space,
The wisdom mind of the Victorious Ones.

7. Things are dreamlike.
In the very moment they appear,
No intrinsic being do they have at all.
And yet their features are not lost;
To their appearance there's no hindrance.
Carefully investigate these false and momentary forms,
In every aspect empty:
They are neither false nor true,
Not existent yet not nonexistent,
Beyond all ontological extremes.
They are like space beyond both thought and word.
Know that they are pure primordially.

8. Thus, by means of such a view,
You gain clear understanding that all things
In saṃsāra and nirvāṇa are like dreams.
I shall now explain how, through your meditation,
You will bring this into your experience.
Adopt a cross-legged posture on a pleasant seat.
Take refuge and engender bodhichitta.
Now think, intensely meditate,
That in the state of emptiness,
Of perfect evenness, all things
Appear like magical illusions.

9. Then visualize above your head,
Upon the center of a lotus and on disks of sun and moon,
Amid a host of deities and dākinīs
Your own root teacher never separate
From the teachers of the lineage.

Make offerings and praise, and pray
That you may train successfully
In seeing all things as a dream.
Then yourself and all phenomenal existence
Dissolve in light that melts into your teacher.
Rest then for a moment in a space-like state of meditation.
Blessings, realization thus will naturally occur.

10. Then meditate according to
The main part of the practice.
Tell yourself repeatedly—grow used to it—that
Outwardly, all mountains, valleys, regions, towns,
The earth, fire, water, wind, and space,
Sentient beings and the rest,
The five sense objects: form, sound, texture, smell, and taste,
And inwardly, the body, faculties of sense, and consciousness—
Are nothing more than dreams.

11. All past things occurring till today
Are mental objects, just like last night's dreams.
Today's appearances, perceived yet nonexistent,
Are but the mind's delusion.
They're just like what you dreamt about last night
And what you'll dream about tonight.
The things that will appear tomorrow
And the night that follows after
Are but dreams in store.
Remember this, that all things that appear—
The joy you want, the pain that you prevent—
Are simply dreams. Not even for an instant
Should you think them true.

12. When moving, sitting, eating, walking, speaking,
Tell yourself with undistracted mindfulness,
"It's all a dream."

Whatever may appear, whatever you may do or think,
Never lose the thought that it is but a dream.
All is without true existence,
Intangible, uncertain, evanescent,
Insubstantial, indefinable.
Train yourself in this great state
In which there's nothing to be grasped.

13. Through thinking that the object to be apprehended
Is a dream, a false appearance,
The cognition of the apprehended is removed,
And the apprehender too, by implication.
For if the object is negated, so too is the subject.

14. This mind that estimates appearances as dreams,
If now and then you really search for it—
Out or in or somewhere in between—
There's no way to identify it,
No point on which to set your bearings.
There is a state of openness like boundless space.
Devoid of the wild frenzy of your memories and plans,
Awareness luminous and empty,
Free of all conceptual construction,
Arises of its own accord.
When the apprehender ceases,
The apprehended also is no more.
When the subject has withdrawn,
All holding of an object vanishes.
Then there is no link with an appearing object.
The framework of discernment falls away.
Then there's simply primal wisdom,
Nondual, self-arisen.

15. When indeed you realize
And grow used to this,

Because the apprehended and the apprehender
Are averted, the assumption
That the object and the mind are real
Subsides and an experience then arises where
There is no apprehension of appearing things
As being this or that.
All that appears arises rootless
And primordially empty.
This is the pristine fundamental nature.

16. By degrees, the apprehension
Of appearing objects as being truly this or that—
That is, impure dependent nature—is arrested
And pure dependent nature is then actualized.
It is like the vanishing of deluded dreams
At the moment when one wakes from sleep.
Then, in the primordial ground,
Manifest enlightenment occurs.

17. Hallucinations are not present in the past;
They are not present in the future;
It is only now that they appear.
They are perceived, yet from the moment of appearing,
They are without existence.
Nonexistent, they appear to the deluded mind
According to its habits.
And yet by nature they're primordially pure.
They resemble dreams.

18. When you are not sleeping, when you are awake,
The things appearing in your dreams do not exist.
Only in your sleep do they occur.
And in the moment they appear, they have no real existence.
In just the same way, you should understand,

The nonexistent things that yet appear
Have neither ground nor root.

19. Meditating strongly in this way by day,
At night as you are sinking into sleep,
Upon a comfortable bed, stretch out on your right side
As the Lord lay down before he passed beyond all sorrow.
Breathing very slowly and with steady gaze,
Visualize within your heart a crystal sphere
In which there is a letter *A*.
White in color and ablaze with light,
It is the size of your own thumb,
Becoming ever smaller as you concentrate on it.
Without distraction, bear in mind that it is like a dream.
In this way, dreamlike luminosity will manifest.

20. At first, when you have frightening nightmares,
Recall that they are dreams.
Your fear will dissipate at once.
To recognize one's dreams as dreams
Is to be concentrated, it is said,
While in the state of dreaming.
This practitioners should understand.

21. Train then to recognize that all dreams are unreal.
Appearances of things without existence
Are no more than the mind's delusion,
Dreamlike and ungraspable.
Since they are neither true nor false,
Know then that they transcend the reach of ordinary mind.

22. Concerning the assumption and the transformation
Of a form while dreaming,
Assume the form of Brahmā, of the Buddha,
Of a bodhisattva, or of something else

According to your wish.
Thus train yourself and place yourself
Within their unreality.

23. Then in successive moments change your form,
According to your wish, from Brahmā into Indra,
Or else from a divine into a human being.
Meditate upon the unreality of all such forms.

24. Then multiply all such appearances
A hundred- or a thousand- or a millionfold.
Train yourself in mastery of antidotes
That subdue all that is to be subdued.

25. Then you may journey in your dreams
To pure fields, various lands and realms,
To Akaniṣṭha and wherever you may wish.
And there you will behold the sugatas,
Listen to their stainless words, and train yourself
In wisdom, concentration, clouds of dhāraṇīs.
Through your training thus with mindfulness
Continually both day and night,
All this will come to pass,
For this is the unfailing quality of your awareness,
Which thus will be made manifest.
All this is the essential pith
Of teachings most profound.

26. Meditating thus by day and night
Upon your dreams,
You will escape the snare
Of thinking that phenomena are truly real.
Through fences, walls, and mountains
You will pass unhindered.
You will gain unnumbered wondrous powers,

Clairvoyance, concentrations.
Innumerable experiences you'll have and realizations,
And sublime primordial wisdom will arise.

27. You will come at last
To the primordial expanse, the nature of the mind,
And gain the dreamlike twofold goal:
The dharmakāya for your own sake
And the rūpakāya for the sake of others.
Meditate therefore that all is like a dream.

2. The Chapter That Is Like a Magical Illusion

1. And thereto also did the Conqueror declare
That all things are like magical illusions,
Explaining that they lack intrinsic being.
Listen! I shall tell you how I have experienced
This quintessential teaching
Of the sūtras, tantras, and the pith instructions.

2. The primordial nature of the mind
Is a spacious, sky-like state
Where primal wisdom is like sun and moon and stars.
And yet when there occurs within this womb of space—
The wondrous sphere of emptiness—
A state of ignorance, conceptualization, dualistic clinging,
The hallucinations of the three worlds
And the six migrations manifest
In the manner of a magical illusion.

3. They appear spontaneously, through the power
Of interdependent causes and conditions—
Just as when a piece of wood or little stone
Is conjured through an incantation
And there appears a magical display,
A horse, an ox, a man or woman,
A mountain or a palace, and the rest.

4. Deluded mind and its habitual tendencies,
Phenomenal existence, the objects of the senses
And the three poisons that fixate on them—
All these occur because of ignorance.
Devoid of real existence, they all appear unceasingly.
They are like conjured apparitions.
From now on be convinced
That they are empty, false reflections.

5. Sure it is that all things in phenomenal existence,
In saṃsāra and nirvāṇa,
Are in their nature equal and they all resemble space.
Understand that all are unborn,
Pure from the beginning.

6. Within the nature unoriginate,
Wherein origination manifests,
The illusion of the character [of luminosity]
Is the ground of purification;
The illusion of impurity
Is the stain that should be purified;
The illusion of the skillful method
Is the purifying remedy;
The illusion of primordial wisdom
Is the perfected fruit.
Through the illusion of an example,
The other four are proved with certainty.

7. By means of an enchantment,
A magical display arises:
A stick and stone appear in form of horse and ox.
Yet at that time the stick and stone themselves
Are neither horse nor ox.
By this example, you should see
That all things, marked by lack of true existence,

Are in themselves but magical displays.
The basis of delusion,
The conditions for delusion and the mode thereof,
The occurrence of delusion as well as its subsiding,
And freedom from delusion in the primal ground—
These correspond respectively to stick and stone,
To the chanting and the working of the spell,
To production of the horse and ox,
Their vanishing, and then the reemergence
Of the stick and stone as previously they were.
By this example thus are step by step explained
Four stages of illusion.

8. The illusion of the "character,"
The mind's luminous nature,
Is the ultimate expanse,
The sugatagarbha, ground of cleansing.

9. Since it is not divided
Into pure and impure,
It's beyond saṃsāra and the state beyond all pain.
It is the space wherein these different states arise,
The basis whence they manifest
According as one knows or fails to know it as it is.
The sugatagarbha is the primal ground,
The fundamental nature.

10. It is like a limpid looking glass,
The base for the arising of reflected forms,
Which, in the moment when such forms appear,
Does not exist as any one of them.
The surface of the glass
Is neither white nor black,
Yet it provides the base
In which both white and black appear.

Awareness is like this.
And knowing this, you will be skilled in everything.

11. Impure illusions are the false appearance
And perception of saṃsāra—
Occurring through our taking
Dualistically what is nondual.

12. The illusion then of skillful means
Thus constitutes the path of remedies.
On the four paths of accumulation,
Joining, seeing, meditation,
The two accumulations
And the practice of two stages
Constitute the means of cleansing.
The stains that should be cleansed
Are thereby swept away like clouds.

13. The illusion of primordial wisdom,
The final path of no more learning,
Consists in the three kāyas,
As well as the activity, spontaneously accomplished,
Of the Victorious Ones.
It is the twofold purity made manifest.

14. The illusion of the example
Is the illusion of dependence.
Just like magic forms arising
Through the substances and chanting of a charm,
All things are understood to be unreal.
This is the instruction of the *Māyājāla*.

15. Just as when a substance is conjoined
With words of wizardry,
The thing that then appears

Is taken as a phantom form,
In just the same way you should understand
That things appearing falsely to migrating beings
Are indeed without existence.
The objects that arise dependently
Because of beings' ingrained deluded habits
Are empty in themselves, ungraspable,
In the very moment they appear.
Understand that they transcend the two extremes
Of nonexistence and existence.

16. Illusory lands and towns that are illusory,
Illusory people and their wealth that is illusory,
Illusory delight and pain, illusory arising and destruction,
Illusory veracity and lies that are illusory—
Just as all these magical illusions
Are perceived and do appear,
In just the same way you should understand
The appearance of the six migrations.

17. Empty from the very first,
All things resemble magical illusions.
Appearing yet without existence,
They are just the same as magical illusions.
Arising from conditions,
They are indeed like magical illusions.
Deceptive and destructible,
They do indeed resemble magical illusions.
In just such terms saṃsāra's false appearances
Are understood as magical illusions.

18. And so it is. Although the six migrations
Have in fact the nature of illusions,
Beings fail to understand
And without respite wander

In the city of saṃsāra without end.
How pitiful! They suffer through their actions,
Source of pain and [temporary] pleasure.
Consider this, O beings:
The things that you mistakenly perceive
Are magical illusions!

19. They arise from nowhere; nowhere do they go;
They are present nowhere—
Such is the true state of things.
From the outset, by their nature, they are pure illusions.
Be sure of this, O you of perfect destiny!

20. Beings are by their nature like illusions;
The nature of enlightenment, it too is an illusion.
The play of an illusion, saṃsāra and nirvāṇa are not two.
Perceive them thus, O you who have good fortune!

21. The Conqueror has said that things are but illusions.
Aside from that, one cannot find
A single atom of reality.
Understand therefore, all you who wish for freedom,
That nothing has true being;
All is of the essence of illusion.

22. The manner of illusion should be understood as follows.
The illusion of enlightenment
Is beyond all change and movement.
It is spontaneously arisen.
It is unfailing, ever space-like, all-pervading;
It is like a wishing jewel, fulfilling all desires.
It utterly displays unbounded excellence and actions.
It is pure and luminous, and free from thought elaboration.

23. The illusion of saṃsāra is untrue, deceptive.
The phenomena thereof have no real features.
Appearing and yet nonexistent,
They resemble magical illusions.
But when deluded thought is cleansed away,
Hallucinations likewise sink into the ultimate expanse.
Just as when the magic ends,
The horse and ox no more appear,
Impure hallucinatory perceptions—
Apprehender, apprehended—
All subside in the primordial ground,
Which, empty in its purity,
Has no intrinsic being.

24. The illusion of the fundamental nature
Refers to ultimate reality devoid of change and movement.
The final nature of all pure and impure things
Is like the space enclosed within a vase.
The vessel may be made of gold or clay,
It may be broken or unbroken,
But its space is neither increased
Nor reduced thereby.
Just so, in the condition of delusion,
The ultimate reality is not diminished,
Nor is it greater in the state of freedom.
It neither worsens nor improves.
This is the fundamental way of being,
The final state of wisdom.
The wise are those who thus have understood.

25. Once you have grasped the view that all is an illusion,
Proceed to meditate upon illusion,
The great state of the absence of intrinsic being.
Perform, as previously, the preliminaries,

And pray that you may realize
That all things are illusions.

26. Regarding the main practice,
You should meditate at all times, day and night,
Considering that all things in their variety,
Both outside and within,
Appear to you like magical illusions
Through their causes and conditions.
They are in truth unreal, intangible,
An unobstructed openness.

27. No matter what defilements may arise,
Attachment or dislike, indulging or rejection,
Look on all of them as magical illusions.
Train yourself to see them all as empty and unreal.
Outwardly, all things are just illusions;
Inwardly, all thoughts are like illusions.
They come from causes and conditions,
And thus they are deceptive and unreal.
They are mere appearances, so meditate on them
Employing the example of a magical illusion.

28. As before, when lying down to sleep,
Relax completely in the state
Of knowing all to be illusory,
Unreal, beyond conceptual construction.
Because you understand deluded dreams—
Whatever may occur—to be illusory,
All fear that might arise
From taking them as true subsides.
Training in them as illusions,
Increase them and transfigure them.
Travel to the buddha fields,

Themselves like magical illusions.
Perform this practice as described before.

29. And by this means, your clinging
To the real existence of saṃsāra
Will dissipate all by itself.
When it subsides through being seen as magical illusion,
The state of nonabiding nirvāṇa is attained.
The twofold aim, illusion-like, is gained all by itself.
So train in the illusory condition of all things.

3. The Chapter That Is Like a Trick of Sight

1. Listen! I shall now explain
The words of the Victorious One
That all things are like tricks of sight.

2. Just as through a certain form
A trick of sight appears,
Likewise in the nature of the mind
And through the power of deluded habit,
The optical illusion of saṃsāra is contrived:
The false appearance of something nonexistent.
However it appears, it is like a trick of sight.

3. Childish beings are deceived thereby;
Unskilled, they cling to it as real.
Caught in the trap, the trick of sight—
The objects of the five sense powers—
They cling to self though there is nothing there.
Just look how they're deceived!

4. Phenomenal existence, universe and beings,
Happiness and sorrow, high and low,
Appear while nonexistent.
They're like shadows in the lamplight,
Or the moon seen double
When one's eyes are pressed,

Or like deep darkness
When there's much affliction.
When left unanalyzed, these things appear;
When analyzed, there is no grasping them;
When closely analyzed, their nature is beyond extremes.
Like space, they are unborn.
Understand this very day,
With sure conviction, their primordial nature.

5. False appearances are groundless
Just like optical illusions.
They are rootless and without true features of their own.
When examined, they are empty;
They have no being and yet seem to be.
It should be understood:
Their primordial nature is to be unborn.

6. Just as in the middle of a desert plain
A small thing seen from far away
May yet seem vast in size,
From just a slight attachment
To a self in that which has no self,
The vast hallucination of saṃsāra manifests.

7. When these hallucinations are investigated,
They are found to be unreal.
When you understand that, just like space,
They cannot be removed,
Just let them be.
And do not cling so foolishly
To this world's real existence—
This world that, like a trick of sight,
Appears without existing.

8. The fundamental state of all phenomena
Is their primordial condition, pure from the beginning.
Do not cling to them; do not conceptualize.
Regarding those appearances that have no self-identity
That could be recognized,
What point is there in getting trapped
Within the cage of partiality and clinging?
Give up all concern for such phenomena.
Understand that what appears
Is void of true existence.

9. When you have an understanding
That all things are just like tricks of sight,
Place your mind in its own nature as it is.
Practice the preliminaries previously described,
And pray that you will clearly see
That all things are like optical illusions.

10. As the main part of the practice,
Train yourself in seeing all things
As optical illusions, tricks of sight.
Of true existence form is empty;
It is like a trick of sight.
Sound is void of sound;
It's like a trick of sight.
Smell and taste and touch
Are all of them like tricks of sight.
The mind and mental objects
All resemble tricks of sight.
Everything is void of true existence.
In this understanding leave your mind relaxed
And free from grasping, free from false assumption.

11. Just as in the daytime,
Likewise when you go to sleep,

Concentrate your mind upon your heart.
Sleep then in the knowledge that
All things are tricks of sight.
And it is certain, as before,
That you will recognize your dreams as dreams.

12. Even the occurrence of experiences and realization
Is like a trick of sight.
Spontaneously the realization comes
That things lack true existence.
And in the state of openness
Devoid of clinging and fixation,
Delusions of accepting and rejecting all collapse.
Powers of vision, preternatural clairvoyance,
All the qualities of concentration
Will be gained. Possessing thus
The treasure of the teaching of the Conqueror,
You will become the guide of every being.
Meditate therefore that everything
Is like an optical illusion.

4. The Chapter That Is Like a Mirage

1. Here too the Conqueror declared
That things resemble mirages.
Listen! I will tell you how this is.

2. Just as during summer
In the middle of the day,
Mirages of water appear upon a plain—
Through the power of the mind's ingrained proclivity
To apprehend and grasp at self,
Saṃsāra's false appearances
Arise just like a mirage.

3. There is no way to grasp at their identity.
They are beyond dichotomies.
They are empty;
All descriptive terms subside.
Unborn, they are like space;
They have no being of their own.
Understand that they are unoriginate,
That they transcend all thought.

4. In the very moment they appear,
Things seem to have beginnings,
And yet, like mirages, they have no origin.
It seems that they remain,

Yet like a mirage, they have no abiding.
They also seem to cease,
And yet, like mirages, they do not cease.
Understand therefore
That, though they do appear,
They are without intrinsic being.

5. All joy and sorrow, pleasure, pain, all good and ill
Are just like mirages—all empty, without self.
All things within phenomenal existence—
Outer, inner—all resemble mirages.
Nonexistent, they appear and are perceived.
Understand that from the outset
They are by their nature pure.
No center do they have, no limit;
They are primordially empty.

6. To apprehend duality where there is no duality
Is like looking at a mirage.
Do not let yourself be caught by clinging,
By taking or rejecting what has no reality.
Watch your mind,
Itself not different from a mirage.
This is the wisdom of the Conquerors
Past, present, and to come.

7. Then, according to the stages of meditative practice,
Begin with the preliminaries as previously explained,
And pray that you may see all things as mirages.

8. As for the main practice, tell yourself
That all things are like mirages.
And then stay free from hopes and fears,
From all engagement with the thoughts
Occurring in your mind.

At night, approach your dreams as previously described,
And they will all arise as mirages.

9. Belief in real existence, clinging to a self
Will naturally subside.
Dhāraṇī clouds, clairvoyance, concentration—
All will burgeon from within.
The enlightened state will swiftly be attained.
Therefore meditate that everything
Is by its nature like a mirage.

5. The Chapter That Is Like the Moon's Reflection on the Water

1. Furthermore, the Victor has declared that everything
Is like the moon's reflection on the water.
This now I shall explain
That you may put this teaching into practice.

2. In the heart of the profound and limpid sea,
The nature of the mind,
The image of spontaneous presence,
Primordially arisen, does indeed abide.
And yet through the turbidity
Stirred up by waves of dualistic clinging,
This presence is not clear,
Disturbed by winds of thought.
Worldly beings manifest
Through ignorance and ego-grasping.
Ignorant, defiled, they do not see primordial wisdom;
They sink in endless and beginningless saṃsāra.

3. Just as in unsullied water
Bright unmoving forms of stars and planets,
Though not really there, are nonetheless perceived,
Within the water of the mind
The forms that have arisen,
Images of false appearances,

Though nonexistent, are perceived.
And beings are tormented.

4. What are they, these appearances?
They are not actual entities—
There is no grasping them.
They do not have, nor do they lack,
Specific character.
Not existent nor yet nonexistent,
They transcend extremes of truth and falsity.
This then is the meaning
When it's said that they are like reflections.

5. The six sense objects, form and all the rest,
Are like the moon's reflection in the water,
For they appear although they are not there.
They do not have intrinsic being
And yet appear unceasingly to those who are deluded.
The eye itself, the visual sense, and visual consciousness—
And equally for all the six sensorial gatherings—
Are just like this same water moon:
Empty, hollow, false, deceptive.
Devoid of an essential core,
They're like the plantain tree.
In every aspect, you should understand,
They are devoid of true existence.

6. The mind unstained,
Unmarred by ontological extremes,
Is also like the water moon.
Experienced yet empty,
It is free of all conceptual constructs.
Primal wisdom, nonconceptual,
Peaceful and profound,
Is utterly ineffable.

Know that from the state of luminosity
It never stirs.

7. When the moon appears in water,
It is not the actual moon.
Just so, when different things appear,
They are neither there nor are they absent.
Refrain from pondering conventional things
Past, present, and to come,
And rest in the unaltered state just as it is,
Devoid of thoughts.

8. The enlightened mind
Is without coming or departing.
It is neither outside nor within.
Transcending thought, it has no partiality.
It is ultimate reality, unlimited and unconfined,
Wherein there is no wide or narrow
And no high or low.
So set aside all anxious search for it.

9. The primordial state does not exclusively abide
Within the state of no-thought.
For it is everything,
And everything is like a water moon.
Saṃsāra and nirvāṇa are equally the same:
They are not truly real, nor are they false.
Settle your mind unaltered in its ultimate condition.

10. Phenomenal existence, saṃsāra and nirvāṇa—
All is but an empty form.
It is just like the moon reflected in a pool—
Primordially empty, spontaneously empty,
Empty by its nature from the very outset.
It is an error to believe

That it's existent or is nonexistent.
Do not subscribe therefore
To any of the different, biased views of tenet systems.

11. As long as there is strong attachment to the self,
There's no escaping from saṃsāra.
The natural mind is uncontrived,
A spontaneous flow in which there is no clinging—
A bare, primordial flow,
Spontaneous openness and freedom,
An immensity unbounded—
What need is there to alter such a nature?

12. When objects of the senses,
Empty from their side,
Appear like moons reflected in the water;
When the mind is likewise empty
Of assumptions and of clinging,
The duality of apprehender-apprehended
Ceases, is no more.
No further link is there between
Sense objects and the mind.
This is the authentic state,
The Great Perfection free from all exertion.

13. All that happens then becomes your helping friend,
And great bliss unconfined is present of itself.
Knowing this, you have no need to travel on the grounds.
For you have gained enlightenment in the primordial ground.

14. To stay within that state when this is understood
Is meditation that resembles an unmoving water moon.
Therefore, you who are so fortunate,
Habituate yourselves to seeing

All that manifests
As untrue, as elusive and intangible.

15. As before, first practice the preliminaries
And pray to see all things
Like moons reflected in the water.
And then the main part is to think
That everything you actually perceive
Is exactly like the moon's reflection
And to place your mind in even meditation.

16. In the nighttime, practice as before.
The only difference lies in your regarding
Dreams as water moons.
Stay within a state where there's no clinging,
Where everything is equal.

17. Swiftly you will gain the everlasting realm,
The nature of the mind.
Whatever you perceive,
You will not grasp at it as real, as this or that.
And luminosity will manifest
As clear and limpid as the moon reflected on the water.
O you who are endowed with perfect fortune,
Meditate upon this well.

6. The Chapter That Is Like an Echo

1. Listen now, and I will lucidly explain
The Victor's word that all is like an echo.

2. Through human voice before a rocky cliff
An echo's sound arises in the form of what was said.
Likewise through conditions do phenomena arise.
They have no being of their own.
Be convinced that they are void of true existence.

3. If, when the echo sounds,
You search for its resounding—
Within you or outside, or somewhere in between—
You do not find it.
If likewise you now mentally investigate
All things that are within you or outside—
The mind and what appears to it—
Nothing, gross or subtle, do you find.
All things are empty; just like space
They have no entity.
If this you understand,
You will not cling or hanker after things.

4. "The relative appears;
The ultimate is not observed."
Yet even to conceive of these two aspects

Is nothing but the mind's distinction.
For in the moment they're perceived,
Phenomena transcend the mind.
The mind is but a fabric
Of conceptual construction
That the mind itself has posited.
And as for things themselves,
The mind does not affect them
By enlarging or diminishing.
They cannot be encompassed
By the webs of thought—
They cannot be identified.
To know them to be so
Is to transcend the mind's construction.

5. The primordial nature of the mind resembles space
Wherein are present of themselves,
Like wish-fulfilling gems, the perfect qualities,
The spotless attributes of buddhahood.
Conditioned through conceptual ignorance,
Saṃsāra's attributes appear without existing, echo-like,
And thus one wanders through this world.
The various perceptions of the six migrations
Appear through beings' habitual tendencies
And through the impure mind's engagement into action.

6. And so all false appearances and the minds of beings
Are groundless, rootless, by their very nature.
Éma! All such things, perceived yet nonexistent—
How laughable, to take such figments for reality!
In truth, all seeming things
Are like the echo's sound.
What does it serve to cling to them,
Believing in their truth?

Stay rather in a state
Where all is equal and elusive,
Where fleeting things sink back
Into great nonreality.
They are neither wide nor narrow,
Neither high nor low—
And how delectable that is!

7. When all fixation falls away
Regarding things that may arise,
Affirmed or else negated,
They are like an echo's sound.
Since they subside
Within a state that's free of reference,
They are all equal,
Free from all one-sidedness.

8. Ha! Now look! All these appearances—
They're just ridiculous!
There's nothing you can grasp at, nothing to define.
Things are loose, intangible,
Vague, uncertain, evanescent—
Not taken to be true, yet variously appearing.

9. For those unskilled who cling to them,
Things are as true as true can be.
For yogis who perceive their falsity,
Things are all elusive and unreal.
For those who think of fleeting things as permanent,
All is fixed and everlasting.
But when belief in permanence has naturally subsided,
All things are empty forms—
Neither wide nor narrow, neither big nor small.
Is not this delectable?

10. In order to grow used
To that which you have understood,
First practice the preliminaries as before
And pray that you may understand
That all is like an echo.
In the main practice, meditate
Reflecting then that everything
Is like an echo's resonance,
Which in the moment of its sounding
Is beyond your grasp.
Reflect like this in all that you experience.

11. Especially all praise and blame,
All reputation, good and bad,
Resound but are an empty resonance
In which there's nothing to be grasped.
It's pointless to accept or to reject them.
Understand that all words are like echoes.

12. Wrath and other states of mind
Have no location, no direction.
They appear without existing;
When looked for, they are nowhere to be found.
Arising from conditions, they are empty
Like an echo's resonance.
And other people's words,
Likewise arising from conditions,
Are also like an echo.
When scrutinized, they're just reverberations,
Occurring yet without existence.
When closely analyzed, they are like space;
They have no solid entity.
They are neither good nor bad.
Excitement and dejection are not found in them.
So do not take these words as something real,

For they are empty, destitute of true existence.
Realize that, in every way, they are like echoes.

13. Through this are quenched
The fires of hate and wrath
And all the habits of beginningless saṃsāra.
Through this, supreme acceptance is attained.
There is no further falling into evil destinies,
And stage by stage is born the wealth of victory.
At night, just as before, approach your dreams
Like echoes, sounding and yet void of sound.
Thus you will achieve acceptance
With regard to all phenomena.
Meditate therefore that all is like an echo.

7. The Chapter That Is Like a City of Gandharvas

1. And also the Victorious One
Declared that everything is like a city of gandharvas.
That you may meditate on this,
Pay heed now to my explanation.

2. In the primordial expanse of luminosity
Appears a city, fair and beautiful, of perfect qualities
Spontaneously present.
It dwells therein beginningless and without end.
No center does it have, no limit.

3. And from this luminous and empty state,
Within the firmament of the unknowing mind,
The six migrations—castles in the clouds—appear,
Which take their origin in dualistic clinging
To the apprehender and the apprehended.
Devoid of ground and basis,
They appear in different forms
Deriving from deluded mind
And its habitual tendencies.

4. When this you see, there manifests
The nature of the mind, the primal state.
But when you fail to see it,
There is just the mind of everyday confusion.

And how are these appearances?
They are ungraspable like castles in the clouds.
Kyé! How else should we describe them?

5. Indeed they are all destitute of real existence;
They are like the cities of the fairies seen
Above a plain as sunlight sinks into the west.
Supported and support
Are simply the deluded mind,
Which sees as it is wont to see.
When closely scrutinized, there's nothing really there.
Left to itself, the vision naturally fades.
So set aside your fear, for you have nothing hard to do.
Understand just how the world and beings
Are from the very outset pure and empty.

6. All appearing objects, empty of true being,
Are like castles in the clouds.
All mental states, by nature empty,
Are like castles in the clouds.
Both sense objects and mind are empty;
They're like castles in the clouds.
The slightest clinging or fixation—
Just leave it where it is!

7. How is this accomplished?
Do not let your mind manipulate phenomena
Appearing yet without existing.
Simply leave them without grasping.
Original delusion is itself the fruit
Of all such grasping and fixation.
And therefore you should know
The state devoid of clinging.

8. The sublime and spotless nature of phenomena,
Phenomena themselves,
And utter peace, the state beyond all sorrow,
Are not existent entities.
Understand that all phenomena,
Things and nonthings both,
All are empty, without true existence.
They resemble castles in the clouds;
They are like the vast abyss of space—
Primordially unborn, the state of utter peace.

9. No desire is found therein.
Ignorance and anger, jealousy and pride
Are not observed. So therefore understand
That these and all thoughts
Are like castles in the clouds.
Defilements, void of real existence,
And enlightenment, the nature of the mind,
Are not two different things.
Know that they're like space;
They are both equal and immaculate.

10. The nature of saṃsāra is nirvāṇa from the outset.
Deluded thoughts subside completely
Like the clouds that melt into the sky.
Know that they subside there whence they came.
Preserve this state of utter peace,
Primordial wisdom, empty, luminous.

11. In the state of unborn nature,
No thoughts, no sense objects are found,
And yet, until the show of their arising
Melts into the ultimate expanse,
Cut through the root of your delusion—ordinary thought.
Action and nonaction are not two;

Not two are taking and rejecting.
And yet, as long as in your mind
You cling to self and real existence,
I urge you to rely upon profound instructions,
Antidotes for your defilements.
Not two are outer things and inner mental states—
Both sink into the nature of the mind.
Wise you are if this you understand.

12. Regarding how to meditate this point,
First perform, as previously, the preliminaries,
And in the main part of the practice
Know with a complete conviction:
All things are like castles in the clouds.

13. Form appears and yet is empty,
Like a castle in the clouds.
Sound, smell, taste, touch, mental objects—
All these six are castles in the clouds.
The mind, its affirmations and negations,
All arising thoughts, are castles in the clouds.
On all this meditate with clarity.
At all times, day and night, reflect just as before
That all appearing things are castles in the clouds.

14. Having seen that all compounded things
Resemble castles in the clouds,
You should settle
In their absence of reality.
Your mind's proliferations all will cease,
And self-arisen, clear, and empty luminosity
Will manifest from deep within.
Even in your dreams
You will see everything
As cities of gandharvas in the clouds.

You will become proficient
In assuming different forms,
Transforming them as previously described.
And as belief in the reality of things subsides,
The dualistic chain of apprehender-apprehended breaks.
All bonds and all habitual tendencies subside
And freedom is achieved.
Meditate therefore upon these castles in the clouds!

8. The Chapter That Is Like an Emanated Apparition

1. The Conqueror has said
That all things are the emanations of the mind.
Listen! I shall tell you what he meant by this.

2. From within the state of primal luminosity,
Through ignorance, through clinging to the self,
There manifest saṃsāra's
Various hallucinatory appearances,
Which are like emanated apparitions.
They are perceived though they do not exist—
And thence come all experiences of joy and sorrow.

3. This is what appears to the minds of beings,
The form of their habitual tendencies.
When these are cleansed,
There manifest spontaneously
The triple kāya of the buddha-element,
Together with the self-experience
Of luminous primordial wisdom.
It is as the *Māyājāla* says:
There is the self-experience of the ordinary mind
And then the self-experience of primordial wisdom.

4. The primordial expanse is source of everything.
When this is recognized and when,

By such a means, defilements have been cleansed,
The self-experience of primordial wisdom manifests.
When this has not been recognized,
Then through deluded clinging to a self,
The mind's subjective vision of the world occurs.
All joys and sorrows of the six migrations
Appear like emanated apparitions.

5. Just as an emanated apparition
Arises without any basis,
Likewise you should understand
That all hallucinatory appearances
Are pure and without any basis.
Just as those who have great power of mind control
Are able to produce an emanated apparition,
Likewise you should understand
That it is through the habits of the minds of beings
That various things appear.
Just as an emanated apparition
Appears according to the emanator's wish,
Likewise you should understand
That things arise from causes and conditions.
Just as an emanated apparition
Is an illusion that arises when nothing's there,
Likewise you should understand
That things are just deluded mind's experience—
Its self-appearance, self-arising,
Wherein the mind is self-engrossed—
And things appear according to its habits.

6. If you do not indulge in any habits,
If you leave things as they are,
You will in no way be deluded.
Abiding in the nature of the ground,
You will remain within the mind's pristine expanse.

7. Now the three poisons, the five poisons—
All derive from thought,
But on examination they are nowhere found.
Defilements are like emanated apparitions;
They lack intrinsic being.
Rest therefore in their unborn and empty nature.

8. Phenomenal existence,
The world and all the beings it contains,
Their bodies and possessions,
Their going, staying, joys, and sorrows all—
Appearing while not really there—
Are like the emanations of the mind,
Without intrinsic being.
They have no origin, they do not cease;
They do not come, they do not go;
They do not pass, they do not change—
Yet variously they all appear.
Understand this well therefore:
They are indeed just emanated apparitions.

9. All deluded thoughts,
All sorrows of the mind,
Are just like emanated apparitions.
They lack intrinsic being and yet appear without obstruction.
Understand their emptiness of true existence.
They are neither in the object nor within the mind itself.

10. The universe composed of the five elements,
The beings that reside in the three worlds,
Whatever one affirms or else denies
Are all, without exception, emanations of the mind.
And the mind itself—though it appears—
Is also void of real existence.

Know that from the outset it is pure,
Just like an emanation, an illusion.

11. Ignorant and childish beings
Perceive and think mistakenly.
All concrete things endowed with features,
All objects that the mind has posited
Are but the outcome of habitual tendencies;
In truth, they have no real existence.
Do not indulge therefore in subject-object clinging,
Speaking of "these things."
Understand instead that all is free of ontological extremes,
Beyond the reach of words.

12. Although phenomena are labeled "this" or "that,"
It's just as with the names for "space" or "rabbit's horns."
Phenomena are not real things.
They are just thoughts without existence
In the fundamental nature.
Understand that they are rootless,
Empty from the outset.

13. All that thought imputes is mind;
It has no factual existence.
All that seems to be an object of the senses
Is just habitual tendency—appearing yet not real.
And since there is no object,
There's no apprehension of an object:
No duality of apprehender and the apprehended.
You cannot say, you cannot think,
You cannot indicate phenomena:
They are beyond the ontological extremes.
No one can identify them saying "this."
Know that they resemble emanated apparitions.
From the outset they are void of self.

14. Just as apparitions emanated forth
Are empty of existence in the moment they appear,
So too are all phenomena
Appearing and yet void of true existence.
Emanated apparitions are beyond extremes
Of being and nonbeing.
Just so are all phenomena
Beyond conceptual thinking.

15. Although things may be variously described—
"They appear," "they are empty," "they are true or false"—
They have no reality at all.
Do not apprehend them, then, as this or that;
Just view them as a limitless expanse.

16. If there is no clinging and fixation,
Things are left just as they are.
What purpose is there in negating or affirming
What is simply words?

17. If you have fixation, saying "this,"
It is not in any way the fundamental nature.
For what can webs of mind's analysis reveal?
Imputed by the mind, your thoughts might indicate
The final truth of emptiness, and yet
This is to cling to an extreme.
How therefore can it be the fundamental nature?

18. "And yet," you may object,
"Because they give an indication,
Will words not lead us to an understanding?"
But emptiness exceeds both words and definitions,
So what is there that words could indicate?
This objection therefore has no meaning.
The nature of the mind cannot be seen

Through concepts and fixated clinging.
Investigations of discursive intellect
Lead only to approximations.

19. But when the blessings of a teacher
Penetrate your heart,
It's like the sun that rises in a cloudless sky.
Through the powerful conjunction
Of dependent factors,
The sublime will manifest.

20. All things then are equal.
There is no discerning them as this or that.
They are a naked state of voidness
Free from ontological extremes, like space itself:
A vast expanse, appearing yet empty,
Like emanated apparitions.
Thus all things come naturally to be realized.

21. Saṃsāra in itself is just deluded thought.
And when the nature of the mind is seen,
It is nirvāṇa—there from the beginning.
It is primal wisdom, free of all fixation,
That, in self-knowing, knows its object.
Nothing that appears is real;
There is no apprehending it as this or that.
The mind finds comfort in a state
Where mind and what appears
Are seen as emanated apparitions.

22. When this is realized, you become
A noble being who beholds the truth.
This is the truth itself;
There's nothing else to indicate.

Everything, spontaneously arising,
Sets in its own place, its very nature.

23. Such realization manifests
To none but those whose hearts
Are touched by blessings
Of a master of a thousand skillful means.
A visible thing, a blazing lamp
Is seen by those with eyes.
How can beings blind from birth
Perceive it even though it's shown to them?

24. Those who have no knowledge of the teaching,
Those who have no understanding of its meaning
Cannot see the sunlight of this excellence.
Others, yet more foolish and pretentious,
Are like reciting parrots.
Caught in the nets of their discursive thoughts,
They will never find the quintessential truth.
Suchness they will never know,
Like beings blind from birth in front of solid objects.
They will never come to realization,
For they take as true the findings of their intellects.
Alas for their pretentious lies,
Alas for their unhappy fortune!
They have no hope of reaching
Quintessential truth.

25. For us, it is the master
Who reveals the nature of the mind,
Sublime primordial wisdom.
Authentic, self-cognizing, primal wisdom
Arises when the mind is left
Unspoiled by tampering and alteration.
When there's neither hope nor doubt—

No clinging, no assumptions—it appears.
More clearly does it manifest
Within the state of emptiness and luminosity
Devoid of center and of boundary.
Thus to be accepted by a holy teacher,
The holder of the blessings of the lineage,
Is indeed of highest moment.

26. For undistracted meditation on the fundamental nature,
As before, first practice the preliminaries,
And in the guru yoga pray that you succeed
In seeing all phenomena as emanated apparitions.
Then, in the main practice, firmly take your stand
Upon the understanding that the mind
Is, by its nature, like an emanated apparition
And that everything appearing to the mind—
This too is, by its nature, like an emanated apparition.
Everything is unborn like an emanation.
With this understanding
Leave the mind at rest,
Devoid of mental agitation.

27. As you rest then in a clear and empty state,
Devoid of mind's elaboration,
There comes a clear and limpid luminosity
Resembling an emanated apparition,
Motionless and free from the duality
Of apprehender-apprehended.
Sense objects appear and are perceived unceasingly,
And yet there is no grasping them as this or that.
There is no fabrication and no alteration.
It is a vivid, limpid, undistracted state of natural bliss,
A state of mind that's bright, devoid of thoughts,
And similar to space itself.
Thus you see the nature of the mind

Devoid of thought's construction.
It's then that mental states
Regarding things that are like apparitions
Subside, themselves like apparitions also.
Craving and aversion, hopes and fears,
All clinging to a self—are all like emanated apparitions.
The ground, the path, the fruit
Are all the state of openness and freedom.

28. Then however you may meditate, it will not fetter you.
Though you meditate on things as if they were existent,
You will be free from the extreme of permanence.
Though you meditate on things as nonexistent,
You will be unstained by nihilism.
Though you meditate in dualistic ways,
You will remain within the state of nonduality.
Though you meditate on self-identity,
You will be not be bound by clinging to a self.
Though you meditate on other things,
You will nonetheless be free of hope and fear.
Though you implement the generation stage,
You will naturally accomplish the perfection stage.
Though you practice the perfection stage,
The stage of generating an appearance is likewise done.

29. Arising and subsiding all occur at once,
And thus from all defilements you are free.
Within the natural state devoid of apprehending thought,
You rest within the wheel of ultimate reality:
The no-time of the triple time.
Meditation and postmeditation—
For you, there is no difference.
You experience them like emanated apparitions.

30. It's then that yogis seem to be
Like aimless lunatics,
Free of clinging, free of care.
They're totally bereft of hope and fear—
They do not alter anything that manifests.
All for them is equal and elusive.
They realize without effort
Wisdom mind, the all-embracing space.

31. And then, both night and day,
The yogi sees all things as emanated apparitions.
In the cakra of great bliss,
There is but a single space of bliss.
In the cakra of enjoyment,
All qualities are savored.
In the cakra of the dharmatā,
The ultimate is ever present.
In the cakra of manifestation,
Appearances are boundless.
In the bliss-preserving cakra,
Bliss is kept both day and night.
So it is that, without any training,
The wind-mind penetrates the crucial place.
The ground of cleansing, factors to be cleansed,
The cleansing agent, the channels main and radial,
Together with the winds, are all primordial wisdom.
The fruit of cleansing—the single taste of all—
Is thus made manifest.

32. You will be able in your dreams
To take on different forms that you can change
And then behold the various buddha fields.
Later these deluded dreams will cease,
And day and night you will remain in luminosity.
Remaining in the concentrations

On bliss, on luminosity, and no-thought,
You will gain the powers
Of vision, preternatural cognition,
Miracles, and other qualities.
Your realization and experience
Will be unbounded, and thus you will achieve
Your own good and the good of other beings.
Therefore, you who are endowed with fortune,
Meditate unceasingly that all things
Have the nature of an emanated apparition.

Conclusion

1. To show that in the eight examples of illusion
Is gathered all the Dharma
That the Buddha has expounded,
Here has been distilled the quintessential sap
Of tantras, commentaries, and pith instructions,
Illumined by the dawning Rays of Spotless Light.[29]

2. By this merit, may all beings, leaving none aside,
See phenomena as unborn, just like magical illusions.
May they, progressing in their practice of the Dharma,
Be graced with riches of the triple kāya of the Conquerors.

3. Like dreams, illusions, mirages, reflections,
Echoes, emanated apparitions—just so are all phenomena.
Through giving up attachment to their true existence,
May beings come to the primordial state endowed
With all the qualities of primal wisdom.

4. May they turn away from towns
Where childish people dwell
Amid their many occupations—
Thick jungles of saṃsāra teeming with defilement.
May they go away to pleasant forest wilds
And there become a jewel that would adorn
The crowns of hundreds, countless, gods.

5. May our minds grow weary of distraction
And take delight in peaceful forest solitudes,
Alone to meditate on profound suchness
And to attain the pure eyes of a noble mind.

6. The forest filled with foliage and flowers,
With fruits and water that is pure,
Is hallowed by the glory of austerity.
In such a place, with life's essential wealth
Of freedoms and advantages,
Assisted by a treasury of beneficial teaching,
May we journey on the path to liberation.

7. So that now our lives should bring forth fruit,
May we in this existence practice virtuous Dharma.
When we have achieved the many qualities
Of this, the path to peace,
May we deliver endless beings from saṃsāra.

8. This text is the essential heart
Of Dharma so profound,
A path where final teachings
Are distilled into their vital point.
You who wish for freedom
Should strive in it sincerely.
Not resting day or night,
Practice it with diligence!

9. O you, the fortunate of future times endowed with faith,
Implement this text with constancy and diligence.
Sure it is that you and others
Will sail across this ocean of existence
And naturally attain the twofold aim of beings.

10. This quintessential meaning
Of the sūtras, tantras, pith instructions
Was well set down upon the slopes of Gangri Thökar
By a yogi who, adorned with spotless rays of light,
Had eyes to see the truth profound
Of all without exception.

11. May this teaching of the Dharma,
The sun graced with a thousand stainless beams,
The light of primal wisdom,
Drive away the gloom of ignorance.
May it completely dry the ocean of saṃsāra.
May the brilliance of the isle of liberation
Spread and shine in all the ten directions.

This concludes the treatise *Finding Rest in Illusion, a Teaching of the Great Perfection*, which was set down in writing on the slope of Gangri Thökar by the yogi Drimé Özer, who touched the feet of Padma, the great master of Oḍḍiyāna.

PART TWO

The Chariot of Excellence

A Commentary on Finding Rest in Illusion, a Teaching of the Great Perfection

In Sanskrit

Mahāsandhimāyāviśrāntasayavrittirataphalanāma

In Tibetan

rDzogs pa chen po sgyu ma ngal gso'i 'grel pa shing rta bzang po ces bya ba

Prologue

Homage to glorious Vajrasattva!

Teacher, Lord of Dharma,
Victorious Ones together with your heirs—
All you who are the sovereigns of the triple world,
From the pure dharmakāya, primordial enlightenment,
You arise in bodies of illusion to display enlightened deeds.
I venerate you with my head bowed down.

Various is the character of beings to be guided,
And various are the means wherewith to guide them.
The vehicles of teaching therefore are past counting,
Yet the essence of them all
Is the illusion of clear luminosity,
Elucidated in this commentary:
The Chariot of Excellence.

Through compassion's wondrous rays of light, there appear bright lamps that scatter the gloom of nescience in an infinite array of worlds. So it is that in this field, our present world, the thousand bhagavan buddhas and so forth, teachers of doctrines both worldly and religious, set forth the countless sections of the Dharma. Of these, the proclamation of the great vehicle, an ocean of unsurpassed methods, is supreme. Now if these methods be gathered into a single, deep, essential point suitable for practice, they are said to be the yoga of the two aspects of illusion defined in terms of eight examples. The definitive key points of the pith instructions of this yoga are established in the treatise *Finding Rest in Illusion*, a teaching belonging to the corpus of the Great Perfection. Here I shall comment on the meaning of its various chapters.

The first point is the expression of homage.

All things emerging from the state of evenness unborn
Are but the great display of primal wisdom
Nondual and illusory.
Through never being parted from this unborn state,
I bow down to the nature of my mind,
The King who from the first is self-arisen.

It is with this verse that the adamantine body of this treatise is laid out. Self-cognizing awareness, the enlightened mind,[30] the buddha-element, the sugatagarbha, is the expanse, or supreme source, of all phenomena of both saṃsāra and nirvāṇa. It is said in the noble *Laṅkāvatāra-sūtra*,

The ultimate expanse from time without beginning
Is the resting place of all phenomena.
Every wandering being possesses it
And therefore has the state beyond all sorrow.

Since it is intrinsically unborn, since it is the state of equality, since it is not an inherently existing thing, and since it transcends the notions of permanence and annihilation, nondual primordial wisdom is unspeakable, unthinkable, and inexpressible. It is self-cognizing awareness, the ultimate truth. As we find in Rāhula's *Praise to the Mother*,

No name, no thought, no explanation is there for the
wisdom that has gone beyond;
Unceasing and unborn, the very character of space.
It is the sphere of primal wisdom self-cognizing:

To this, the mother of the buddhas past, present, and to
come, I bow.

Although it is without intrinsic existence, it is the ground for the arising of both saṃsāra and nirvāṇa. As it is said in the *Songs of Realization*,

The nature of the mind is the sole seed of everything.
Existence and nirvāṇa both emerge from it.
I bow down to this mind that like a wish-fulfilling gem
Is giver of the fruits one may desire.

The expression of homage is followed by the promise to compose the treatise.

That you may understand
The perfect teaching of the Conqueror
That all things are by nature the two aspects of illusion,
Here I have distilled the sappy essence
Of the sūtras, tantras, pith instructions.
Listen! I shall set it forth as I myself experience it.

The Buddha has taught that phenomenal existence, all things in saṃsāra and nirvāṇa, are like magical illusions. They appear and yet they do not exist. As it is said in the *Middle-Length Prajñāpāramitā*,

O Subhūti, phenomena are like dreams, like magical illusions. Even nirvāṇa is like a dream, like a magical illusion. And if there were anything greater than nirvāṇa, that too would be like a dream, like a magical illusion.

And in the *Questions of Bhadra the Magician*, the Buddha said,

Understand, O Bhadra, all things each and every one
Resemble magical illusions.

Since the phenomena of saṃsāra appear to the [ordinary] mind, in being the full development of the strong habitual tendencies lodged therein, they are referred to as illusions of mistaken perception.[31] By contrast, the phenomena of nirvāṇa appear to primordial wisdom, being the spontaneous radiance of awareness. They are the display of kāyas and wisdoms. They are spontaneously present and are beyond [the condition] of entities and substances endowed with properties. They are, for this reason, referred to as illusions that are perfectly pure.[32] As it is said in the tantra entitled *Māyājāla*,

> In the second aspect of illusion, that of perfect purity,
> There is no self nor something other that belongs to self,
> For it is, by its nature, the expanse of utter purity.

This shows the reason for embarking on the composition of the present treatise. And the body of this treatise will be explained in terms of eight vajra points.[33]

The First Vajra Point: Dream

With the help of the first point one should come to a definite understanding that all phenomena are dreamlike in the sense that they appear even though they have no intrinsic being. To begin with, and by means of the view, one must come to a clear conviction with regard to the ground nature, which appears but lacks inherent existence, the supreme dharmadhātu beyond the extremes of one and many.[34]

1. The ground's expanse beyond all change,
The vast sky of the nature of the mind,
Is empty, luminous, and free from mind's elaboration.
Therein like the sun, the moon, and all the stars,
The pure, unstained phenomena of buddhahood
Are present of themselves:
The threefold kāya never sundered
From the five primordial wisdoms,
And all the qualities of luminosity naturally complete.
This primal, fundamental, natural state
Is said to be the entirely pure illusion of the ground.

The illusory ground, the source of both saṃsāra and nirvāṇa, is awareness, the enlightened mind, primordial luminosity, the sugatagarbha. Since its nature is empty, it is like the sky. Since its character is luminous, it is like the sun and moon. And since its cognitive potency is the basis of manifestation, it is like the limpid surface of a mirror.[35] Therein are spontaneously present all the qualities of the kāyas and wisdoms. They are the great and primordial manifestation. They are the attributes of the ultimate expanse from time without beginning, like the sun, the moon, the planets, and the stars within the sky's expanse. As the *Tantra of the Self-Arisen Awareness* says,

> The nature of this space is like the sky itself. Its character is spontaneously luminous, and its knowing power is present as the essence of awareness. As such, it is the ground for the arising of every perfect attribute.

This is the ground for the unfolding of saṃsāra and nirvāṇa; it is the essence of primordial luminosity. It is what is referred to as the "perfectly pure illusion of the ultimate expanse."[36]

Now the way in which the delusory appearance of ordinary beings occurs in this ground is as follows:

> **2. Within this ground,**
> **Through coemergent ignorance**
> **(Like sleep that brings forth dreams,**
> **Which are like clouds of momentary illusion),**
> **And through conceptual ignorance**
> **(The mind impaired by apprehension**
> **Of duality where there is no duality)**
> **There appear the various false appearances of**
> **The six migrations similar to dreams.**

When people sleep, they have good or bad dreams. Now the ground expanse of all appearance is awareness, which—conditioned by the sleeping state—deviates into the experience of dreams that are the outcome of habitual tendencies. These visions appear clearly even though they are without existence and the dreamer takes them as true. This is similar to what happens when in the state of luminosity of the primordial expanse, the appearances of the ground[37] manifest as objects. Because [their true status] is veiled by coemergent ignorance,[38] they are not recognized as the self-experience of awareness. And since, because of conceptual ignorance, they are apprehended in a dualistic manner, the cognition that discerns them evolves into an apprehending subject and an apprehended object, and the various hallucinatory appearances of the six classes of beings arise in the manner of dreams. Beings of the lowest kind wander in the three lower realms. Those of the middle order wander in the human and celestial worlds of the desire realm, while those of the highest kind wander in the form and formless realms. As it is said in the *Sum of Precious Noble Qualities*,

> All living beings low, middle, and supreme
> Arise from ignorance, the Sugata has said.

Because the ground awareness is confused by sleeplike ignorance and discursive thought, the hallucinatory appearances of the three worlds now manifest in the manner of dreams. As it is said in the *Guhyagarbha Tantra*,

> *Emaho!* Through the activity of thought,
> There arise from the sugatagarbha
> Different bodies and possessions
> And various experiences of sorrow and of joy.

Yet how, it may be asked, do they appear?

> **3. Though nonexistent, yet appearing still,**
> **Beings feel different pains and pleasures—**
> **Habits gained through long protracted time.**
> **Places, bodies, property, and more**
> **Are but their mind's experience.**
> **Joys and pains, the wages of both good and evil deeds,**
> **Resemble drawings traced in varying forms.**
> **And from one delusion many more are spawned.**
> **Apprehended thus in multiplicity,**

These false appearances arise in seamless continuity.
***Éma!* Existence is, by nature, like a dream.**

All the phenomena of saṃsāra and nirvāṇa appear clearly and yet have no existence. Because the habitual tendency to take them as truly existent things is very strong, the result is that, for each of the six classes of beings, there appear a whole variety of objects: dwelling places, bodies, possessions, joys, and sorrows. It is through the various wholesome and unwholesome actions performed through the agency of the individual mind that the multiplicity of hallucinatory appearances arises. And through the apprehension of such appearances as inherently existing there arises a continuous transmigration within saṃsāra from one existential state to another. When, on the other hand, one understands that the different kinds of action are dreamlike, one understands that phenomena too cannot be other than dream visions. As it is said in the *Sūtra of the Wise and the Foolish*,

> Wandering beings resemble dreams;
> Like dreams also are their deeds.
> The one who acts, the one who reaps the fruit—
> All of them are similar to dreams.

And other than hallucinatory appearance, there is absolutely nothing else, as now the root text tells us:

4. Within the single nature of the self-arisen mind,
Through ignorance's sleep,
A dualistic, subject-object apprehension
Of false appearances occurs.
These dream visions manifold and various
Are nothing other than the mind itself—
Illusions that arise through false perception.
This the Conqueror himself has said.

When awareness sinks momentarily into the sleep of the duality of apprehender and something apprehended, the dreamlike states of the six classes of beings occur. In all such hallucinatory samsaric appearances, there is not even an atom of a truly existent phenomenon, whether inside or outside the mind.

As it is said in the *Laṅkāvatāra-sūtra*,

> Objects are without existence; they are but the mind.
> The mind deluded by habitual tendency
> Is what indeed appears as objects.
> To see external things is a mistake.

And it is said in the *Avataṃsaka*, "*Kyé!* Offspring of the Conqueror! The three worlds are the mind alone."

Some misunderstand this text and think that the universe and the beings it contains are simply one's own mind. This is not the meaning, however. Instead, this scripture teaches that the things that appear extramentally are but the subjective experiences of one's mind; they do not exist otherwise. It also teaches that the three worlds are but the distinct groupings of the subjective experiences of beings for whom they are the common consensus. Other than that, they have no existence. The intended purpose of this statement was to refute the belief of certain śrāvakas in the real existence of sense objects outside the mind, such as material things endowed with specific characteristics. On the other hand, if all things were simply one's own mind, it would follow that when one person fell into delusion, all would be deluded, and when one person achieved liberation, all would be liberated. It would follow that all beings would be a single person. It would be impossible to have more than a single man or woman. And it would mean too that just as one's mind could know and assess an object, that same object could know and assess the mind. All such consequences would follow, as was shown in *The Great Chariot*.[39] Here, therefore, all outer appearances of any kind are considered to be simply the mind's subjective experience. They exist neither as the mind itself nor as inert matter separate from the mind. It is consequently shown that they are like dream visions that appear while being nonexistent.

In brief, all the mind's hallucinatory experiences may be referred to as "illusions of mistaken perception." As it is said in the *Longer Māyājāla Tantra*,

> All the various things appearing to the mind
> Are called illusions of erroneous perception.

There is an example that illustrates the fact that in the very moment that hallucinatory appearances are perceived, these same appearances are devoid of intrinsic being.

> **5. To those intoxicated by datura**
> **Various things appear—**
> **Hallucinations one and all.**
> **Through the intoxication likewise**
> **Of the sleep of ignorance,**
> **The six migrations manifest**
> **To the deluded mind.**
> **Now therefore you should understand:**
> **They are not truly there.**

The things seen by those who have consumed datura are regarded as false even by ordinary worldly people. In the same way, the wise should understand that the hallucinatory appearances of saṃsāra are just the products of the sleep of ignorance—which, though unreal, appear unceasingly. As it is said in the *Samādhirāja-sūtra*,

> Just as a young woman dreaming
> That she has a son who later dies
> Rejoices at his birth and mourns his death—
> Understand that all things are like this.

And in the *Questions of Kumarāprabha* it is said,

All things in their variety
Are unborn by their nature.
Insubstantial, they resemble dreams;
They have no true existence.

Thus a clear conclusion is reached that, on the level of the primordial ground, dreamlike phenomena have the character of space.

6. From deluded thought
Derives perception equally deluded,
And thence delusory appearances.
Not true, not false, not both,
Beyond the ordinary mind,
They should in truth be named
"Awarencss, self-arisen, self-cognizing."
They are without identity, without existence,
A vast expanse where all extremes subside.
Know them to be similar to space,
The wisdom mind of the Victorious Ones.

All the hallucinatory appearances of samsaric existence occur through the ingrained habit of mistaken perception. This derives from the continuum of interconnected moments of thought. The root of the appearance of the five aggregates, the eighteen constituents, and the twelve sense fields[40] is the ordinary mind's mistaken discursive activity expressed in terms of karma and defilement. The nature of the mind, on the other hand, is like space, which does not exist in any way. In effect, it is the primordial ground, as the *Uttaratantra* says:

Earth is based on water, water based on wind,
And wind indeed is based on space.

But space itself is not based on the elements
Of wind or water or of earth.

Likewise aggregates, the elements, and senses
All are based on karma and defilement.
And karma and defilement both
Depend upon the mind's improper use.

And the mind's improper use
Depends upon the mind's own purity.
But the nature of the mind itself
Does not depend on any such phenomena.[41]

Now it will be shown that saṃsāra, which appears even though it lacks intrinsic being, is primordially a state of purity and equality similar to space.

7. Things are dreamlike.
In the very moment they appear,
No intrinsic being do they have at all.
And yet their features are not lost;
To their appearance there's no hindrance.
Carefully investigate these false and momentary forms,
In every aspect empty:
They are neither false nor true,
Not existent yet not nonexistent,
Beyond all ontological extremes.
They are like space beyond both thought and word.
Know that they are pure primordially.

Like the visions of a dream, all things belonging to phenomenal existence simply appear on the conventional level; they are just empty forms, clearly appearing and yet without existence. And on the ultimate level, they transcend both truth and falsity, both existence and nonexistence. They are like space. In their failure to understand this, all beings cling to these clearly appearing and yet nonexistent forms as if they were truly real and are thus victims of false perception. Yet in the moment of being perceived, these forms do not in the slightest way move from the dharmatā, their ultimate nature. This is referred to as the "various display arising from the space-like dharmakāya, the wisdom of the sugatas." As it is said in the *Ratnolka-sūtra*,

> Phenomena are like the Sugata,
> But those with childish minds, who cling to them as real,
> Experience what has no existence in the world.
> But those trained in the view will understand.

And as it is said in the *All-Creating King*,

> All things thus, the world and living beings—
> Phenomenal existence—all are unoriginate.
> This unborn nature, you should know,
> Is that which is the all-creator.

The view of the intrinsically pure ground, which is dreamlike and objectless, has thus been established.

Now we will discuss the path, which is also dreamlike, appearing but without intrinsic being.

> **8. Thus, by means of such a view,**
> **You gain clear understanding that all things**
> **In saṃsāra and nirvāṇa are like dreams.**
> **I shall now explain how, through your meditation,**
> **You will bring this into your experience.**
> **Adopt a cross-legged posture on a pleasant seat.**
> **Take refuge and engender bodhichitta.**
> **Now think, intensely meditate,**

That in the state of emptiness,
Of perfect evenness, all things
Appear like magical illusions.

Having thus understood that phenomena are without intrinsic being, just like the things one sees in a dream, one should rest in this understanding in a state of meditative evenness. In order to do this, one should adopt a cross-legged position on a comfortable seat and in a pleasant place. One should take refuge in the Three Jewels and engender the attitude of wishing to gain enlightenment for the sake of beings. One should then reflect as follows: All phenomena, appearing in their different ways, are primordially unborn and yet in the present situation they appear. They are all the same in that from the very moment they appear, they are without real existence. According to the common vehicle, they are equal in being included in the two truths. According to the uncommon vehicle (that of Secret Mantra), they are equal in that everything that appears as the universe, the support, is the immeasurable palace of the deity, while the supported, the beings that the universe contains, are deities. By reflecting on these four ways of being equal, one should meditate that phenomena are the maṇḍala of Samantabhadra. They appear and yet are without intrinsic being, just like the visions of a dream. As it is said in the *Guhyagarbha Tantra*,

Through two equalities and two superior equalities,
[All things are] the maṇḍala of Samantabhadra's buddha field.

Subsequently, one should implement the profound path of guru yoga.

9. Then visualize above your head,
Upon the center of a lotus and on disks of sun and moon,
Amid a host of deities and ḍākinīs

Your own root teacher never separate
From the teachers of the lineage.
Make offerings and praise, and pray
That you may train successfully
In seeing all things as a dream.
Then yourself and all phenomenal existence
Dissolve in light that melts into your teacher.
Rest then for a moment in a space-like state of meditation.
Blessings, realization thus will naturally occur.

One should visualize oneself as the noble Avalokita in his four-armed form. The palms of his first two hands are joined. In his second right hand, he holds a mālā of pearls and in his second left hand he holds a white lotus. Smiling and arrayed in precious ornaments and silken robes, he is seated in cross-legged posture. In his heart, in the center of a lotus and a moon disk, the syllable HRĪ is encircled by the six-syllable mantra. The universe and beings are the body of the Great Compassionate One. All sounds are the resonance of his speech: the mantra OṂ MAṆI PADME HŪṂ HRĪ. This should be recited one hundred times, and one should then imagine that all the buddhas, bodhisattvas, and teachers of the lineage dissolve into one's own root teacher seated upon the lotus, sun, and moon disks above the crown of one's head, who then emanates and reabsorbs dense clouds of countless retinues of dākas and dākinīs. As one visualizes this, one should recite the following text three times:

In the guru, yidam, dākinī,
In the Buddha, Dharma, Saṅgha,
With respect and homage, I take refuge.
I make outer, inner, secret offerings.
My sins and obscurations I confess of body, speech, and mind,
And I rejoice in every wholesome deed.
Requesting them to turn the wheel of teaching,

I implore the buddhas not to pass beyond all sorrow.
Through this virtue may supreme enlightenment be gained.

Reciting this melodiously, one should take refuge as many times as one can in one's teacher and the Three Jewels. Then one should pray as follows:

Bless me with success in seeing everything as dreams.
Bless me that I understand that all is but illusion.
Bless me that I see the hollowness of false appearance.
Bless me that my clinging to a self disintegrates.

One then imagines that the whole of phenomenal existence dissolves into oneself and that, melting into light, one dissolves into the heart of one's teacher, who, also melting into light, mingles with space itself. Recognizing then that the empty luminosity that pervades the whole of space is the dharmakāya teacher, one should relax in this spacious experience and rest in meditation for as long as it lasts. This is a supreme source of merit. As it is said in the *Supreme and Wish-Fulfilling Bliss Tantra*,

It is far better to recall your teacher for a single instant
As a jewel to ornament the cakra in your crown
Than to meditate upon a hundred thousand deities
For as many kalpas as the grains of dust in the entire
universe.

With the completion of these preliminaries, one should remain in the meditative concentration in which all phenomena are like a dream.

10. Then meditate according to
The main part of the practice.
Tell yourself repeatedly—grow used to it—that

Outwardly, all mountains, valleys, regions, towns,
The earth, fire, water, wind, and space,
Sentient beings and the rest,
The five sense objects: form, sound, texture, smell, and taste,
And inwardly, the body, faculties of sense, and consciousness—
Are nothing more than dreams.

One should develop the skill of seeing that all phenomenal appearances are unreal. From a high position one's view is very vast, and all that one sees—all the mountains, valleys, towns, and regions, everything included in the sphere of the five outer objects of the senses, together with living beings, with their bodies, sense powers, and consciousness, and all their mental states—all these are like the visions of a dream. And just like dream visions, all such things, apart from simply appearing, have no intrinsic being. They are unreal. One should think this deeply and sincerely and grow used to it, without a single moment of distraction.

Similarly,

11. All past things occurring till today
Are mental objects, just like last night's dreams.
Today's appearances, perceived yet nonexistent,
Are but the mind's delusion.
They're just like what you dreamt about last night
And what you'll dream about tonight.
The things that will appear tomorrow
And the night that follows after
Are but dreams in store.
Remember this, that all things that appear—
The joy you want, the pain that you prevent—
Are simply dreams. Not even for an instant
Should you think them true.

Past phenomena, yesterday's perceptions, are like last night's dreams. Present phenomena, today's perceptions, are just like the dreams that will occur tonight. Future phenomena, the perceptions that are in store, are like tomorrow night's dreams. They are destitute of intrinsic being and yet they appear unceasingly. They appear and yet they are unreal. In the very moment of their perception they are simply not there. Remembering that all acceptance and rejection, all happiness and sorrow, are in no way different from the things one dreams about, one should understand that they are unreal.

Again,

12. When moving, sitting, eating, walking, speaking,
Tell yourself with undistracted mindfulness,
"It's all a dream."
Whatever may appear, whatever you may do or think,
Never lose the thought that it is but a dream.
All is without true existence,
Intangible, uncertain, evanescent,
Insubstantial, indefinable.
Train yourself in this great state
In which there's nothing to be grasped.

Wherever one may go, in whichever place one finds oneself and in no matter whose company, whatever food one may consume, whatever one may say or think, whatever one does, whatever perceptions may arise—in that very instant it is actually a dream and the dream is itself unreal. Now there is no grasping at what is unreal. Something that cannot be grasped is intangible, and what is intangible is uncertain. Something that is uncertain is evanescent, and what is evanescent is insubstantial. And whatever is insubstantial is indefinable. Reflecting that all things are without existence even though they appear clearly, one should habituate oneself to this thought without distraction and with one-pointed determination.

When one understands that an appearing sense object[42] is only a dream image, one will naturally conclude that this very object as apprehended is without intrinsic existence. Consequently, the root text goes on to say,

> **13. Through thinking that the object to be apprehended**
> **Is a dream, a false appearance,**
> **The cognition of the apprehended is removed,**
> **And the apprehender too, by implication.**
> **For if the object is negated, so too is the subject.**

It should be understood that the things that appear as the various objects of the senses are simply dreams. One should know that the first moment of cognition, which arises as the apprehended object, is a dream and that the aspect of apprehending cognition (the apprehender), which subsequently experiences that object, also manifests as a dream. Consequently, when it is understood that the apparent object [out there] is devoid of real existence, the dualistic, subject-object structure whereby the object is assessed also manifests as something unreal.[43] For if the object is negated, the subject is by implication also negated.

The root text goes on to explain that by arresting the apprehender, the apprehended is also arrested:

> **14. This mind that estimates appearances as dreams,**
> **If now and then you really search for it—**
> **Out or in or somewhere in between—**
> **There's no way to identify it,**
> **No point on which to set your bearings.**
> **There is a state of openness like boundless space.**
> **Devoid of the wild frenzy of your memories and plans,**
> **Awareness luminous and empty,**
> **Free of all conceptual construction,**
> **Arises of its own accord.**
> **When the apprehender ceases,**
> **The apprehended also is no more.**

When the subject has withdrawn,
All holding of an object vanishes.
Then there is no link with an appearing object.
The framework of discernment falls away.
Then there's simply primal wisdom,
Nondual, self-arisen.

When the mind that perceives the appearing object to be a dream is itself subjected to an inquiry as to its arising, its dwelling place, its cessation, and indeed its very identity, it is found to be a cognition that does not exist as anything at all, that is empty and free of all points of reference. Then, as the inner apprehender subsides, even though the outer appearing object continues to be perceived, it manifests as the self-experience of awareness, empty and ungraspable. This state is referred to as "primordial wisdom devoid of the duality of an apprehender and something apprehended: awareness, the enlightened mind." As it is said in the *Guhyagarbha*,

In many forms this nature shows itself,
Yet secret is its character.
It is completely secret by its very nature.

When this experience occurs, one's view and meditation transcend the ordinary mind. For they are free of the duality of apprehended and apprehender.

15. When indeed you realize
And grow used to this,
Because the apprehended and the apprehender
Are averted, the assumption
That the object and the mind are real
Subsides and an experience then arises where
There is no apprehension of appearing things
As being this or that.
All that appears arises rootless

And primordially empty.
This is the pristine fundamental nature.

The terms "apprehended" and "apprehender" here refer to the discerning cognition that apprehends the appearing object. Therefore, when these two poles of experience are no more, this is referred to as "the subsiding of the assumption that the appearing object is real." At that time, there arises an experience in which there is no apprehension of what appears as being this or that. And by one's watching the nature of this experience, there arises a state that is primordially empty, rootless, and bare: the primordial fundamental nature. This is referred to as the "vision of the exhaustion of phenomena in the ultimate nature." As it is said in the *Lotus Crown Tantra*,

> The experience of "exhaustion" is free from every object,
> Free from every apprehending thought.
> It is like the pure and open sky:
> A suchness free of center and circumference.

As one grows used to this, the hallucinatory appearance of objects and the cognitions of apprehender and apprehended related to them—the impure dependent nature, in other words—subside. There then arises the pure dependent nature and thence a freedom in the primordial expanse.[44]

16. By degrees, the apprehension
Of appearing objects as being truly this or that—
That is, impure dependent nature—is arrested
And pure dependent nature is then actualized.
It is like the vanishing of deluded dreams
At the moment when one wakes from sleep.
Then, in the primordial ground,
Manifest enlightenment occurs.

When sick people are cured of jaundice, they no longer see white conches as yellow. In the same way, when the apprehension of an appearing object as being this or that is halted, hallucinatory appearances are also halted. When one awakens from the sleep of assuming the reality of the apprehended and the apprehender, the dream of the impure dependent nature subsides. It is then that pure buddha fields appear in one's perceptions. This is the pure self-experience of one's own mind. It is like seeing a white conch shell as white. Although this outer appearance is not an experience of something other—other than one's own mind's self-experience—it is nevertheless referred to as "other," and one says accordingly that the pure dependent nature[45] is actualized. This resembles the four kinds of mastery occurring on the three pure grounds. It is said in the *Sūtrālaṃkāra*,

> Because the mind, the apprehenders, and conceptual
> thought[46]
> Are all transformed, four kinds of mastery take place—
> In nonconceptuality, in buddha fields,
> In primordial wisdom, and activities.
>
> These four kinds of mastery are gained
> On the three levels, the Immovable and upward.[47]
> On one of these, two masteries are gained,
> And one each on the other two.

Subsequently, when manifest enlightenment occurs, from the ultimate expanse that transcends both appearance and nonappearance (for these are of a single taste within the dharmakāya) the two form bodies appear spontaneously and work for the benefit of beings.

The root text goes on to show that in the very moment that hallucinatory appearance and perception manifest, they are without existence.

17. Hallucinations are not present in the past;
They are not present in the future;
It is only now that they appear.
They are perceived, yet from the moment of appearing,
They are without existence.
Nonexistent, they appear to the deluded mind
According to its habits.
And yet by nature they're primordially pure.
They resemble dreams.

The hallucinatory appearances of saṃsāra have no existence in the primordial expanse. Neither do they exist at the end when freedom is gained. In the present moment, when self-experience of awareness within the ultimate expanse is misperceived, such appearances seem truly to exist, and yet in the very moment of being perceived, they have no existence either as things singular or plural. They are simply clear appearances of what does not exist. It is because they appear to the mind as existing things—even though they are destitute of such existence—that they are referred to as hallucinatory appearances or perceptions. They are like things seen in a dream.

But how, one may ask, are they similar to dreams?

18. When you are not sleeping, when you are awake,
The things appearing in your dreams do not exist.
Only in your sleep do they occur.
And in the moment they appear, they have no real existence.
In just the same way, you should understand,
The nonexistent things that yet appear
Have neither ground nor root.

An object of desire that one dreams of is present neither at the moment when one goes to bed nor at the moment when one wakes. It appears to one only while one is asleep. In the same way, although the hallucinatory appearances and perceptions [of samsaric existence] have no existence either at the time of the ground or at the moment of the result, they nevertheless appear now at the time of the path. But even now, while they are being perceived, all such hallucinatory experiences are completely without any real ground or root. One should understand that they are mere empty reflections. As it is said in the *Samādhirāja-sūtra*,

> People yearning for the things they crave
> Behold such objects even in their dreams.
> They then enjoy them but must lose them when they wake.
> Understand that all things are like this.

We now come to an explanation of the night practice for those who have grown used to seeing everything as dreamlike.

> **19. Meditating strongly in this way by day,**
> **At night as you are sinking into sleep,**
> **Upon a comfortable bed, stretch out on your right side**
> **As the Lord lay down before he passed beyond all sorrow.**
> **Breathing very slowly and with steady gaze,**
> **Visualize within your heart a crystal sphere**
> **In which there is a letter *A*.**
> **White in color and ablaze with light,**
> **It is the size of your own thumb,**
> **Becoming ever smaller as you concentrate on it.**
> **Without distraction, bear in mind that it is like a dream.**
> **In this way, dreamlike luminosity will manifest.**

When one has, during the day, trained assiduously and with success in regarding everything as a dream, one should lie down relaxed in the posture of a sleeping lion. One should breathe very slowly so that the movement of the breath is no longer felt. With eyes open and with a steady gaze, one should visualize in one's heart a white letter *A* brightly shining with rays of light that emanate and then are gathered back. One should concentrate on this letter, which at first is the size of your thumb and becomes smaller and smaller until it is the size of a single horsehair. Remembering that this is itself a dream, one falls asleep. For those whose concentration is stable, a limpid and clear state of luminosity devoid of center and circumference will arise. Those whose concentration is not yet stable will find that their dreams will become clearer than before and that it will be easy for them to recognize their dreams for what they are. By means of such a practice,

> **20. At first, when you have frightening nightmares,**
> **Recall that they are dreams.**
> **Your fear will dissipate at once.**
> **To recognize one's dreams as dreams**
> **Is to be concentrated, it is said,**
> **While in the state of dreaming.**
> **This practitioners should understand.**

When in the course of dreaming one finds oneself in dangerous situations, such as walking along a precipice, being caught in avalanches, confronted by mastiffs or enemies, and one knows them to be dreams, this is defined as the achievement of a concentration based on keen aspiration, whereby dreams are for the first time recognized as dreams. Such an accomplishment is the supreme antidote whereby every kind of fear is overcome. When one is able to recognize one's dreams as dreams,

> **21. Train then to recognize that all dreams are unreal.**
> **Appearances of things without existence**
> **Are no more than the mind's delusion,**
> **Dreamlike and ungraspable.**
> **Since they are neither true nor false,**
> **Know then that they transcend the reach of ordinary mind.**

The dissipation of one's fear that comes through the recognition that one is dreaming is not, of course, enough. One must understand that all dreams are unreal. One should reflect that just as dreams are unreal, so too are all phenomena, for they appear while being nonexistent. As it is said in the sūtra entitled *Ornament of the Light of Wisdom*, "Dream visions, O Mañjuśrī, are perceived and yet have no existence. Likewise all phenomena are perceived and yet do not exist."

It is of the highest importance to understand the unreality of dreams [while one is dreaming]. Therefore, to begin with, the following training is prescribed:

> **22. Concerning the assumption and the transformation**
> **Of a form while dreaming,**
> **Assume the form of Brahmā, of the Buddha,**
> **Of a bodhisattva, or of something else**
> **According to your wish.**
> **Thus train yourself and place yourself**
> **Within their unreality.**

By assuming thus the form of a buddha, a bodhisattva, a śrāvaka, a pratyekabuddha, a world-protecting ruler, or a peaceful or wrathful deity, one should come to the understanding that it is [precisely] because such forms are unreal that they can appear.

Then comes the transformation of these forms.

> **23. Then in successive moments change your form,**
> **According to your wish, from Brahmā into Indra,**
> **Or else from a divine into a human being.**
> **Meditate upon the unreality of all such forms.**

Telling oneself that since all such manifestations are able to transform into each other, they are themselves without true existence, one should transform them according to one's wish.

Finally, there comes the increase of such forms.

24. Then multiply all such appearances
A hundred- or a thousand- or a millionfold.
Train yourself in mastery of antidotes
That subdue all that is to be subdued.

One should then multiply these assumed and subsequently transformed appearances a hundredfold or a thousandfold. One should change them all into a single form or change a single form into many—training oneself thoroughly in their lack of real existence. One should transform oneself into a garuḍa (an enemy of the nāgas) or into Hayagrīva (the bane of the *gyalpo* and *senmo* spirits), subduing them by soaring or devouring. This is an extraordinary ancillary cause for the acquisition of various powers and for the ability to display miracles.

Now if in the course of this, one's body becomes twisted, contracted, or swollen, this occurs through the dislocation of the channels and winds, through a failure to gain mastery of the processes of the assumption and transformation of one's form. When this happens, one should lie down comfortably, breathe slowly, and allow one's awareness to clarify. This is a crucial point for gaining experience [in the mastery of one's dreams].

When the training in the unreality of one's dreams is complete, the root text goes on to say,

25. Then you may journey in your dreams
To pure fields, various lands and realms,
To Akaniṣṭha and wherever you may wish.
And there you will behold the sugatas,
Listen to their stainless words, and train yourself
In wisdom, concentration, clouds of dhāraṇīs.
Through your training thus with mindfulness
Continually both day and night,
All this will come to pass,
For this is the unfailing quality of your awareness,
Which thus will be made manifest.

All this is the essential pith
Of teachings most profound.

Having successfully trained in the assumption and transformation of one's form while in the dream state, one may wish to see other countries, the dwellings of the nāgas and the devas, the other cosmic continents, and Sukhāvatī and the other buddha fields, places where one has never been before. During the daytime one should nourish a keen aspiration and wish to visit them, and at night one should adopt the posture for falling asleep as was mentioned above. And reflecting that all regions and all worlds are present within the cakra of enjoyment in one's own throat, and that the entire three thousandfold universe is as it were inserted into a tiny grain, one should fall asleep without being distracted from such a thought. So it is that one will behold whatever one wishes. Such visions depend upon a single key point: from the very beginning, awareness is endowed with every perceivable quality.

At this time too, it is important to habituate oneself to the unreality of all such things. This unreality is the same thing as the absence of intrinsic existence, which itself is synonymous with the transcendent perfection of wisdom. Through one's training in it, all excellent qualities will be accomplished. As it is said in the *Abridged Prajñāpāramitā*,

> The perfect realization of the lack of real existence in all things
> Is transcendent wisdom, so the Conqueror has said.

And in the *Middle-Length Prajñāpāramitā* it is said,

> If you wish to look upon the pure buddha fields that in every respect exceed the dwellings of the gods and humankind, you should train in the perfection of wisdom. If you wish to place the great thousandfold universe inside a tiny grain without thinking that this tiny

> grain grows bigger or that the universe contracts, simply train in the perfection of wisdom.

This is the very essence of the path and should be regarded as the highest yoga of the Mahāyāna.

Now follows a description of the result achieved through the meditation in which everything is seen to be a dream:

> **26. Meditating thus by day and night**
> **Upon your dreams,**
> **You will escape the snare**
> **Of thinking that phenomena are truly real.**
> **Through fences, walls, and mountains**
> **You will pass unhindered.**
> **You will gain unnumbered wondrous powers,**
> **Clairvoyance, concentrations.**
> **Innumerable experiences you'll have and realizations,**
> **And sublime primordial wisdom will arise.**

The result of primordial wisdom gained at such a point is that, truly established on the path to liberation, one will gain all that one desires, and one will be cared for by ḍākas and ḍākinīs endowed with accomplishment. Maintaining good health, one will not be troubled by many illnesses. Completing the path of accumulation, one will easily realize that phenomena are without intrinsic being and with concentration one will meditate on it. When one completes the path of joining, one will have a mastery of miraculous powers and the experience of many kinds of preternatural knowledge.[48] Signs will appear indicating that one has fully understood the dreamlike quality of phenomena, and one will accomplish the qualities of a stable virtue. As it is said in the *Abhisamayālaṃkāra* [regarding the stages of warmth and peak of the path of joining],

> Even in one's dreams are all things seen as dreams.
> Twelve signs are said to indicate

That one has gained the culmination of the training.
And if one takes as an example
All the virtue gained from making offerings
To as many buddhas as beings who live in Jambudvīpa,
The increase of the merit is sixteenfold.[49]

As one trains progressively, the sublime nonconceptual primordial wisdoms of the paths of seeing and meditation—not achieved hitherto—are gained, and the path of no more learning is subsequently actualized.

27. You will come at last
To the primordial expanse, the nature of the mind,
And gain the dreamlike twofold goal:
The dharmakāya for your own sake
And the rūpakāya for the sake of others.
Meditate therefore that all is like a dream.

Through training on the dreamlike path to enlightenment, the dreamlike final result will appear although it lacks intrinsic being: the perfection of all the qualities of elimination and realization of buddhahood.[50] As it is said in the sūtras,

> The roots of virtue are like illusions and dreams. The thirty-seven factors leading to enlightenment[51] are also like illusions and dreams. And omniscient primordial wisdom is also like an illusion and a dream.

When one's own aim has been accomplished, namely, the sky-like expanse of the dharmakāya, it is through its spontaneous cognitive power that the two rūpakāyas or form bodies will manifest for others like the sun and moon and benefit them for as long as saṃsāra lasts.

As the *Uttaratantra* tells us,

The Knower of the World in great compassion
Looks on those within the world
And, without stirring from the dharmakāya,
Manifests in various emanations.

He takes birth in Tuṣita
And from that realm comes down
And, entering a womb, takes birth.
He grows in skill in all the arts,

Delighting in the company of queens.
He then renounces all and practices austerities.
Going to the seat of his enlightenment,
He subjugates the māras and achieves complete
enlightenment.

He turns the wheel of Dharma
And passes to the state beyond all sorrow.
These then are the deeds the Buddha demonstrates
In impure fields, as long as this saṃsāra lasts.[52]

In conclusion,

May all the dreamlike beings in saṃsāra
Who strayed from their primordially pure nature
Gain freedom from the four great streams of sorrow.
May they reach the state endowed
With all the qualities of great bliss.

May I be a guide for all without exception
And lead them from saṃsāra,
This great empty, dreamlike form,
This mighty ocean difficult to cross,
This mass of suffering's fire that reaches
Even to the summit of existence.

This concludes the chapter that is like a dream, a commentary on the first vajra point of *Finding Rest in Illusion, a Teaching of the Great Perfection.*

The Second Vajra Point: Magical Illusion

Phenomena are thus revealed as being, in their dreamlike nature, devoid of origin. The root text then explains that they should be understood as a mere, unceasing, illusory display.

1. And thereto also did the Conqueror declare
That all things are like magical illusions,
Explaining that they lack intrinsic being.
Listen! I shall tell you how I have experienced
This quintessential teaching
Of the sūtras, tantras, and the pith instructions.

We find in the *Middle-Length Prajnapāramitā*, "Phenomena are like magical illusions.[53] They are not born; they do not cease. They do not come; they do not go." As it is said in the sūtra entitled the *Irreversible Wheel*,

Things resemble magical illusions.
Even buddhahood is like a magical illusion.

We also find in the tantra entitled the *Terrifying Lightning of Wisdom*,

All these illusion-like phenomena
Are merely names. They're empty of intrinsic being.

This is taught in many of the sūtras and the tantras. On the basis of three kinds of evidence that occurred in my own experience, which itself unfolded in the light of my teacher's pith instructions, I shall speak of magical illusion classified according to ground, path, and result.

First, the root text explains how hallucinatory appearances occur within the illusion of the ground, a state similar to space:

2. The primordial nature of the mind
Is a spacious, sky-like state
Where primal wisdom is like sun and moon and stars.
And yet when there occurs within this womb of space—
The wondrous sphere of emptiness—
A state of ignorance, conceptualization, dualistic clinging,
The hallucinations of the three worlds
And the six migrations manifest
In the manner of a magical illusion.

The nature of the mind, the self-arisen primordial wisdom, is primordially pure and space-like. Within this state, which does not exist as anything at all, there move the five winds, of which the life-supporting wind is the root.[54] This leads to the manifestation of the self-experience of awareness in the state of luminosity. When this is not recognized, it is misapprehended as an outer universe together with its inner contents, including one's own body. All this appears variously as a mere magical illusion. As it is said in the tantra entitled the *Mirror of Vajrasattva's Heart*, "In various ways, the beings of the three worlds stray from the ground, which in itself is nothing at all."

But how do these hallucinatory appearances, which are like magical illusions, occur? The root text goes on to say,

3. They appear spontaneously, through the power
Of interdependent causes and conditions—
Just as when a piece of wood or little stone

Is conjured through an incantation
And there appears a magical display,
A horse, an ox, a man or woman,
A mountain or a palace, and the rest.

When a magical illusion is created of horses, oxen, and so on, there is a material cause, namely, a piece of wood or a pebble, and also a condition for the illusion, that is to say, the visual consciousness manipulated through the magic spell. On this basis, a hallucinatory experience of horses and oxen is produced. This manifests as the subjective experience of the mind, arising through the interdependent conjunction of causes and conditions. The hallucinatory appearances of saṃsāra are similar to this.

4. Deluded mind and its habitual tendencies,
Phenomenal existence, the objects of the senses
And the three poisons that fixate on them—
All these occur because of ignorance.
Devoid of real existence, they all appear unceasingly.
They are like conjured apparitions.
From now on be convinced
That they are empty, false reflections.

The underlying cause for all this is awareness itself. The condition, on the other hand, is ignorance, owing to which, awareness is distorted by the duality of the [subjective] apprehender and the apprehended (which thus becomes the object). It is thus that hallucinatory appearances, the universe and its animate contents, appear differently for different kinds of beings. Because of the three poisons, the various realms of saṃsāra, high and low, are experienced and seem real. But it should be understood that in fact they are nothing but false appearances—empty reflections—and that within awareness, the enlightened mind, there is no movement or change. The *Samādhirāja-sūtra* says,

Just as in the midst of crowds,
The forms displayed by a magician—
Horses, oxen, chariots, and the like—
Appear in various forms yet lack reality,
Understand that all things are like this.

And as the root text goes on to say, the illusions that appear while lacking all intrinsic being are like space.

5. Sure it is that all things in phenomenal existence,
In saṃsāra and nirvāṇa,
Are in their nature equal and they all resemble space.
Understand that all are unborn,
Pure from the beginning.

All phenomena are by their nature devoid of existence. In themselves, they are like space. The *Middle-Length Prajñāpāramitā* says, "In themselves, phenomena are like space. One can find in them no center and no boundary." And likewise we find in the *Samādhirāja-sūtra*,

All things disintegrate, O Son of the Victorious One,
All existents are primordially empty.
Extremists hold a lesser emptiness.
But there is no debate between the learned and the childish.

In this regard, some say that phenomena are empty by virtue of a preclusion of something that they do not possess[55] but that they are not empty of themselves.[56] This is like saying that the sun is empty of darkness but is not empty of rays of light. This is a lesser kind of emptiness, however, through which no freedom would ever be possible from the belief in the true existence of things. Examined according to the argument of "neither one nor many," the sun is empty of inherent existence; being thus, it is also empty of rays of light. It is empty and yet it appears. This is the very principle and essence of Madhyamaka, the Middle Way. As the *Bodhicittavivaraṇa* says,

> As fire is by its nature hot
> And treacle by its nature sweet,
> So too are all phenomena
> Said to be empty by their nature.

The *Prajñāpāramitā-sūtra* says, "Form is empty of form itself." And the shorter commentary on the *Abhisamayālaṃkāra* declares,

> Since of its very nature every thing is empty,
> It's said that there are twenty kinds of emptiness.

But the fact of being empty does not imply that phenomena are nothing at all. For emptiness is inseparable from appearance. Therefore in emptiness, all phenomena are tenable. It is as Nāgārjuna has said,

> Where emptiness is granted
> Everything is likewise granted.[57]

Emptiness has many divisions. For example, there is the emptiness of mutual exclusion (as a pillar is empty of being a pot); there is the emptiness of what is not possessed (as in the case of "thing" being empty of "nonthing"); there is the emptiness of specific characteristics (as in the case of rabbit's horns); and there is emptiness of an intrinsic nature (as in the case of a reflection). All these, however, are no more than the asseverations of philosophers. But here we say that all things in phenomenal existence, in saṃsāra and nirvāṇa, even though they appear to the mind, are, in their own nature, nonexistent. They should be understood as being primordially empty—empty in transcending all ontological extremes. As it is said in the *Laṅkāvatāra-sūtra*,

Since all things, each and every one,
Are by their nature unoriginate,
They are like space devoid of substance
And stainless in their emptiness.

We also find in the tantra named *Questions of Subāhu*,

Phenomena are like reflections—
Clear, unsullied, pure,
Ungraspable, ineffable.
Without intrinsic being, they have no abiding.

When one has ascertained that phenomena are empty, one may well go on to ask how saṃsāra manifests within the expanse of emptiness, and how one is to train upon the path, and what is freedom like when one reaches the end of the path.

First the root text gives an answer to this in summary form:

6. Within the nature unoriginate,
Wherein origination manifests,
The illusion of the character [of luminosity]
Is the ground of purification;
The illusion of impurity
Is the stain that should be purified;
The illusion of the skillful method
Is the purifying remedy;
The illusion of primordial wisdom
Is the perfected fruit.
Through the illusion of an example,
The other four are proved with certainty.

Thus it is briefly explained. Now those who are learned bring others to a state of understanding by means of examples. There are four kinds of illusion (that of luminous character and so on), and these occur in four situations: the ultimate pure expanse, the state of straying from this, the purification of delusion, and the perfected result. And so that these four kinds of illusion may be understood, I will first explain their meaning through the illusion of an example [mentioned at the end of the stanza] and will then ascertain the definition of each of them. This example is as follows:

7. By means of an enchantment,
A magical display arises:
A stick and stone appear in form of horse and ox.
Yet at that time the stick and stone themselves
Are neither horse nor ox.
By this example, you should see
That all things, marked by lack of true existence,
Are in themselves but magical displays.
The basis of delusion,
The conditions for delusion and the mode thereof,
The occurrence of delusion as well as its subsiding,
And freedom from delusion in the primal ground—
These correspond respectively to stick and stone,
To the chanting and the working of the spell,
To production of the horse and ox,
Their vanishing, and then the reemergence
Of the stick and stone as previously they were.
By this example thus are step by step explained
The four stages of illusion.

The awareness of the ground of delusion[58] is the illusion of [luminous] character.[59] Delusion is not intrinsically present in the ground, but since coemergent ignorance may occur in relation to the ground of delusion, it is possible for delusion to arise, in the same way that although the horse or ox is not perceived [in a stick or stone], it is nevertheless always possible for it to be so—to use the terms of the example given earlier. When awareness rises up from the ultimate expanse as the appearance of the ground, conceptual ignorance manifests as the root of the dualistic structure of apprehended and apprehender. This produces the illusion of impurity (illusory impurity), the stain that is to be purified. Awareness is now obscured by deluded thoughts; this being so, it is in the form of these thoughts that hallucinatory appearances occur, even though they are not actually present. Then, when these hallucinatory appearances are actually perceived, awareness is altered by the duality of apprehended and apprehender, and consequently various forms manifest as the mind's subjective experience. It is just as when, through the operation of the spell, the actual magical illusion is produced and the stick and stone appear as a horse and an ox.[60]

Subsequently, as one trains in awareness while on the path, the assumption of the true existence of phenomena is curtailed, and this happens through the illusion of skillful means. This corresponds to the ending of the illusory magical charm. Finally, deluded thoughts come to an end, as a result of which hallucinatory appearances and perceptions cease. This is freedom in the primordial state, which occurs when awareness returns to the primordial ground. And this is the illusion of primordial wisdom. The spell, which is the ignorance producing the duality of apprehended and apprehender, is arrested. And the hallucinatory samsaric appearances of horses and oxen consequently cease. And just as the stick and stone reappear when the illusion is dissipated, in the self-experience of awareness there manifest the kāyas and wisdoms, which are the "genuine form" of the ground. This constitutes the immovable, immutable realization, from which there can be no further change. It corresponds to the stick and stone that reappear when the magical illusion is destroyed. This passage reveals the difficult points of the tantras' immensely powerful vajra words.

Now that the correspondence between the example and the four kinds of illusion has been demonstrated, a definition of each of the latter is given. First,

8. The illusion of the "character,"
The mind's luminous nature,

Is the ultimate expanse,
The sugatagarbha, ground of cleansing.

Awareness, the enlightened mind, is present from the very beginning, spontaneous and unconditioned. It pervades the whole of saṃsāra and nirvāṇa without diminution or increase, without becoming smaller or greater. As it is said in the *Candrapradīpa-sūtra*, "The sugatagarbha pervades all beings." And we find in the *Uttaratantra*,

Because the kāya of perfect buddhahood is all-pervading,
Because in suchness there is no division,
Because they have potential for enlightenment,
All beings have at all times buddha essence.[61]

The sugatagarbha is sheer luminosity, primordial and immaculate. As the *Prajñāpāramitā in Eight Thousand Lines* declares, "As for the mind, the mind does not exist. The nature of the mind is luminosity." And as we find in the *Two-Part Hevajra Tantra*,

Beings indeed are buddhas,
And yet they are obscured by adventitious veils.
When these have been discarded, they are buddhas.

And the *Pramāṇavārttika* says,

The nature of the mind is luminosity.
The stains on it are adventitious.

In the condition of sentient beings, the buddha-element, or sugatagarbha, is the defiled buddha-element. This same element, in the condition of the bodhisattvas, is both pure and impure. At the time of buddhahood, it is completely pure. And yet, although it is qualified in these three different ways, in itself it remains unchanging either for better or for worse. It is said in the *Uttaratantra*,

As impurity, impurity-and-purity,
And utter purity
Are described respectively
Beings, bodhisattvas, tathāgatas.[62]

And in the *Sūtrālaṃkāra* it is also said,

This suchness is in every being
Without distinction, and yet when it is purified,
[It is tathāgata.]

And,

As it was before, so later it will be.
It is unchanging suchness.

The root text describes the buddha-element, the sugatagarbha, the nature of self-cognizing awareness as follows:

9. Since it is not divided
Into pure and impure,
It's beyond saṃsāra and the state beyond all pain.
It is the space wherein these different states arise,
The basis whence they manifest
According as one knows or fails to know it as it is.
The sugatagarbha is the primal ground,
The fundamental nature.

Awareness is, in its own nature, neither saṃsāra nor nirvāṇa, for in it there is nothing to be either accomplished or eliminated. As we find in the *Ratnakūṭa*, "O Kāśyapa, the ultimate expanse, completely pure by nature, is neither saṃsāra nor nirvāṇa. For it is not a truly existing thing." Within this nature, which does not exist as anything at all, there is a radiance that supplies the ground for unceasing manifestation. If this radiance is recognized for what it is, nirvāṇa ensues; if it is not recognized, the hallucinatory appearances of saṃsāra, which are like magical illusions, arise. As it is said in the *Songs of Realization*,

> The nature of the mind is the sole seed of everything.
> Existence and nirvāṇa both emerge from it.

The root text then gives an example of how—because it does not exist as anything at all—awareness provides the basis for the arising of anything at all:

> **10. It is like a limpid looking glass,**
> **The base for the arising of reflected forms,**
> **Which, in the moment when such forms appear,**
> **Does not exist as any one of them.**
> **The surface of the glass**
> **Is neither white nor black,**
> **Yet it provides the base**
> **In which both white and black appear.**
> **Awareness is like this.**
> **And knowing this, you will be skilled in everything.**

The pure surface of a mirror does not exist as any of the reflections that appear in it. Yet it is the ground upon which all such reflections appear. And although what appears in it may be white or black, the surface of the mirror is not so. Thanks to such an example, one should understand that awareness, which is similar to a reflecting surface, does not exist as anything at all and yet it provides the basis for the appearance of every kind of manifestation. In the very moment that appearances arise, whether of saṃsāra or of nirvāṇa, awareness itself is not stained or colored by them. It is therefore said of hallucinatory appearances that even though they do arise, awareness is not stained by them, provided it is not impaired by one's clinging to such appearances. Practitioners who are beyond the acceptance and rejection of sense objects are said to be "great yogis skilled in the natural flow of awareness." It is as the mighty yogi Tilopa has said,

> Appearance does not fetter you; clinging to it does.
> Therefore cut your clinging, Nāropa.

And as Śāntideva has proclaimed,

> It's not indeed our purpose to disprove
> Experience of sight or sound or knowing.
> Our aim is here to undermine the cause of sorrow:
> The thought that such phenomena have true existence.[63]

The second [of the four kinds of] illusion is the illusion to be purified.

> **11. Impure illusions are the false appearance**
> **And perception of saṃsāra—**
> **Occurring through our taking**
> **Dualistically what is nondual.**

The hallucinatory appearances of the universe and beings, together with deluded thought patterns, are the stains that obscure the sphere of luminosity, which has the nature of awareness. These deluded thought patterns are the cause, true origins, whence there arises the result, true sufferings [the hallucinatory appearances].[64]

The third kind of illusion is the illusion of the purification of these stains.

> **12. The illusion then of skillful means**
> **Thus constitutes the path of remedies.**
> **On the four paths of accumulation,**
> **Joining, seeing, meditation,**
> **The two accumulations**
> **And the practice of two stages**

Constitute the means of cleansing.
The stains that should be cleansed
Are thereby swept away like clouds.

The practice of the basic level on the path of accumulation is the implementation of the four close mindfulnesses. The practice of the middle level is the implementation of the four genuine restraints, while training in the four bases of miraculous power is the practice of the greater level. On the path of joining, the five powers are applied through the stages of warmth and peak, while the five irresistible forces are applied on the stages of acceptance and the supreme mundane level. On the path of seeing, one implements the seven elements leading to enlightenment, and on the path of meditation, one follows the eightfold noble path.[65] Therefore, all together, one implements the thirty-seven elements leading to enlightenment, the two accumulations of merit and of wisdom, and the two stages of generation and perfection. It is thus that one journeys along the path to suchness. Since this system of paths and grounds of realization is so important, I shall supply a rough explanation of it taken from the sūtras.[66]

As it is said in the *Sūtra of Dṛdhramati*,

> Once Dṛdhramati asked the Buddha, "Lord, how is one to meditate on the four close mindfulnesses?"
>
> And the Lord replied and said, "Bodhisattvas, O Dṛdhramati, should meditate with close mindfulness upon their bodies. How should they do this? They should examine separately how this body began in the past, how it will end in the future, and how it is in the present. Alas, this body, having arisen from causes and conditions, is impermanent and changing like a magical illusion. Bodhisattvas should not regard their bodies as their property. Instead, they should give essential meaning to these bodies of theirs, which in themselves are bereft of such essential meaning. Now, how are they

to give their bodies an essential meaning? They do so by practicing in such a way as to acquire the body of a tathāgata. This is the meaning of the close mindfulness of the body.

"Now what, you may ask, O Dṛdhramati, is the meaning of close mindfulness of one's feelings? Of all the feelings that may occur, there are those that are pleasant and that make one happy. There are those that are unpleasant and that make one sad. Finally, there are those that are neutral and that leave one indifferent. I for my part have trained in seeing them as being like illusions without intrinsic existence. And I set forth the Dharma so that beings may sever the stream of their feelings. Why so? Because happiness arises when the nature of feeling is understood; suffering arises when its nature is misunderstood. Therefore, when one understands that the feelings regarding all one's concerns, all one's cogitations, and all that is labeled as phenomena are but magical illusions, this is the close mindfulness of feeling.

"Now what, O Dṛdhramati, is the close mindfulness of the mind? States of mind, having arisen, must cease; they are impermanent. The attitude of the enlightened mind, which I generated in the beginning, does not stay. It does not abide anywhere. So it is that the mind cannot see the mind. The character of the mind is to be like a magical illusion. Magical illusions are themselves deprived of any truly existent characteristics. Since the mind too is deprived of any truly existent characteristics, you should not cling to it. This is the close mindfulness of the mind.

"Now what, O Dṛdhramati, is the close mindfulness of phenomena? Phenomena are empty; they are devoid of characteristics and are beyond all expectation.[67] One cannot find even an atom of a truly existent phenomenon. The nature of phenomena is perfectly perceived when one pauses and observes phenomena. On the other hand, one will not perceive such a nature in something that is not a phenomenon. Regarding what is known as the close mindfulness of phenomena, we may speak as follows. The manifold things that the Buddha designated as such are mere names. Neither things nor names are to be found either in the mind or in the extramental world. No ontological extreme is found in them. Thus they are beyond the ontological extremes; they lack intrinsic being. Such is the close mindfulness of phenomena."

Then Dṛdhramati asked, "How is one to understand the four genuine restraints?" And the Lord answered, saying,

"Dṛdhramati, there are four genuine restraints on the path of the bodhisattva. In order not to generate sin and nonvirtue that have not yet arisen, this path consists in cultivating keen interest and perseverance, in being diligent, and in perfectly focusing and settling one's mind.

"In order to dispel sin and nonvirtue when these have arisen, this path consists in cultivating keen interest and perseverance, in being diligent, and in perfectly focusing and settling one's mind.

"In order to generate positive states that have not yet arisen, the bodhisattva path consists in cultivating keen interest and perseverance, in being diligent, and in perfectly focusing and settling one's mind.

"In order to generate positive states when these have arisen, to stabilize them when they have arisen, to intensify them when they have been stabilized, and to prevent them from decline and from being dissipated, the bodhisattva path consists in cultivating keen interest and perseverance, in being diligent, and in perfectly focusing and settling one's mind.

"Dṛdhramati, the phenomena referred to as sin and nonvirtue are all the factors that run counter to discipline, concentration, and wisdom. The factors that run counter to discipline are discipline that has declined and anything that provokes its decline. The factors that run counter to concentration are whatever provokes mental distraction and impairs concentration. The factors that run counter to wisdom are states whereby the mind is utterly obscured and which arise through perverse views and through clinging to the supremacy of one's beliefs.

"And in order to reject all such nonvirtuous phenomena, the proper mental activity consists in cultivating keen interest and perseverance, in being diligent, and in perfectly focusing and settling one's mind. This is the first genuine restraint.

"Moreover, the phenomena labeled nonvirtuous are desirous attachment, angry hatred, and ignorant stupidity. These are the causes whence all negativities arise. The proper and appropriate mental activity is to remove attachment through reflection on the impurity [of the object], to remove hatred through love, and to remove ignorance through the understanding of dependent origination. The understanding of [the nature] of each of these defilements leads to their removal, thanks to which all that has been removed will no longer be found. This then is the second genuine restraint.

"In order to generate positive states not yet arisen, the cultivation of keen interest and perseverance has been mentioned, together with diligence, perfect focus, and the settling of the mind. To practice with keenness and mental focus on the boundless positive states to be accomplished is the root of all virtuous deeds. This is the third genuine restraint.

"In order to stabilize all the positive states already arisen and to prevent them from decline and from being dissipated, one should dedicate them to the attainment of enlightenment. Why? Because when the roots of virtue do not remain confined within the three worlds but are dedicated to the attainment of omniscience, they will never be exhausted. This is the fourth genuine restraint."

Dṛdhramati then asked, "Lord, how is one to understand the four bases of miraculous power, the 'four miraculous legs'?" And the Lord answered and said,

"Dṛdhramati, the bodhisattva path has four 'miraculous legs.' And what are these four? There is the miraculous leg of concentration endowed with the factor of keenness that eliminates what is contrary [to concentration]. There is the miraculous leg of concentration endowed with the factor of endeavor that eliminates what is contrary [to concentration]. There is the miraculous leg of concentration endowed with the factor of one-pointed mindfulness that eliminates what is contrary [to concentration]. And there is the miraculous leg of concentration endowed with the factor of conduct[68] that eliminates what is contrary [to concentration].

"Dṛdhramati, phenomena are not real; they are like magical illusions. Now regarding such phenomena, which are nowhere to be found or apprehended, one will feel neither animosity nor fear. On the contrary, one will feel joy, happiness, and keenness. This is the concentration based on keenness.

"Dṛdhramati, those who have the keenness of one-pointed faith will abandon all exertion in mundane matters and, resisting all that causes indolence, will cultivate endeavor. This is the concentration based on endeavor.

"Dṛdhramati, those who cultivate continuous endeavor will not find their minds anywhere. They will rest one-pointedly in luminosity, the nature of their minds. This is the concentration based on one-pointed mindfulness.

"Dṛdhramati, those who have one-pointed concentration will at all times act with concentration, whether they are walking, moving, sitting, or lying down. And this is the concentration based on conduct.

"Dṛdhramati, how is it that these concentrations are referred to as 'miraculous legs'? It is because these concentrations cause one to abandon everything that is wrong and, having done so, to act with probity and to accomplish excellence, and because they therefore cause one to progress along the path, that they are referred to as 'miraculous legs.'"

Then Dṛdhramati asked, "What, O Lord, are the five powers?" And the Lord answered and said,

"Dṛdhramati, the bodhisattva path has five powers. And what are these five? They are the power of faith, the power of diligence, the power of mindfulness, the power of concentration, and the power of wise discernment.

"What is the power of faith or confidence? It is to be profoundly confident in the correct worldly view regarding conduct in saṃsāra. This means to be apprehensive about the fully ripened effects of one's acts and thus to avoid negative actions even at the cost of one's life; it means to engage in the ways of a bodhisattva; it means to have joy and confidence untroubled by doubt when one hears about emptiness, the absence of characteristics, and the absence of expectation, and when one hears about the qualities of a buddha, such as the ten strengths and the four fearlessnesses. This is the power of faith or confidence.

"What is the power of diligence? It is to develop the power of diligence with regard to the teachings and their implementation—this is the power of diligence.

"What is the power of mindfulness? It is, through the power of mindfulness, not to allow the teachings gathered through one's diligence to go to waste—this is the power of mindfulness.

"What is the power of concentration? It is to be free of distraction and to concentrate one-pointedly on the teachings that, through the power of mindfulness, have not been wasted—this is the power of concentration.

"What is the power of wise discernment? It is to examine with wisdom the teachings on which one is one-pointedly concentrated and to understand that phenomena, like magical illusions, have no real existence—this is the power of wise discernment."

Dṛdhramati then asked, "Lord, what are the five irresistible forces?" And the Lord replied and said,

"Dṛdhramati, there are five irresistible forces on the bodhisattva path: the irresistible force of faith or confidence, the irresistible force of diligence, the irresistible force of mindfulness, the irresistible force of concentration, and the irresistible force of wise discernment.

"What is the irresistible force of faith or confidence? It is not to allow yourself to be deterred from the object of your faith and aspiration by anyone at all. Indeed, if a demon appeared in the guise of the Buddha himself and tried to influence you and turn you away from such an object, declaring it to be nonvirtuous and wrong, he would be powerless to make you separate from it and forsake it. It would be easier for the great elements to be changed into something else than for you, endowed with the force of faith, to be turned from the object of your devotion. That indeed is the irresistible force of faith.

"What is the irresistible force of diligence? It is to exert yourself in any of the virtuous practices with a steadfast force—in such a way that, until it has been accomplished, nothing can turn you from it. That is the irresistible force of diligence.

"What is the irresistible force of mindfulness? When you are closely mindful of something, your mind cannot be distracted from it and cannot be overwhelmed by defilement. Since all defilements are vanquished by this power of mindfulness, one speaks of the irresistible force of mindfulness.

"What is the irresistible force of concentration? When you have mindfulness and carefulness, you are never overwhelmed by defilement and wherever you may be, you will be preserved from distracting activities. You will not have an attitude of clinging to sense objects such as form, and you will not be preoccupied with such phenomena. When you are free from thoughts regarding any phenomenon, a force is acquired that preserves you from all distracting activities. One speaks then of the irresistible force of concentration.

"What is the irresistible force of wise discernment? When, through the force of wisdom a complete knowledge has been gained of all worldly and transworldly phenomena, you will be able to liberate beings from saṃsāra. Since such liberation derives from the force of wise discernment and primordial wisdom, one speaks of the irresistible force of wise discernment.

"Why, finally, does one speak of the five irresistible forces? It is because the five powers previously discussed are now stabilized and fully developed. One therefore speaks of the five irresistible forces."

We also find in the *Questions of Matisambhava*,

Matisambhava once asked, "Lord, how is one to understand the seven elements of the path to buddhahood?" And the Lord replied and said,

"Matisambhava, since the bodhisattvas are without thoughts and mental activity, for them phenomena are empty by way of their specific characteristics. To see that phenomena lack intrinsic being is the element of correct mindfulness leading to enlightenment.

"Matisambhava, since everything, virtuous, nonvirtuous, or neutral, is destitute of real existence, anything designated as a phenomenon is nowhere to be found. It is like a magical illusion. This is the element of perfect discernment leading to enlightenment.

"Matisambhava, since ideas about phenomena have fallen away, the bodhisattvas experience neither acceptance nor rejection with regard to the phenomena of any of the three realms or of nirvāṇa. They are free from clinging to the realization of the path, and yet, on account of their joyful and nonconceptual aspiration, they do not set diligence aside. This is the element of correct diligence leading to enlightenment.

"Matisambhava, since pleasure and displeasure have fallen away, the bodhisattvas will take no delight in anything produced by causes and conditions, and they will eliminate all their defilements. This is the element of correct joy leading to enlightenment.

"Matisambhava, since they do not find even an atom of true existence in the phenomena on which they focus, the bodhisattvas will experience extreme flexibility of body. And since their minds have also acquired an extreme flexibility with regard to all phenomena, they remain in a state of stainless, nonconceptual concentration. This is the element of correct flexibility leading to enlightenment.

"Matisambhava, since all clinging to phenomena has fallen away, or since the bodhisattvas have understood what phenomena are, they will have minds that have no conceptions with regard to anything. With their minds settled in meditative evenness, they will have an understanding of all phenomena. This does not occur when the mind is not so settled. Only those whose minds settle in meditative evenness will attain the state of buddhahood; those whose minds do not settle in meditation will not attain to it. Therefore to rest thus in meditative evenness, free from clinging [to phenomena], is the element of correct concentration leading to enlightenment.

"Matisambhava, those who forbear to dwell upon phenomena, who do not depend on them, who are not attached to them or bound by them, will have minds free of any fixation on phenomena liable to produce happiness, sorrow, or indifference. They will not be attracted by worldly things and will enjoy the evenness of mind that sees all phenomena correctly as they are. They indeed will come to joy. This is the element of correct evenness leading to enlightenment.

"So it is, O Matisambhava, that you should view the seven elements leading to enlightenment."

Then Matisambhava again asked, "Lord, how should one view the eightfold path of the bodhisattvas?" And the Lord replied and said,

"Matisambhava, right view consists in seeing the equality of all phenomena. Wrong view is to believe in self, in personhood, in mind possession, in a life principle, and in a [nihilistic] emptiness. Moreover, right view is to be free of referents of a view, from the tiniest thing to nirvāṇa itself, and to be free of all views superior, medium, or inferior.

"Matisambhava, those who discard conceptual understanding are skilled in deep insight, or vipaśyanā, based on calm abiding, or śamatha. Moreover, to abandon, to abandon wholly, to abandon utterly all thoughts of phenomena as good or bad; to be without thought, to be wholly without thought, and to be utterly without thought, is right thought.

"Matisambhava, to refrain from harming oneself and others with one's speech, and to teach with surety that all phenomena are equal—by means of speech that does not provoke defilement either in oneself or others, is right speech.

"Matisambhava, an action that exhausts karma and does not produce karma is right action. Through it, defilement subsides; defilement is not inflamed. It is an action that eliminates defilement; it is not an action that generates defilement. This action is free from all deeds, whether white, black, or a mixture of the two, and does not produce such deeds. This is right action.

"Matisambhava, right livelihood is unstained by defilement. Livelihood that does no harm either to oneself or others and that allows for the perfect practice of the Dharma is right livelihood.

"Matisambhava, the practice of the Dharma, which is profound and unconditioned and beyond conceptual construction, constitutes right effort. Therefore, to focus the mind perfectly, to have strong interest and diligence, not to be discouraged, and to realize the ultimate truth is right effort.

"Matisambhava, thanks to mindfulness, all defilements are deprived of an opportunity to attack. Thanks to mindfulness of the elements leading to enlightenment, to mindfulness of the four boundless attitudes, and to mindfulness of the six transcendent perfections, negative forces find no occasion to attack. Thanks to mindfulness, one's path will not deviate. Thanks to mindfulness, placed like a guard upon the gate, every unvirtuous impulse of the mind and mental factors will be deprived of the opportunity for attack. This is right mindfulness.

"Matisambhava, since the 'self-identity' of phenomena is the state of equality, all phenomena partake of this same state. Since their self-identity is a state of purity, all phenomena are pure. Since their self-identity is the state of emptiness, all phenomena are empty. To remain perfectly absorbed in this is right concentration. The instants of mind are thus endowed with primordial wisdom. Omniscient wisdom consequently occurs, and thence the manifest state of perfect buddhahood. This is right concentration.

"Matisambhava, it is thus that you should understand the eightfold path of the bodhisattvas."

So it is that all the elements of the path arise without their having any intrinsic being. They are like magical illusions. It is said in the *Prajñāpāramitā-sūtra in Eighteen Thousand Lines*,

> O Devaputra, the states of close mindfulness are like dreams; they are like illusions. In the same way, the genuine restraints, the miraculous legs, the powers, the irresistible forces, the elements leading to enlightenment, and the eightfold noble path are all dreamlike. They are like illusions. Similarly, the four fearlessnesses, the four distinct perfect knowledges, great love, great compassion, and the eighteen distinctive qualities of a buddha—all are like dreams. They are like illusions.

Moreover, in itself, the path consists in the skillful means that is the union of śamatha and vipaśyanā and in extraordinary realizations. Therefore it is the supreme remedy for the obscuring veils. As it is said in *The Way of the Bodhisattva*,

> Penetrative insight joined with calm abiding
> Utterly eradicates afflictive states.[69]

And we find in the *Letter to a Friend*,

> Lacking wisdom, concentration fails,
> And without concentration, wisdom too.
> For someone who has both, saṃsāra's sea
> Fills no more than the print left by a hoof.[70]

On the paths of accumulation and joining, beings are engaged in aspirational practice. It is through aspiration that one appraises the ultimate truth, that is, emptiness endowed with supreme qualities. It is likewise through aspiration that one places restraints upon the sense doors, that one principally engages in the accumulations of merit and wisdom, that—by curtailing one's sleep during the first and last periods of the night—one practices śamatha and vipaśyanā. As one trains in the extraordinary union of skillful means and wisdom, completing and perfecting the three levels of the path of accumulation, a concentration in harmony with this wisdom will arise in one's mind as a presage of the appearance of nonconceptual primordial wisdom. This is referred to as warmth [the first stage of the path of joining]. And as one goes on to perfect the stages of peak, acceptance, and the supreme mundane level, gross defilements will be suppressed and one will approach the first moment of the arising of primordial wisdom on the noble path [of seeing].

Subsequently, on the path of seeing, one will behold in direct reality nonconceptual primordial wisdom, the nature of the four truths. It is at this time that one aspect of the buddha-element,[71] namely, the adventitious obscurations arising through conceptual imputation (which is one of the items to be abandoned), is purified or removed.

In this regard, it may be said that each of the four truths (of suffering, origin, path, and cessation) exhibits four instants (understanding, acceptance, subsequent understanding, and subsequent acceptance), so that in the four truths there are, all together, sixteen instants. In the instant of understanding, one sees the specific characteristics of each of the truths. In the instant of acceptance, the seeing of these characteristics provokes a state of fearlessness. In the instant of subsequent understanding, one realizes that the characteristics specific to each of the four truths are a state of emptiness. In the instant of subsequent acceptance, one experiences no fear when seeing these characteristics as space. Partaking of the same mental substance, these aspects manifest—four for each truth, in the instants needed for the accomplishment of a given action—as the vision of the nature of the four truths: an illusion-like empty appearance. Thus for the four truths there arise, in successive order, four understandings, four acceptances, four subsequent understandings, and four subsequent acceptances. As it is said in the *Abhisamayālaṃkāra*,

> The truth of suffering and the rest display
> The nature of the instants
> Of understanding and subsequent understanding,
> Acceptance and subsequent acceptance.

It is then that one hundred twelve obscurations are eliminated by seeing.[72] These are, first, the six defilements of imputed character: ignorance, desire, anger, pride, doubt, and views. Concerning these views, there are five of them: the view of the transitory composite, the view of extremes, wrong views, the view of doctrinal superiority, and the view of ethical and yogic superiority. When these views are added to ignorance and the remaining four defilements that are not views [that is, desire, anger, pride, and doubt], we come to a total of ten root defilements. In the realm of desire, these ten defilements are present for each of the four truths, which makes forty all together. In the form and formless realms there is no anger, with the result that in those realms there are nine defilements for each of the four truths, and this makes thirty-six for each of these realms. If we add to these the forty factors just mentioned, we arrive at a grand total of one hundred twelve obscurations to be eliminated by seeing.

They are eliminated in the following way. By the path that gives rise to the wisdom of the path of seeing,[73] gross obscurations are indirectly eliminated. And when this wisdom arises, the subtle obscurations are directly eliminated. Finally, when wisdom is fully arisen, all the seeds of the obscurations that are eliminated through seeing are neutralized.

There are, in addition, the four hundred fourteen stains on the nine grounds of the path of meditation, and these are eliminated in the course of preparation, main practice, and conclusion of the successive grounds. The defilements that are eliminated on the path of meditation are latent; they are innate or coemergent. These defilements may be classified sixfold as ignorance, desire, anger, pride, the view of the transitory composite, and the view of extremes. In the desire realm, each of these six defilements has three degrees of intensity (great, middle, and small), each of which can be further divided into three levels (great of the great, middle of the great, small of the great, and so on). When they are divided thus into nine degrees of intensity, these six defilements, by virtue of this ninefold division, result in fifty-four defilements.

In the four samādhis of the realm of form, there is no anger. Consequently, when each of the remaining five defilements is subdivided according to these nine degrees of intensity, there are forty-five defilements for each level of samādhi. Therefore for the four levels of samādhi, there are, all together, one hundred eighty defilements.

Likewise in the formless realm, according to its four levels of infinite space, infinite consciousness, utter nothingness, and the peak of existence, there are also one hundred eighty defilements. Consequently in the two higher realms, each with its one hundred eighty defilements, there are, all together, three hundred sixty defilements. If we add to this the fifty-four defilements of the desire realm, we come to a grand total of four hundred fourteen obscurations that are eliminated by [the path of] meditation.

As for the manner in which the elimination occurs, the "path of preparation"[74] and the "path that is free of obstacles" both—as a first stage—eliminate the immediate cause [of the six root defilements]. The "special path," on the other hand, is what actually eliminates them [and in so doing, is the real and active antidote], while the "path of total freedom" eliminates them by banishing [their propensities] far away and by arresting subtle defilements.

Each of the ten grounds of realization is associated principally with the practice of one of the ten transcendent perfections[75]—with the other nine in attendance on it. For example, on the ground of Perfect Joy, one chiefly practices the perfection of generosity with the remaining nine perfections as accompaniments. As we find in *Distinguishing the Middle from Extremes*,

> On each of the ten grounds, it should be understood,
> One predominates; the others do not do so.

Concerning the qualities of the ten grounds, the following teaching is found in the *Questions of Kumāraprabha*:

> "O child of noble family, the sign that bodhisattvas are dwelling on the first ground is that, when they wish, they can—in one, two, or three instants[76]—perfectly achieve and be absorbed in a hundred concentrations. They are able to behold a hundred buddhas and perceive that they are blessed by them. They can cause a hundred universes to tremble and shake and can travel to a hundred buddha fields. They can illuminate a hundred universes and bring a hundred beings to maturity. They are able to remain for a hundred kalpas and, through their concentration, gain access to a hundred past kalpas and a hundred future ones. They can open a hundred doors of Dharma. They can display a hundred bodies, each with its surrounding retinue of a hundred bodhisattvas that, practicing with right diligence, all possess the same qualities as the [first-ground] bodhisattvas themselves.
>
> "O child of noble family, the bodhisattvas residing

on the second ground of realization can—in one, two, or three instants—perfectly achieve and be absorbed in a thousand concentrations. They are able to behold a thousand buddhas and perceive that they are blessed by them. They can cause a thousand universes to tremble and shake and can travel to a thousand buddha fields. They can illuminate a thousand universes and bring a thousand beings to maturity. They are able to remain for a thousand kalpas and can gain access to a thousand past kalpas as well as a thousand future ones. They can open a thousand doors of Dharma. They can display a thousand bodies and display for each of them a retinue of a thousand bodhisattvas.

"O child of noble family, the bodhisattvas residing on the third ground of realization can—in one, two, or three instants—perfectly achieve and be absorbed in a hundred thousand concentrations. They are able to behold a hundred thousand buddhas and perceive that they are blessed by them. They can cause a hundred thousand universes to tremble and shake and can travel to a hundred thousand buddha fields. They can illuminate a hundred thousand universes and bring a hundred thousand beings to maturity. They are able to remain for a hundred thousand kalpas and can gain access to a hundred thousand past kalpas as well as a hundred thousand future ones. They can open a hundred thousand doors of Dharma. They can display a hundred thousand bodies and display for each of them a retinue of a hundred thousand bodhisattvas.

"O child of noble family, the bodhisattvas residing on the fourth ground of realization can—in one, two, or three instants—perfectly achieve and be absorbed in a billion concentrations. They are able to behold a billion buddhas and perceive that they are blessed by them. They can cause a billion universes to tremble and shake and can travel to a billion buddha fields. They can illuminate a billion universes and bring a billion beings to maturity. They are able to remain for a billion kalpas and can gain access to a billion past kalpas as well as a billion future ones. They can open a billion doors of Dharma. They can display a billion bodies and display for each of them a retinue of a billion bodhisattvas.

"O child of noble family, the bodhisattvas residing on the fifth ground of realization can—in one, two, or three instants—perfectly achieve and be absorbed in a thousand billion concentrations. They are able to behold a thousand billion buddhas and perceive that they are blessed by them. They can cause a thousand billion universes to tremble and shake and can travel to a thousand billion buddha fields. They can illuminate a thousand billion universes and bring a thousand billion beings to maturity. They are able to remain for a thousand billion kalpas and can gain access to a thousand billion past kalpas as well as a thousand billion future ones. They can open a thousand billion doors of Dharma. They can display a thousand billion bodies and display for each of them a retinue of a thousand billion bodhisattvas.

"O child of noble family, the bodhisattvas residing on the sixth ground of realization can, if they wish—in one, two, or three instants—perfectly achieve and be absorbed in a hundred thousand billion concentrations. They are able to behold a hundred thousand billion buddhas and perceive that they are blessed by them. They can cause a hundred thousand billion universes to tremble and shake and can travel to a hundred thousand billion buddha fields. They can illuminate a hundred thousand billion universes and bring a hundred thousand billion beings to maturity. They are able to remain for a hundred thousand billion kalpas and can gain access to a hundred thousand billion past kalpas as well as a hundred thousand billion future ones. They can open a hundred thousand billion doors of Dharma. They can display a hundred thousand billion bodies and display for each of them a retinue of a hundred thousand billion bodhisattvas.

"O child of noble family, the bodhisattvas residing on the seventh ground of realization can, if they wish—in one, two, or three instants—perfectly achieve and be absorbed in one million one hundred thousand billion concentrations. They are able to behold one million one hundred thousand billion buddhas and perceive that they are blessed by them. They can cause one million one hundred thousand billion universes to tremble and shake and can travel to one million one hundred thousand billion buddha fields. They can illuminate one million one hundred thousand billion universes and bring one million one hundred thousand billion beings to maturity. They are able to remain for one million one hundred thousand billion kalpas and can gain access to one million one hundred thousand billion past kalpas as well as one million one hundred thousand billion future ones. They can open one million one hundred thousand billion doors of Dharma. They can display one million one hundred thousand billion bodies and display for each of them a retinue of one million one hundred thousand billion bodhisattvas.

"O child of noble family, the bodhisattvas residing on the eighth ground of realization can, if they wish—in one, two, or three instants—perfectly achieve and be absorbed in as many concentrations as there are atoms in the hundred thousand of the three thousandfold universe multiplied by ten. They are able to behold as many buddhas as there are atoms in the hundred thousand of the three thousandfold universe multiplied by ten and perceive that they are blessed by them. They can cause a similar number of universes to tremble and shake and can travel to a similar number of buddha fields. They can illuminate as many universes as there are atoms in the hundred thousand of the three thousandfold universe multiplied by ten and bring the same number of beings to maturity. They are able to remain for as many kalpas as there are atoms in the hundred thousand of the three thousandfold universe multiplied by ten and can gain access to the same number of past kalpas as well as the same number of future ones. They can open the same number of doors of Dharma. They can display the same number of bodies and display for each of them a retinue of the same number of bodhisattvas.

"O child of noble family, the bodhisattvas residing on the ninth ground of realization can, if they wish—in one, two, or three instants—perfectly achieve and be absorbed in as many concentrations as there are atoms in ten times one hundred thousand measureless[77] buddha fields. They are able to behold as many buddhas as there are atoms in ten times one hundred thousand measureless buddha fields and perceive that they are blessed by them. They can cause a similar number of universes to tremble and shake and can travel to the same number of buddha fields. They can illuminate the same number of universes and bring the same number of beings to maturity. They are able to remain for the same number of kalpas and can gain access to the same number of past kalpas as well as the same number of future ones. They can open the same number of doors of Dharma. They can display the same number of bodies and display for each of them a retinue of the same number of bodhisattvas.

"O child of noble family, the bodhisattvas residing on the tenth ground of realization are able, if they wish—in one, two, or three instants—to gain the acceptance of

> the great import of the Dharma, the great light of the Dharma, the measureless cloud of Dharma. They can uphold it perfectly, and teach it perfectly without being attached to it. Why is this? It is because the bodhisattvas on this ground are endowed with an inconceivable cloud of Dharma of primordial wisdom proceeding from the space-like dharmakāya. This ground is therefore called the Cloud of Dharma."

In this regard, some say that all the qualities of the grounds and paths are but visions that develop and transform in one's dreams and that they are not present during the daytime—for it is said in the *Brāhmānanda-sūtra*,

> All the qualities of grounds and paths
> Will be understood at the time when one is dreaming.

But this is untenable. For in this sūtra, an extraordinary dream is discussed which involves traversing the grounds and paths. And this example demonstrates the attainment of all such grounds of realization. It does not teach that the qualities of the grounds cease to exist during the day. On the contrary, these qualities are ever present, day and night. The detailed description of these qualities should be understood according to the teaching of the great charioteers. This concludes the exposition of the magical illusion of the path of skillful means.

Now the root text goes on to describe the accomplishment produced by these skillful means. [This is the fourth of the four kinds of illusion.]

> **13. The illusion of primordial wisdom,**
> **The final path of no more learning,**
> **Consists in the three kāyas,**
> **As well as the activity, spontaneously accomplished,**

Of the Victorious Ones.
It is the twofold purity made manifest.

In the final moment of the tenth ground, the vajra-like concentration overwhelms all the propensities that lead to evil states. Manifest enlightenment then occurs: all the qualities of elimination and realization are perfected. From within the state of the twofold purity of the dharmakāya, wherein the ultimate expanse and primordial wisdom are inseparable, the two form bodies spontaneously appear and work for the benefit of beings for as long as saṃsāra lasts. The tantra entitled *Wisdom Unsurpassed* has this to say:

Unconditioned space and primal wisdom
Are inseparable.
Defilements and phenomena are pure.
Such is the dharmakāya
Endowed with twofold purity,
Unchanging and unborn,
Beyond all attributes.
The buddhas are the dharmakāya;
They are beyond all physical presence,
Yet by dint of causes and conditions—
Of bodhichitta previously engendered,
Of merits, prayers of aspiration,
And the generation stage—
The twofold rūpakāya
Spontaneously manifests.

All this may be applied to the supreme Sage. In the Śrāvakayāna, it is believed that the Buddha began as an ordinary being and in his very lifetime actualized the five paths, thereby attaining enlightenment on the vajra seat of Bodhgaya. In the *Abhidharmakośa* we find,

If one serves one's parents (even though they are not noble),
Those tormented by disease, and those who teach the
Dharma;
If one serves the bodhisattvas in their last samsaric birth,
The merit gained is limitless, the teachings say.

According to the expository vehicle of the Mahāyāna, the Buddha is believed to have gained enlightenment innumerable kalpas in the past and to have displayed his enlightenment for the sake of beings in our world. In the *White Lotus Sūtra*, the Buddha is recorded as saying, "O child of noble family, I gained enlightenment billions of kalpas in the past." And in the *Sūtra of the Meeting of the Father and the Son*, the Buddha says, "As Indraketu, I attained buddhahood innumerable measureless kalpas in the past."

In the Yoga system of the Secret Mantrayāna, it is said that the prince Siddhārtha journeyed to the realm of Akaniṣṭha.[78] There he received the blessing of as many buddhas as there are seeds in a pod of sesame and attained enlightenment by means of the five factors of awakening.[79]

In the Anuttarayoga [father] tantras it is said that the prince Siddhārtha attained enlightenment in Akaniṣṭha, after requesting empowerment from the great Vajradhara Vairocana. And it was his emanation that displayed his enlightenment in this world of Jambudvīpa. As we find in the *Secret Essence of the Moon Tantra*,

Discarding the pure levels of the realms of form,[80]
In Akaniṣṭha, beauteous Dense Array,
'Tis there the Buddha gained enlightenment,
While here, his emanation gained enlightenment.

The tantra called the *Gathering of Great Meaning* declares,

In the supreme secret place of Akaniṣṭha,
The mighty one among the host of bodhisattvas
Received empowerment within the palace of the dharmatā,

And as Samantabhadra he was blessed—
The body of the indestructible expanse,
The vajra of enlightened mind.
And in that instant he achieved
Full manifest enlightenment, becoming Vajradhara
Of the essence unsurpassed.
In great bliss self-arisen did he wake.

In the mother tantras, it is believed that the eleven buddhas of great desire[81] requested the four empowerments complete in the center of the palace of the Vajra Queen in Akaniṣṭha, and relying on the supreme mistress, they achieved the thirteenth level of the vajra holder. As it is written in the tantra entitled *Supreme Nonabiding*,

Relying on the female karmamudrā,
All eleven buddhas
Gained the state of Vajradhara.

These are just brief excerpts from the teachings of the various vehicles. Now, the tradition of the glorious *Māyājāla Tantra* (of the nondual class)[82] states on the other hand that, by the time the path of learning is completed, the buddha-element is freed from the cloud-like stains or obscurations that conceal it. And it is this buddha-element that is referred to as enlightenment. All the many excellent qualities [now actualized] of the buddha-element are the very constituents of buddhahood. And, with the kāyas and wisdoms inseparable, the two goals are perfectly achieved. As it is said in the *Longer Māyājāla Tantra*,

Stainless, pure enlightenment
Is changeless and is free from stain.
It is the very form of every perfect quality.
Five kāyas and five wisdoms are spontaneously present.

And as we find in the *Guhyagarbha*, "At that time, the five kāyas are completely manifest."

A question may be asked about the location of Akaniṣṭha, the place where enlightenment is achieved. Some believe that it is the Akaniṣṭha found in the pure levels [of the form realm], but this is untenable, invalidated by the fact that the Buddha forsook these pure levels. Others hold that Akaniṣṭha is located beyond the pure levels, as a lonely place is at a distance from a town. This is also untenable and is invalidated by the fact that it is said, in terms of spatial extension, that Akaniṣṭha is boundless.

For our part, we say that Akaniṣṭha is the pure self-experience of primordial enlightenment. It is the Akaniṣṭha of awareness—the kāyas and the wisdoms that are found in the one ultimate expanse. The tantra entitled *Wisdom Unsurpassed* says,

> The nature of the mind, great coemergent bliss,
> Is Akaniṣṭha, place of supreme purity.

And in the *Praise of the Dharmadhātu*, we find,

> Beauteous Akaniṣṭha, I declare,
> Is the three wisdoms
> Brought together into one.

Within this sphere of Akaniṣṭha, the five families of the rūpakāya appear to the bodhisattvas. The saṃbhogakāya Vairocana Mahāsāgara is the support for infinite universes. He is surrounded by the bodhisattvas residing on the ten grounds, and the place itself is called the Dense Array of Ornaments. It manifests within the wheel of indestructible continuity, for since the perception of the noble beings on the grounds of realization is pure, there is no hallucinatory experience of movement and change. And in a small buddha field located within this Dense Array, infinite universes seemingly come into being and pass away, for the perceptions of the minds of beings also seem to come into being and pass away.

In this regard, some say that if the buddha field of Dense Array is not destroyed, likewise these universes should not be destroyed. For they are said to be located in the field of Dense Array, and both these universes and Dense Array are qualified as bases for destruction.[83]

In reply to this objection, it may be argued that it is strange that such people fail to differentiate between the support and the supported, and between different orders of perception or experience. When it is said that it is not the support or basis (Dense Array) that is destroyed but the supported (the infinite universes within a small buddha field located in Dense Array), the destruction of the latter and the nondestruction of the former are both tenable, for they represent two different orders of experience. The one is said to be destroyed and the other is said not to be destroyed according to the perceptions of beings who assume the reality of arising and destruction, and the perceptions of noble beings who see that there is no coming into being and no passing out of being. This is how the distinction is made. Though both these spheres are termed "universes," or bases for destruction,[84] nevertheless, from the perspective of support and supported, the support or basis [namely, Dense Array] is not destroyed, while the supported [the infinite universes within Dense Array] *is* destroyed. If one understands what was said above, the buddha field of the Dense Array of Akaniṣṭha can be regarded as a "universe" or basis for destruction [for it is the support of those lesser universes that *are* subject to destruction].

The *Vajra Peak Tantra* says,

> Akaniṣṭha is the beauteous field of Dense Array.
> This field of Dense Array is indestructible.
> It is the place wherein the Dharma sprang
> Of the saṃbhogakāya buddhas.

The three kāyas—the saṃbhogakāya, the dharmakāya, and the nirmāṇakāya—are inseparable in their nature and possess inconceivable qualities such as the ten strengths and the four fearlessnesses. This is referred to as the illusion of primordial wisdom. It is said in the *Māyājāla*,

> The kāyas of the sugatas
> Are the illusion of primordial wisdom, unmoving
> luminosity.

And the sūtra entitled the *Teaching of the Inconceivable* declares,

> The earth and sky could be encompassed
> By measuring it in points like tips of hair.
> But if one were to lecture for a measureless kalpa's length,
> One still could not describe the ocean of the Buddha's
> qualities.
> For these are endless and ineffable,
> Beyond the reach of thought.

Now that the four kinds of illusion have been explained, we now turn to the illusion of the example, the illusion of dependent arising.

> **14. The illusion of the example**
> **Is the illusion of dependence.**
> **Just like magic forms arising**
> **Through the substances and chanting of a charm,**
> **All things are understood to be unreal.**
> **This is the instruction of the *Māyājāla*.**

Things appear and yet they lack intrinsic being. It is just as when, through the chanting of a word of power, a stick and a stone appear as a horse and an ox. It is thus that one should understand that phenomena arise in dependence on appropriate causes and conditions. As it is said in the sūtra entitled the *Ornament of the Light of Wisdom*, "Magical illusions, O Mañjuśrī, appear and yet do not exist. Likewise all phenomena appear and yet do not exist."

In this respect, the glorious nondual tantra, the *Great Māyājāla in One Hundred Thousand Lines*, says,

> Illusory are all phenomena.
> Luminous character, skillful means,
> Primordial wisdom, the impure—
> These four kinds of illusion all occur
> Within the space of self-arisen primal wisdom.

The root text now declares that these phenomena are magical illusions beyond the ontological extremes:

> **15. Just as when a substance is conjoined**
> **With words of wizardry,**
> **The thing that then appears**
> **Is taken as a phantom form,**
> **In just the same way you should understand**
> **That things appearing falsely to migrating beings**
> **Are indeed without existence.**
> **The objects that arise dependently**
> **Because of beings' ingrained deluded habits**
> **Are empty in themselves, ungraspable,**
> **In the very moment they appear.**
> **Understand that they transcend the two extremes**
> **Of nonexistence and existence.**

By the recitation of a magic spell, sticks and little stones may be made to appear in the form of horses and oxen. If the onlookers do not perceive the sticks and stones and see horses and oxen instead, it follows that their perceptions are mistaken or hallucinatory. And this is what samsaric appearances are like. All the things that one perceives do indeed seem to be truly existent entities composed of partless particles. But the fact is that they are the clear appearances of what has no existence. In themselves, partless particles cannot be perceived. And since apart from such particles there is nothing of which gross objects can be composed, the latter are pure hallucinations. In themselves, planks of wood, stones, earth, and water do not constitute a house. It is rather the gathering together of all such items that appears in such a form. On the other hand, no house can appear in dependence on [imperceptible] partless particles. Therefore, since the house appears and is perceived, it is a pure hallucination. Similarly, if one examines one's friends and the joy one takes in them; if one examines one's enemies and the displeasure they provoke; and if one examines all the ways one talks and thinks and all the actions one undertakes, not one of them actually exists [as a real entity]. But for as long as one does not examine such things, they do indeed seem real. They are, in other words, hallucinations, clear appearances of what does not exist. If one investigates these hallucinations, they have no true existence; they are just like space. One should recognize that they are magical illusions beyond the ontological extremes—just empty reflections. As it is said in the *Sūtra of the Teaching of the Inconceivable*,

> Phenomena resemble magical illusions.
> By nature they are without origin.
> Empty, they have no real features.
> They are beyond conception and beyond expression.

The root text goes on to say that everything is just an illusory display:

> **16. Illusory lands and towns that are illusory,**
> **Illusory people and their wealth that is illusory,**
> **Illusory delight and pain, illusory arising and destruction,**
> **Illusory veracity and lies that are illusory—**
> **Just as all these magical illusions**
> **Are perceived and do appear,**
> **In just the same way you should understand**
> **The appearance of the six migrations.**

Like the things that a magician causes to appear, it is thus that one should understand beings and their happiness and suffering, arising and cessation, coming and going, the various regions of the six classes of beings, all one's possessions and experiences, one's enemies and friends. As it is said in the *Stages of Understanding*,

> Various forms and various possessions,
> All the many things that do appear
> Are clearly seen yet lack intrinsic being.
> They are like tricks of magic and like things seen in a dream.

All phenomena are thus on a level in being by nature magical illusions.

> **17. Empty from the very first,**
> **All things resemble magical illusions.**
> **Appearing yet without existence,**
> **They are just the same as magical illusions.**
> **Arising from conditions,**
> **They are indeed like magical illusions.**
> **Deceptive and destructible,**
> **They do indeed resemble magical illusions.**
> **In just such terms saṃsāra's false appearances**
> **Are understood as magical illusions.**

The elements of earth, air, fire, and water, which appear as the universe and beings contained therein, together with all the experiences of the mind, are all primordially pure; they resemble magical illusions. Magic horses and oxen are nothing but sticks and stones; they are empty of being horses and oxen. In the same way, the hallucinatory experiences [of saṃsāra] are groundless, no more than the mind's subjective experience. They do not exist in fact. In the very moment that the magical illusion is perceived, no actual horse or ox is present, even though it seems to be. Likewise, in the very moment that all the various phenomena are perceived, they are not really there; they are like magical illusions. And as the coincidence of the condition (the magic spell) and of the material cause (the stick and the stone) gives rise to the appearance of the horse and ox, in just the same way, thanks to the coincidence of the condition (the various karmic actions) and of the cause (the ignorance and so on consisting in the duality of apprehending subject and apprehended object), beings circle in the six existential states and must suffer manifold experiences, even though they are nothing but magical illusions. When one's eyes are tricked by a charm, a stick and a stone may appear as a horse and an ox, and the mind is thus deceived. In the same way, the appearances of form, touch, taste, and smell deceive the mind. One should therefore understand that such hallucinatory appearances are just like magical illusions.

The root text continues with advice to cultivate compassion toward those who fail to understand that phenomena are like magical illusions:

> **18. And so it is. Although the six migrations**
> **Have in fact the nature of illusions,**
> **Beings fail to understand**
> **And without respite wander**
> **In the city of saṃsāra without end.**
> **How pitiful! They suffer through their actions,**
> **Source of pain and [temporary] pleasure.**
> **Consider this, O beings:**
> **The things that you mistakenly perceive**
> **Are magical illusions!**

Although saṃsāra in all its variety is from the very beginning an illusion, through ignorance and clinging to self, beings are unaware that phenomena are false—appearing so clearly and yet devoid of real existence. And they doggedly believe in their real existence. So it is that they wander constantly in the city of saṃsāra, which is without beginning or end. And all these beings, who owing to their individual karmic destiny experience different hallucinatory appearances, are regarded by the noble ones as objects of compassion. This is why one should train on the relative level in compassion, the cause of one's concern for beings in saṃsāra that is like a magical illusion. As it is said in the *Sūtrālaṃkāra*,

> Their compassion touches sentient beings
> Who burn with lust or fall into the power of their enemies. . . .
>
> Who are weighed down with heavy shackles
> And are addicted to what poisons them. . . .
> Strengthless, wandering on mistaken paths.

Beings who are burning with defilement, who are beset and hindered by demonic forces and who are fettered by afflictions and false views, those who are outside the Dharma, as well as those who are beguiled by the taste of samādhi—and also the śrāvakas, the pratyekabuddhas, and beginners on the bodhisattva path—all such beings are the object of the compassion of the noble ones.

The root text now addresses those who have understood that all is like a magical illusion, instructing them to train in it:

> **19. They arise from nowhere; nowhere do they go;**
> **They are present nowhere—**
> **Such is the true state of things.**
> **From the outset, by their nature, they are pure illusions.**
> **Be sure of this, O you of perfect destiny!**

From the very beginning, phenomena are devoid of intrinsic being. Those who are intelligent should understand that while phenomena appear, they do not exist in any inherent sense. Things are the display of emptiness. As the *Stages of Light* says,

> Sense powers lack intrinsic being.
> They are illusions, they are emptiness.

Everything, the root text goes on to say, is the illusory and subjective experience of the mind:

> **20. Beings are by their nature like illusions;**
> **The nature of enlightenment, it too is an illusion.**
> **The play of an illusion, saṃsāra and nirvāṇa are not two.**
> **Perceive them thus, O you who have good fortune!**

The appearance of beings is an illusion; the appearance of buddhas is an illusion. All the phenomena of both saṃsāra and nirvāṇa simply appear in awareness, but they have no existence in awareness. It should be understood that their illusory display is simply the self-experience of awareness. As it is said in the *Prajñāpāramitā in Eighteen Thousand Lines*, "Devaputra, saṃsāra is like a dream; it is like a magical illusion. Nirvāṇa too is like a dream; it is like a magical illusion."

One must come to the conclusion that phenomena are none other than magical illusions.

> **21. The Conqueror has said that things are but illusions.**
> **Aside from that, one cannot find**
> **A single atom of reality.**
> **Understand therefore, all you who wish for freedom,**
> **That nothing has true being;**
> **All is of the essence of illusion.**

Phenomena are simply magical illusions. They do not exist in any other way. As it is said in the *Middle-Length Prajñāpāramitā*,

> Subhūti, all things are like dreams, like magical illusions. Since whatever seems to be a thing is in fact without origin, it is said to be like a dream, like a magical illusion. You ought not to say that phenomena are different from dreams, that they are different from illusions, or that

> dreams and magical illusions are different from phenomena. For all phenomena are themselves none other than magical illusions.

The various kinds of illusion may be condensed into three, which are as follows. Regarding the illusion of perfect freedom, the root text says,

> **22. The manner of illusion should be understood as follows.**
> **The illusion of enlightenment**
> **Is beyond all change and movement.**
> **It is spontaneously arisen.**
> **It is unfailing, ever space-like, all-pervading;**
> **It is like a wishing jewel, fulfilling all desires.**
> **It utterly displays unbounded excellence and actions.**
> **It is pure and luminous, and free from thought elaboration.**

If the adventitious stains that mask the ultimate expanse (which is pure by its very nature) are removed, the dharmakāya buddha manifests endowed with twofold purity. And from within this state, the rūpakāya spontaneously appears. This is referred to as the illusion of enlightenment.[85] It is said in the *Sūtra Like a Magical Illusion*,

> Enlightenment has the nature of a magical illusion,
> And primal wisdom too is like a magical illusion.
> Existent entities and nonexistent entities subside.
> No examples can describe immaculate enlightenment.

The illusion of the various [multiplicity of] things[86] is next described:

> **23. The illusion of saṃsāra is untrue, deceptive.**
> **The phenomena thereof have no real features.**
> **Appearing and yet nonexistent,**

They resemble magical illusions.
But when deluded thought is cleansed away,
Hallucinations likewise sink into the ultimate expanse.
Just as when the magic ends,
The horse and ox no more appear,
Impure hallucinatory perceptions—
Apprehender, apprehended—
All subside in the primordial ground
Which, empty in its purity,
Has no intrinsic being.

When the magic spell is broken, the illusory horse and ox no longer appear. It is just the same with illusory, hallucinatory appearances. When ignorance and the cognitions involving the duality of apprehender and apprehended are purified, the appearing objects, hallucinatory as they are, occur no more. They are said to "sink into the ultimate expanse," disappearing like the magical horse and ox. This is why hallucinatory appearances are devoid of true characteristics; like magical illusions, they are devoid of intrinsic being.

The text goes on to describe the illusion of the ultimate expanse of saṃsāra and nirvāṇa:

24. The illusion of the fundamental nature
Refers to ultimate reality devoid of change and movement.
The final nature of all pure and impure things
Is like the space enclosed within a vase.
The vessel may be made of gold or clay,
It may be broken or unbroken,
But its space is neither increased
Nor reduced thereby.
Just so, in the condition of delusion,
The ultimate reality is not diminished,
Nor is it greater in the state of freedom.
It neither worsens nor improves.
This is the fundamental way of being,

The final state of wisdom.
The wise are those who thus have understood.

The illusion of the fundamental nature,[87] the ultimate reality of all things, is awareness, the enlightened mind. The pure appearances that occur in the state of enlightenment and the impure hallucinatory appearances, together with the deluded thoughts occurring in the state of saṃsāra, are all contained within awareness. Positive thoughts appear in awareness; evil thoughts also appear in awareness. Variegated appearances appear in awareness. There is no alternative to this. As ultimate reality, awareness pervades all things. For example, a golden vessel and an earthenware vessel both contain space. The vessels may appear to be precious or tawdry, but the space contained in them is neither good nor bad. In the same way, whereas nirvāṇa and saṃsāra seem to be good and bad respectively, it is important to understand that within awareness, they are neither good nor bad. As we find in the *Sūtrālaṃkāra*,[88]

> Just like space pervading different vessels,
> Likewise dharmatā pervades them both.

If one has this understanding, one sees that awareness, namely, the spontaneously present enlightened mind, is indeed the actual foundation of everything. And without accepting or rejecting, without affirming or negating, one becomes quite naturally adept in the ultimate reality of things. And thus one comes to be known as a great sage.

Moreover, the space contained within a vessel [remains constant]. It is not greater when the vessel remains whole, nor is it lessened when the vessel breaks. In the same way, in the state of delusion or freedom, awareness neither worsens nor improves; it neither decreases nor increases. It is simply the ultimate reality of things.

Thus far, then, we have established the view of the magical illusion-like ground. The root text now goes on to explain the practice of the path.

> **25. Once you have grasped the view that all is an illusion,**
> **Proceed to meditate upon illusion,**
> **The great state of the absence of intrinsic being.**
> **Perform, as previously, the preliminaries,**
> **And pray that you may realize**
> **That all things are illusions.**

Yogis who have understood that phenomena are illusory go on to train in it. They take refuge and generate the attitude of bodhichitta and reflect upon the illusory character of all things. They visualize themselves as deities with their teachers above their heads and recite the seven-branch prayer just as before. They then pray to their teachers that they might be able to train with success in the illusory nature of everything. During that time, it is imperative to have unbounded devotion. The reason for this is that meditation on a deity together with other practices related to the view and meditation do not, in themselves, confer freedom. For this depends on other factors such as the application of the various activities, as well as progress in one's general practice. By contrast, simply through devotion to one's teacher, one easily progresses on the grounds and paths. As it is said,

> If to you the master is at all times present,
> From all the buddhas you are never parted.

And,

> Through six months of unwavering devotion,
> The ground of Vajradhara will be reached.

Some people claim that when one practices guru yoga, one should not visualize one's teacher in human form. One should visualize him or her in the form of a deity, the main figure in the maṇḍala, and so on. For it is said in the *Vajra Garland Tantra* and the *Vajra Tent Tantra* that the teacher is the very embodiment of the maṇḍalas of the five enlightened families. This is completely wrong. The explanation to the effect that the teacher is the embodiment of the maṇḍala of the thirty-two deities and that—as the *Vajra Tent Tantra* says—the teacher is the embodiment of the five enlightened families, is meant to show that one's teacher is the Buddha in truth. These texts do not imply that the teacher's form is to be changed. This means that if, while practicing guru yoga, one meditates on one's teacher in the form of a yidam deity, this is in fact meditation on a yidam. It is not guru yoga, for it does not produce the kind of devotion that comes when one focuses on one's own teacher. This is a very important mistake. One should indeed meditate on one's teacher in his or her present form. For it is not taught that one will gain enlightenment through devotion to the yidam—however excellent that may be—for in the latter case, one must still pass through the approach and accomplishment stages.[89]

When one's devotion to one's teacher is at its best, it is there and then that accomplishment is gained. Once again, this is said in the *Fifty Classes of Tantra*:

> Through six months of unwavering devotion,
> The ground of Vajradhara will be reached.

Again, others say that it is enough to supplicate the Three Jewels and that it serves no purpose to pray to one's teacher. On the contrary, one's teacher is the very embodiment of the Three Jewels. As we find in the *Saṃvarodaya*,

> Your teacher is the Buddha and your teacher is the Dharma;
> Your teacher likewise is the Saṅgha.

Your teacher is the all-accomplisher.
For us there's nothing greater than the teacher.

In other words, the teacher is supreme and one should meditate on his or her actual physical form—as the text just cited proves.

If to you the master is at all times present,
From all the buddhas you are never parted.

If devotion fails and wrong ideas arise, one should alter one's state of mind. If the teacher seems to have strong desire and attachment, one should remind oneself that authentic teachers do not have the slightest attachment in themselves but make a show of it as a means of training those who do have desire. Reflecting that true teachers have the "vajra desire" spoken of in the tantras, and considering how extraordinary this is, one should again generate feelings of devotion. In the same way, when teachers seem angry, ignorant, proud, jealous, or avaricious, one should reflect that they are in fact free of all such defilements. One should think that it is oneself who possesses such defects and that one's teacher is in fact demonstrating them only as a means of removing them from one's mind. True teachers demonstrate vajra anger, vajra ignorance, vajra pride, vajra jealousy, vajra miserliness of which the tantras speak. Reflecting on how extraordinary this is, one should generate even stronger devotion and confess one's faults. It is thus that one will surely gain accomplishment.

The root text continues,

26. Regarding the main practice,
You should meditate at all times, day and night,
Considering that all things in their variety,
Both outside and within,
Appear to you like magical illusions
Through their causes and conditions.

They are in truth unreal, intangible,
An unobstructed openness.

Sitting in a high and open place, one should meditate on the understanding that whatever one sees, hears, and thinks is the illusory, subjective experience of one's own mind. And one should rest in the thought-free state.

Then, as one arises from this state, one's practice in the postmeditation period should be as follows:

27. No matter what defilements may arise,
Attachment or dislike, indulging or rejection,
Look on all of them as magical illusions.
Train yourself to see them all as empty and unreal.
Outwardly, all things are just illusions;
Inwardly, all thoughts are like illusions.
They come from causes and conditions,
And thus they are deceptive and unreal.
They are mere appearances, so meditate on them
Employing the example of a magical illusion.

Attachment and aversion, friends and enemies, happiness and suffering—all the outer appearances of sense objects and all the inner experiences of the mind take their origin in extraneous conditions and are therefore illusory. They are false and deceptive and are therefore illusory. They appear without really existing and are therefore illusory. By reflecting in this way, one should come to the understanding that these illusions are but the radiance of emptiness. As *The Way of the Bodhisattva* tells us,

With things that in this way are empty,
What is there to gain and what to lose?

What is there to give me joy and pain?

And,

> May beings like myself discern and grasp
> That all things have the character of space![90]

With regard to one's practice at nighttime, the root text goes on to say,

> **28. As before, when lying down to sleep,**
> **Relax completely in the state**
> **Of knowing all to be illusory,**
> **Unreal, beyond conceptual construction.**
> **Because you understand deluded dreams—**
> **Whatever may occur—to be illusory,**
> **All fear that might arise**
> **From taking them as true subsides.**
> **Training in them as illusions,**
> **Increase them and transfigure them.**
> **Travel to the buddha fields,**
> **Themselves like magical illusions.**
> **Perform this practice as described before.**

Assuming the recumbent posture of a lion, one should relax in the state of the illusoriness of all things. Phenomena are empty and beyond the reach of conceptual elaboration. Then one should visualize the central channel with its upper extremity in the Brahmā aperture and the lower end in the secret center. Within this channel that is white and fine, like an inflated membrane, one should concentrate on a bright flame that then becomes increasingly fine until it disappears. And in this state, one should fall asleep. At first, one should recognize one's dreams as simply magical illusions, getting used to their lack of real existence. Then one should multiply the things that one is dreaming about and transform them, and travel to the buddha fields as previously described.

It could be argued that since dreams are delusions within delusion, no purpose is served by recognizing them as such, in training in them and multiplying them. But as the scriptures say,

> Through delusion is delusion purified,
> And countless benefits accrue from this.
> If for one night a yogi recognizes that he dreams,
> For fifteen days he will be happy.
> The gods, the nāgas, and gandharvas all
> Will make him offerings and praises.
> Dākas and dākinīs will surround him in reality.
> To recognize one's dreams to be illusions
> Is a boat in which to cross the ocean of the lower realms.

And as one meditates on this path, the result will be as the root text describes:

> **29. And by this means, your clinging**
> **To the real existence of saṃsāra**
> **Will dissipate all by itself.**
> **When it subsides through being seen as magical illusion,**
> **The state of nonabiding nirvāṇa is attained.**
> **The twofold aim, illusion-like, is gained all by itself.**
> **So train in the illusory condition of all things.**

With regard to results in the immediate term, when one meditates day and night on the fact that all things are the illusory body of the deity (which is neither permanent, nor discontinuous, nor both),[91] one will acquire all the qualities of the path of learning. And in the ultimate term, one will gain the saṃbhogakāya while in the bardo state and pass beyond all sorrow. As it is said in the *Later Tantra of Secret Primal Wisdom*,

> All buddha fields within the ten directions—
> The dream body accomplishes them.

Thence arise—not otherwise—
The first ground's perfect qualities.
And since upon the eighth ground
The impure deluded tendencies
Of the daytime and of dreams do not occur,
There is no need to say that they are absent
On the ground endowed with lotuses.[92]

And in the *Arrangement of Samayas* it is said,

When daytime things arise for you
As empty, magical illusions,
And when at night in dreams
You see all things as deities—
If you do not stray from this,
Within a single instant in the bardo,
You will gain enlightenment
In the saṃbhogakāya state
And pass beyond all sorrow.
No need to say what will occur
When you remain continually thus.
Such is luminosity, illusion-like.
Do not speak of it in any other way.

It is said in the *Longer Tantra of the True Arising of Primordial Wisdom*,

The dharmadhātu, an illusion, is the ground of all.
If you practice meditation, which is like illusion,
With regard to things that are illusion-like,
You will accomplish buddhahood that is like an illusion.
The five paths and twelve grounds
Are not traversed in any other way.
Such is the fruit for others and oneself,
In which the vast and the profound are never separate.

In conclusion,

The illusory display of all phenomena
Is deep in nature, vast in character.
May beings understand it perfectly
As the adamantine state of nonduality
And thus accomplish the illusion of enlightenment.

The state of the enlightened attitude
Is like the sky, immense and pure,
Endowed with light of sun and moon,
The luminosity illusion-like.
Through the myriad lights of wisdom and of love,
Arising through that concentration
Where space and light are blended,
May the ignorance of wandering beings be dispelled.

And like the disk of the full autumn moon
Reflected in the water cleansed of all impurity,
May all the qualities of excellence be perfect
In the firmament of vajra essence,
Pure and ultimate reality.

This concludes the chapter that is like a magical illusion, a commentary on the second vajra point of *Finding Rest in Illusion, a Teaching of the Great Perfection.*

The Third Vajra Point: Trick of Sight

Now that it has been demonstrated that phenomena, which are by nature like magical illusions, are an unceasing display, we must now show how these same phenomena come from nowhere—just like optical illusions or tricks of sight.[93]

1. Listen! I shall now explain
The words of the Victorious One
That all things are like tricks of sight.

Phenomena appear and yet they have no intrinsic being; they arise from nowhere just like [something seen in] an optical illusion. It is said in the *Middle-Length Prajñāpāramitā-sūtra*, "Subhūti, phenomena are like tricks of sight; by their nature, they come from nowhere." This teaching, condensed into an essential instruction, is divided into three parts corresponding to ground, path, and result. First, by means of the view, we establish the ground, which, like a trick of sight, comes from nowhere:

2. Just as through a certain form
A trick of sight appears,
Likewise in the nature of the mind
And through the power of deluded habit,
The optical illusion of saṃsāra is contrived:
The false appearance of something nonexistent.
However it appears, it is like a trick of sight.

Shadows are cast by material forms. They arise in the shape of these forms but are different in kind. In similar fashion, there is the radiance of awareness of the primordial ultimate expanse—empty, luminous, spontaneously present. This corresponds to the material form. Not recognizing this radiance, beings stray into the duality of apprehended and apprehender, and there appear, concomitant with the radiance of awareness, the five aggregates, the five elements, the five defilements, the five sense objects, the five material sense organs, and so on. They are different in kind from the radiance of awareness, for they manifest as a host of hallucinatory appearances that afflict, obstruct, and are impure, and as karma and the five defilements. So it is that there are the three worlds and six migrations wherein beings circle through the coming together of causes and conditions. As it is said in the *All-Creating King Tantra*, "Just like shadows cast by material forms, even so are manifold hallucinatory experiences." And as the *Abridged Prajñāpāramitā* says, "When the conditions are assembled, the deceptive mechanism of karma manifests."

On the basis of false appearance, beings turn [and wander] in a further level of hallucinatory experience.

> **3. Childish beings are deceived thereby;**
> **Unskilled, they cling to it as real.**
> **Caught in the trap, the trick of sight—**
> **The objects of the five sense powers—**
> **They cling to self though there is nothing there.**
> **Just look how they're deceived!**

Childish beings, who do not understand that saṃsāra is like an optical illusion, constantly take it as something real. Their mental consciousness strongly clings to apparent but hallucinatory sense objects: form, sound, smell, taste, textures—all of which are perceived but are without real existence. Beings are engrossed in sense objects; they hold to "I" and "mine" and thus turn constantly in saṃsāra. They are like children who lose themselves in their games.

If one does not understand that the apparent world is devoid of intrinsic reality, one is deceived by it. And even among those engaged upon the path, there are many who are just like childish people! As *The Way of the Bodhisattva* tells us,

> Children can't help crying when
> Their sandcastles come crumbling down.
> My mind is so like them
> When praise and reputation start to fail.[94]

It is thus that childish beings are attached to appearances that are in fact just tricks of sight. Therefore, the root text continues with an exhortation—addressed to practitioners—to understand the nature of phenomena and realize their lack of intrinsic being:

> **4. Phenomenal existence, universe and beings,**
> **Happiness and sorrow, high and low,**
> **Appear while nonexistent.**
> **They're like shadows in the lamplight,**
> **Or the moon seen double**
> **When one's eyes are pressed,**
> **Or like deep darkness**
> **When there's much affliction.**
> **When left unanalyzed, these things appear;**
> **When analyzed there is no grasping them;**
> **When closely analyzed, their nature is beyond extremes.**
> **Like space, they are unborn.**
> **Understand this very day,**
> **With sure conviction, their primordial nature.**

Phenomenal existence, the universe and beings, happiness and suffering, the high and the low, are all like tricks of sight. Such optical illusions, which appear even though they do not exist, are produced in relation to certain forms and are not different from them in respect of their arising, duration, and subsiding. They are like a shadow that is cast, like a second moon, like darkness, and so on. In brief, this means respectively that, on the basis of an actual form, another form appears as a copy, a second form manifests, and another form arises in the manner of a reflection. In contrast with the actual form, these secondary forms are categorized as optical illusions because they are not causally effective. Likewise, if all phenomena are examined, they are like tricks of sight, for although they appear, they have no intrinsic being. If they are left unexamined, they seem to be perfectly fine. If on the other hand they are minutely investigated, even the partless particles and the subtle moments of consciousness that support [the experience of] coarse, extended phenomena are found to be without any identifiable nature. They are like space; they do not have any existence at all. It is said in the *Middle-Length Prajñāpāramitā*, "Since like tricks of sight, all phenomena are devoid of intrinsic being, they are by nature primordially empty."

But in what way are they empty? The root text continues,

> **5. False appearances are groundless**
> **Just like optical illusions.**
> **They are rootless and without true features of their own.**
> **When examined, they are empty;**
> **They have no being and yet seem to be.**
> **It should be understood:**
> **Their primordial nature is to be unborn.**

Samsaric phenomena appear like tricks of sight; they do not have any true characteristics of their own. When they are examined, they are empty; they are none other than the mere subjective experience of one's mind. And this condition of theirs is their primordial state. This primordial state is the emptiness of phenomena—the fact that, while they appear within the self-cognizing mind, they have no existence from their own side. It does not mean that phenomena are investigated as to their past. Therefore, everything that appears is just the subjective experience of one's own mind. It is like a trick of sight. Everything should be understood as the mind's radiant display, which has no existence within awareness, the fundamental nature. As it is said in the *Ornament of the Light of Wisdom*, "Mañjuśrī, an optical illusion is perceived even though it has no intrinsic being. Likewise, all phenomena are perceived and yet have no intrinsic being."

Within the nature [of the mind], which is rootless, and because of subtle ignorance, which is difficult to discern, hallucinatory appearances arise ever more vividly and extensively.

> **6. Just as in the middle of a desert plain**
> **A small thing seen from far away**
> **May yet seem vast in size,**
> **From just a slight attachment**
> **To a self in that which has no self,**
> **The vast hallucination of saṃsāra manifests.**

When a small thing appears to be great in size, this is a hallucination. For example, in an immense desert and at a distance, a crow may appear to be as big as a yak, and a yak may look as large as a mountain. This impression occurs because the desert is dry and one is in a distressed state, overcome by the heat, and furthermore the object is very far away. It is the same in the case of the appearances of saṃsāra. Because of the subtle ignorance of self-grasping, which is the root, one becomes habituated to conceptual ignorance and to the dualism of apprehending subject and apprehended object. By this means, one provides the cause, and through various actions, one provides the conditions, for the various hallucinatory appearances—of the outer universe and the beings it contains—which pervade the whole infinity of space. All this derives from a subtle root hard to discern. Yet if this same root is examined, it is found to be the utterly pure nature of the mind, which is itself rootless. As it is said in the *Guhyagarbha Tantra*,

The rootless nature of the mind
Is the root of all phenomena.

Because the ground and root are subtle, they are hard to discern and cannot be indicated with words. However, if one leaves the mind alone [without contrivance], it will clarify in the same way that muddy water does when it is left to stand.

7. When these hallucinations are investigated,
They are found to be unreal.
When you understand that, just like space,
They cannot be removed,
Just let them be.
And do not cling so foolishly
To this world's real existence—
This world that, like a trick of sight,
Appears without existing.

No one is able simply to annul an optical illusion. But if the form that triggered the trick of sight in the first place is removed, the optical illusion will no longer occur. In the same way, it is not possible simply to remove the hallucinatory appearances of saṃsāra for the simple reason that they are not actually existent things. On the other hand, it is through halting one's apprehension and clinging to such appearances that the latter will disappear. When all apprehension or clinging is left to settle in its own nature, all this will be brought to an end. As it is said in one of the sūtras, "How can the duality of apprehender and apprehended remain when all conceptuality collapses?"

The root text goes on to show that whatever appears cannot be conceived of, expressed, or found:

8. The fundamental state of all phenomena
Is their primordial condition, pure from the beginning.
Do not cling to them; do not conceptualize.

Regarding those appearances that have no self-identity
That could be recognized,
What point is there in getting trapped
Within the cage of partiality and clinging?
Give up all concern for such phenomena.
Understand that what appears
Is void of true existence.

Everything within phenomenal existence is like an optical illusion. It appears and yet is devoid of intrinsic being. With regard to the phenomena that appear in the world, one should overcome the partiality of accepting or rejecting them, the assumption of their true existence, and all attachment and aversion and so on. And with regard to the ideas that appear in the tenet systems, one should discard all partisan attitudes in distinguishing between cause and effect, appearance and emptiness, the two truths, and the aggregates, elements, and sense fields. They appear to perception, but if one does not indulge in clinging to them, one will come to the understanding that they are all simply a "vivid, naked, free state of openness." This is what is meant when one speaks of "the fundamental way of being" of phenomena. It is said in the *Treasury of Precious Nonorigination*,

Do not think of anything; do not ponder anything.
Do not alter anything; stay naturally relaxed.
This uncontrived condition is the treasury of
nonorigination:
The path that all the buddhas take, past, present, and
to come.

This concludes the section on the establishment of the ground. We now turn to the practice of the path.

9. When you have an understanding
That all things are just like tricks of sight,

Place your mind in its own nature as it is.
Practice the preliminaries previously described,
And pray that you will clearly see
That all things are like optical illusions.

Understanding that all phenomena are like optical illusions, one should remain in a state of meditative evenness. As a preliminary to this, one should practice guru yoga, as explained above, and one should pray to one's teacher for help in seeing that everything is like a trick of sight.

The root text continues:

10. As the main part of the practice,
Train yourself in seeing all things
As optical illusions, tricks of sight.
Of true existence form is empty;
It is like a trick of sight.
Sound is void of sound;
It's like a trick of sight.
Smell and taste and touch
Are all of them like tricks of sight.
The mind and mental objects
All resemble tricks of sight.
Everything is void of true existence.
In this understanding leave your mind relaxed
And free from grasping, free from false assumption.

The six objects, form and so on; the six organs, the eyes and so on; and the six consciousnesses such as the consciousness of sight—all things, whether they are appearing phenomena or mental designations, are devoid of true existence, just like optical illusions. When one reaches such an understanding, one should settle in a state of meditative evenness free of thoughts and recollections. As it is said in the sūtra, "All thinking is nonvirtuous. It is a virtue to refrain from thinking. When there is no recollection, when there is no cogitation, then it is that one recalls the Buddha."

The teaching for the night practice is as follows:

> **11. Just as in the daytime,**
> **Likewise when you go to sleep,**
> **Concentrate your mind upon your heart.**
> **Sleep then in the knowledge that**
> **All things are tricks of sight.**
> **And it is certain, as before,**
> **That you will recognize your dreams as dreams.**

One should first visualize within one's heart a ball of five-colored light, and finally one should fall asleep in a state that is free of all reference. One will understand that all the things that appear in one's dreams are nothing but optical illusions. One can then assume different forms in one's dreams and transform them just as previously described.

The results of practice on the path are as follows:

> **12. Even the occurrence of experiences and realization**
> **Is like a trick of sight.**
> **Spontaneously the realization comes**
> **That things lack true existence.**
> **And in the state of openness**
> **Devoid of clinging and fixation,**
> **Delusions of accepting and rejecting all collapse.**
> **Powers of vision, preternatural clairvoyance,**
> **All the qualities of concentration**
> **Will be gained. Possessing thus**
> **The treasure of the teaching of the Conqueror,**
> **You will become the guide of every being.**
> **Meditate therefore that everything**
> **Is like an optical illusion.**

The immediate result of this practice is the realization that all things are like optical illusions, and on the basis of such an understanding, one will have the meditative experience of the collapse of hallucinatory appearance. And this will certainly propel one out of saṃsāra. Meditative concentration will be accomplished and likewise various powers of vision, preternatural clairvoyant knowledge, and various miraculous abilities. As it is said in the *Abridged Prajñāpāramitā*,

> Through meditative stability the lower pleasures of the senses are discarded.
> All kinds of perfect knowledge, clairvoyance, concentration—all are truly gained.

Meditative experience is like smoke, whereas realization is like fire. Realization consists in the assimilation of the fact that the nature of awareness is a state of groundless openness. If one remains without distraction in this realization, the meditative experiences of bliss, luminosity, and no-thought will manifest. Realization is the perfect assimilation of the ultimate status of phenomena. As one grows accustomed to this state, one experiences in one's body and mind the signs of "warmth,"[95] and this is referred to as meditative experience.

As for the ultimate result of this practice, it is through the full understanding of phenomena as tricks of sight that one comes to the realization of their fundamental nature, which is groundless and empty. One is consequently released from saṃsāra and one attains to the state beyond sorrow. As we find in the *Abridged Prajñāpāramitā*,

> Through wisdom, having perfectly cognized the nature of phenomena,
> The three worlds one will utterly transcend.

In conclusion,

Certain that phenomena are empty forms,
Appearing yet unreal,
Nonexistent yet perceptible,
May beings come to perfect peace
Within the vast and unoriginate expanse
Devoid of mind's elaborations.

The dualistic play
Of apprehender-apprehended,
Like an optical illusion,
Teeters on the brink of dissolution.
And when hallucinatory appearance—
The dark of ignorance—dissolves,
The sun of self-arisen luminosity
Rises from within.
May others see, as I have done,
The way things truly are.

Because phenomena in their variety
Appear to be, they may seem also not to be.
May the deluded clinging
To these two alternatives collapse all by itself!
Within the state of nondual evenness,
Of utter freedom and transparent openness,
May beings all together gain their freedom—all without exception.

This concludes the chapter that is like a trick of sight, a commentary on the third vajra point of *Finding Rest in Illusion, a Teaching of the Great Perfection.*

The Fourth Vajra Point: Mirage

Now it will be shown that just as phenomena are said not to come from anywhere, neither do they depart. They are like mirages.

1. Here too the Conqueror declared
That things resemble mirages.
Listen! I will tell you how this is.

All things in phenomenal existence, both saṃsāra and nirvāṇa, appear and yet lack intrinsic existence. They are like mirages. As we find in the *Middle-Length Prajñāpāramitā*, "O Subhūti, since phenomena are primordially free from 'departing,' they are like mirages." The meaning of this statement will be explained in three sections according to the ground, path, and result.

First of all, by means of the view, one will arrive at a clear conviction that the ground is itself like a mirage, devoid of all "departing."

2. Just as during summer
In the middle of the day,
Mirages of water appear upon a plain—
Through the power of the mind's ingrained proclivity
To apprehend and grasp at self,
Saṃsāra's false appearances
Arise just like a mirage.

During the summer, when one is on a wide plain, and the sun is shining and one's eyes are affected by the heat—when, in other words, there is a connection between the floating vapors and one's phlegmatic humor—the appearance of a stretch of water appears, even though there is no water there. In the same way, although the nature of awareness is primordially pure, it happens that through a subtle thought of self and the radiance of awareness appearing as sense objects, there occurs upon the "even plain of emptiness" hallucinatory appearances similar to the water seen in a mirage. And consequently one wanders in the six migrations of the three worlds. Nevertheless, it is important to understand that they are like mere reflections without any existence of their own. They do not exist even though they clearly appear. As it is said in the *Samādhirāja-sūtra*,

> At midday in the summertime,
> Those tormented by their thirst
> May see a mirage of a stretch of water.
> Understand that all things are like this.

The root text then goes on to show that in the very moment that phenomena are perceived, they are devoid of intrinsic being.

> **3. There is no way to grasp at their identity.**
> **They are beyond dichotomies.**
> **They are empty;**
> **All descriptive terms subside.**
> **Unborn, they are like space;**
> **They have no being of their own.**
> **Understand that they are unoriginate,**
> **That they transcend all thought.**

If one examines the infinitesimal particles, directional location, color, shape, and so on, of whatever appears, one will conclude that outer and inner phenomena are like space. The noble sūtra *Lamp of the Three Jewels* declares that "Phenomena are like the Sugata." And we find too in the sūtra the *Irreversible Wheel*,

Ignorance resembles space itself;
Phenomena have no real features.

Since phenomena are empty in the very moment that they appear, the root text goes on to declare that they are devoid of intrinsic being.

4. In the very moment they appear,
Things seem to have beginnings,
And yet, like mirages, they have no origin.
It seems that they remain,
Yet like a mirage, they have no abiding.
They also seem to cease,
And yet, like mirages, they do not cease.
Understand therefore
That, though they do appear,
They are without intrinsic being.

In the very moment that phenomena appear in all their variety, they have no real existence of their own. The outer universe is formed; plants and so forth grow therein; beings—the living content of the universe—are born and give rise to thought. But in the very moment that all these things seem to arise, they are devoid of origin, because the objects that come into being and the experience of arising itself do not exist in the nature of awareness. Likewise, in the very moment that phenomena seem to remain in existence as solid entities, there is neither the act of remaining nor indeed anything that remains. Finally, in the very moment that the universe seems to be evacuated and destroyed, and the minds of beings seem to vanish, the universe does not cease, and neither do the minds of beings. It should be understood therefore that, like the water seen in a mirage, phenomena appear and yet are devoid of intrinsic being. As it is said in the *Scripture of Summarized Wisdom*,

Emaho! A wondrous and a marvelous thing,
A secret all the perfect buddhas know!
Without being born are all things born,
And in the moment of their birth, they are unborn!

Emaho! A wondrous and a marvelous thing,
A secret all the perfect buddhas know!
Without remaining, all things yet remain,
And in the moment of remaining, they do not remain!

Emaho! A wondrous and a marvelous thing,
A secret all the perfect buddhas know!
Without their coming or their going, all things come and go,
And in the moment that they come and go, they're free of coming and of going!

When this view has been understood, it should be reflected in one's personal behavior.

5. All joy and sorrow, pleasure, pain, all good and ill
Are just like mirages—all empty, without self.
All things within phenomenal existence—
Outer, inner—all resemble mirages.
Nonexistent, they appear and are perceived.
Understand that from the outset
They are by their nature pure.
No center do they have, no limit;
They are primordially empty.

All outer and inner phenomena are devoid of intrinsic being. This being so, all friends and enemies, all that one accepts or else rejects, should be brought onto the path as being similar to mirages that naturally subside. It should be understood that from the very first, they are nothing but the manifestation of the radiance of emptiness.

Consequently,

6. To apprehend duality where there is no duality
Is like looking at a mirage.
Do not let yourself be caught by clinging,
By taking or rejecting what has no reality.
Watch your mind,
Itself not different from a mirage.
This is the wisdom of the Conquerors
Past, present, and to come.

To cling in the ordinary way to oneself and others, accepting or rejecting accordingly, is quite simply absurd. For phenomena are like mirages: they have no intrinsic reality even though they appear. As it is said in the sūtra the *Ornament of the Light of Wisdom*, "A mirage, O Mañjuśrī, appears but is unreal. Likewise phenomena appear but are unreal."

Concerning the practice on the path, the root text goes on to say,

7. Then, according to the stages of meditative practice,
Begin with the preliminaries as previously explained,
And pray that you may see all things as mirages.

One should practice guru yoga as before, invoking the teacher and praying especially for success in seeing that all things are mirage-like.

Then,

8. As for the main practice, tell yourself
That all things are like mirages.
And then stay free from hopes and fears,
From all engagement with the thoughts

Occurring in your mind.
At night, approach your dreams as previously described,
And they will all arise as mirages.

Bearing in mind that whatever occurs in the course of the day is just a mirage and does not really exist, one should be relaxed without being carried away by the mind's proliferation outward, and without the mind's becoming engaged with inner preoccupations or withdrawing one-pointedly within. One should continually maintain the recognition that everything is but the radiance of awareness. At night, one should lie down as previously described and fall asleep visualizing just the central channel. By this means, mirage-like dreams will be recognized for what they are, and one will be able to assume many forms in the course of them, transforming them at will. And even when sleeping, one will be aware of all the sights and sounds occurring in one's vicinity. Innumerable visions will occur—smoke, mirages, fireflies, and so on.[96]

As for the result of the practice, the root text says,

9. Belief in real existence, clinging to a self
Will naturally subside.
Dhāraṇī clouds, clairvoyance, concentration—
All will burgeon from within.
The enlightened state will swiftly be attained.
Therefore meditate that everything
Is by its nature like a mirage.

The immediate result of this practice is that, through understanding that all phenomena are like mirages, one will experience neither desire nor aversion for them, and one will acquire the power of dhāraṇī, concentration, powers of vision, and all kinds of preternatural knowledge.

The dhāraṇī or power of memory is so called because it consists in an unforgetting recollection whereby one retains all the words and meanings of the teaching. As it is said in the tantra entitled the *Perfect Accomplishment of Susitikara*,

> Dhāraṇī or the power of memory is of three kinds:
> Recollection of the words, the meaning,
> And the words and meaning both together.
> The term *dhāraṇī* is employed[97]
> Because this memory retains its contents
> Free from all decline.

Concentration is a one-pointed state of awareness, limpid and clear. It is also a state of meditative evenness that may be focused on any object. As we find in the *Samādhirāja-sūtra*,

> Those who place their minds
> Upon the Lord of all the world,
> Endowed with beauteous, golden form,
> Are "bodhisattvas who repose in even meditation."

Powers of vision consist, for example, in the ability to perceive whatever is impeded from sight. Clairvoyance or preternatural knowledge is the knowledge of one's previous existences and so on; it is the preternatural perception of anything at all.

In conclusion,

Born from the great ocean
Of the qualities of perfect freedom,
Chief of holy beings residing in the fields
Of fathomless immensity,
O mighty Lord who go in bliss,
The source and wellspring of all happiness,
May we become like you
And quaff the draft of immortality.

Upon the precious ground of a pure field,
Within a palace measureless, of ravishing delight,
The Dharma's drum resounds.
May those of pure and limpid mind
Behold this place of Amitābha, Boundless Light.

Things that appear in their variety
Are by their very nature pure.
May we discern their unborn empty nature
And, annulling in a single stroke
The false hallucinations of saṃsāra,
May we come to spotless peace,
The state beyond all sorrow!

This concludes the chapter that is like a mirage, a commentary on the fourth vajra point of *Finding Rest in Illusion, a Teaching of the Great Perfection.*

The Fifth Vajra Point: Reflection of the Moon

Having shown in this way that phenomena do not come and do not go, it is now time to discuss the aspect of their appearance, showing how, like the moon reflected in water, they do appear even though they have no intrinsic existence.

1. Furthermore, the Victor has declared that everything
Is like the moon's reflection on the water.
This now I shall explain
That you may put this teaching into practice.

All the phenomena of saṃsāra and nirvāṇa may be perceived. They are not nothing[98] but are like the moon reflected in water. The *Middle-Length Prajñāpāramitā-sūtra* says, "O Subhūti, phenomena appear; they are not nothing. They are like the moon reflected on the water." The implementation of this teaching will be described under the three headings of ground, path, and result.

First, we will consider the ground, which appears while lacking intrinsic being.

2. In the heart of the profound and limpid sea,
The nature of the mind,
The image of spontaneous presence,
Primordially arisen, does indeed abide.
And yet through the turbidity
Stirred up by waves of dualistic clinging,

This presence is not clear,
Disturbed by winds of thought.
Worldly beings manifest
Through ignorance and ego-grasping.
Ignorant, defiled, they do not see primordial wisdom,
They sink in endless and beginningless saṃsāra.

The nature of the mind is like a pure ocean. Within this support for the kāyas, which are inseparable from the wisdoms, are found the attributes of enlightenment as numerous as the grains of sand in the Ganges. They are present of themselves primordially. Nevertheless, with coemergent ignorance as the cause, and with conceptual ignorance stirring up the waves of dualistic clinging, the perfect qualities of the ultimate expanse, the luminous reflections of the stars and planets, do not appear. Instead, because of karma and defilement, there manifest all sorts of hallucinatory appearances, and as a result beings go turning in saṃsāra. As it is said in the *Longer Māyājāla Tantra*,

Being limpid and of vast immensity,
Containing the reflections of primordial wisdom,
The ultimate expanse is like a pure and limpid sea.
But agitated by the winds of ignorance
And the dualistic play of apprehender-apprehended,
It becomes disturbed and turbid.

To show that this manifold, hallucinatory display is like the moon reflected in water, the root text continues:

3. Just as in unsullied water
Bright unmoving forms of stars and planets,
Though not really there, are nonetheless perceived,
Within the water of the mind
The forms that have arisen,
Images of false appearances,

Though nonexistent, are perceived.
And beings are tormented.

Just as in a pool of clear water the reflections of the stars and planets appear, likewise, within the clear water of the mind, and through the doors of the limpid sense powers, outer and inner phenomena (form and the other five sense objects) appear in the manner of reflections. But the mind is deluded and takes such objects to be really existing. In the terms of the comparison, the mind and the sense powers are like the pure water, whereas the appearance of the sense objects—which are the awakening of the habitual tendencies stored in the mind from time without beginning—are represented by the stars and planets. These sense objects are neither the mind nor something other than the mind. Manifesting in the manner of reflected images, appearing objects come before the dualistically oriented mind. And reacting to them with craving and aversion, as things to be accepted or rejected, beings are caught thereby. As the *Samādhirāja-sūtra* says,

The moon arises in the limpid sky,
And though her form appears upon the limpid sea,
The moon into the water does not pass.
Understand that all things are like this.

This teaches us that the [seemingly extramental] appearing objects of perception, the solidification of habitual tendencies, appear as secondary images to the sense faculties lodged within the five sense doors. If they are not grasped by the mental consciousness, one is not defiled.

Since the universe and beings are surely understood to be like the reflection of the moon in the water, their lack of intrinsic being is proclaimed.

4. What are they, these appearances?
They are not actual entities—

There is no grasping them.
They do not have, nor do they lack,
Specific character.
Not existent nor yet nonexistent,
They transcend extremes of truth and falsity.
This then is the meaning
When it's said that they are like reflections.

When all phenomenal appearances are understood in terms of the example of the moon reflected in the water, one will see that all such things do not exist even at the level of infinitesimal particles. They are empty forms. It will be understood that they cannot be established as either entities or nonentities, as either existent or nonexistent, as either true or false. One will laugh to think how amazing phenomena are—and how different they are from the way they seemed to be in the past. And realizing now that though such things are perceived, they are devoid of intrinsic being, one will have the highest respect for the Lord Buddha. As it is said in the *Supreme Essence*, "Because phenomena are empty by their nature, they are like the reflection of the moon in water."

The root text goes on to make the same point:

5. The six sense objects, form and all the rest,
Are like the moon's reflection in the water,
For they appear although they are not there.
They do not have intrinsic being
And yet appear unceasingly to those who are deluded.
The eye itself, the visual sense, and visual consciousness—
And equally for all the six sensorial gatherings—
Are just like this same water moon:
Empty, hollow, false, deceptive.
Devoid of an essential core,
They're like the plantain tree.
In every aspect, you should understand,
They are devoid of true existence.

The six sense objects (form and so on), the six sense doors (the eyes and so on), the six sense faculties (the visual receptor and so on), and the six sense consciousnesses (of sight and so on) are all said to be as unreal as the moon reflected in the water. Why is this? It is because they are mere appearances; they are without any being of their own; they appear unceasingly; and although they are nonexistent, they arise like hallucinatory visions. Since they are perceived while being nonexistent, they are deceptive; since there are mere reflections, they are hollow; since they appear while being untrue, they are false; and since they are without essential core, they are like the plantain tree. It should be understood that phenomena are a mere display of empty form. As it is said in the *Questions of Rāṣṭrapāla*,

> Phenomena are lacking in intrinsic being.
> Deceptive, hollow, false,
> They are like plantain trees devoid of essence.

It is not only phenomena that are like a "water moon." Even the dharmadhātu, utterly pure awareness, the enlightened mind, defined as self-cognizing primordial wisdom, is without intrinsic being even though it is experienced.

> **6. The mind unstained,**
> **Unmarred by ontological extremes,**
> **Is also like the water moon.**
> **Experienced yet empty,**
> **It is free of all conceptual constructs.**
> **Primal wisdom, nonconceptual,**
> **Peaceful and profound,**
> **Is utterly ineffable.**
> **Know that from the state of luminosity**
> **It never stirs.**

The moon that is reflected in the water is not a concrete object endowed with specific (efficacious) characteristics. It is neither present nor absent, and yet it is perceived unhindered. In the same way, the pure nature of the mind is not a concrete entity endowed with specific character. It transcends all conceptual extremes of existence and nonexistence. And yet, thanks to the blessings of a teacher, it may be experienced by self-cognizing awareness as the great and unceasing state of emptiness and luminosity. As we find in the *Lalitavistara*,

> Deep and peaceful, thought-free, luminous, unmade:
> The nectar truth, this now I have discovered.
> Were I to teach it, none would understand;
> And so I will remain, not speaking, in the forest.[99]

The root text then encourages us to remain in the state of suchness beyond ontological extremes:

> **7. When the moon appears in water,**
> **It is not the actual moon.**
> **Just so, when different things appear,**
> **They are neither there nor are they absent.**
> **Refrain from pondering conventional things**
> **Past, present, and to come,**
> **And rest in the unaltered state just as it is,**
> **Devoid of thoughts.**

In the same way that the moon reflected in the water is not the real moon, when phenomena appear in a certain way, it is not in that way that they exist. Therefore, with regard to whatever appears, one should remain in a state uncluttered by any thoughts or ideas concerning it. As we find in the *All-Creating King Tantra*,

> *Kyé!* The nature of the mind *just as it is*!
> This state *just as it is* is effortless great bliss.

Endowed with every aspect, it's completely free of them!
Leave the mind unaltered *as it is*.

The root text then has this to say about leaving the mind in the unaltered, natural state:

8. The enlightened mind
Is without coming or departing.
It is neither outside nor within.
Transcending thought, it has no partiality.
It is ultimate reality, unlimited and unconfined,
Wherein there is no wide or narrow
And no high or low.
So set aside all anxious search for it.

The indwelling, self-arisen primordial wisdom neither comes nor goes. It is neither outside nor within and is thus inconceivable. One should not try to identify it. Unlimited and unconfined, it is neither vast nor restricted, neither high nor low, and this is why one should avoid getting caught in the cage of intellectual meditation. As we find in *The Way of the Bodhisattva*,

The ultimate is not the object of the mind;
The mind is said to be the relative.[100]

Since all appearances are without intrinsic being, there is no point in examining them.

9. The primordial state does not exclusively abide
Within the state of no-thought.
For it is everything,
And everything is like a water moon.
Saṃsāra and nirvāṇa are equally the same:
They are not truly real, nor are they false.
Settle your mind unaltered in its ultimate condition.

Since whatever appears transcends all ontological extremes, saṃsāra and nirvāṇa are equal. One should not purposefully meditate on their emptiness. Instead, one should understand this point in accordance with the sūtras. As the *Ornament of the Light of Wisdom* stipulates, "O Mañjuśrī, the moon reflected in the water appears and yet it lacks intrinsic being. Phenomena also appear and yet are lacking in intrinsic being."

The root text goes on to advise us to refrain from mental assumptions and from clinging to ontological extremes:

10. Phenomenal existence, saṃsāra and nirvāṇa—
All is but an empty form.
It is just like the moon reflected in a pool—
Primordially empty, spontaneously empty,
Empty by its nature from the very outset.
It is an error to believe
That it's existent or is nonexistent.
Do not subscribe therefore
To any of the different, biased views of tenet systems.

Since they are groundless, phenomena are primordially empty. Since they are devoid of intrinsic being, they are spontaneously, naturally empty. Since they are without real characteristics, they are by nature empty from the very outset. And in their emptiness they are all equal. It serves no purpose to evaluate them according to different one-sided and partial tenet systems, in terms of their existence, authenticity, level, or any other criterion. One should be able to affirm that they are all like space, free from ontological extremes. As is it said in the *Laṅkāvatāra-sūtra*,

As long as one engages with the ordinary mind,
There is no end to boundless vehicles of teaching.
But when this mind collapses,
There are no more vehicles, no going and no coming.

What is the difference between the presence and the absence of realization?

11. As long as there is strong attachment to the self,
There's no escaping from saṃsāra.
The natural mind is uncontrived,
A spontaneous flow in which there is no clinging—
A bare, primordial flow,
Spontaneous openness and freedom,
An immensity unbounded—
What need is there to alter such a nature?

If there is even the slightest apprehension of, and clinging to, anything as being "this" or "that," one continues to be trapped in the samsaric state. As the *Songs of Realization* says,

Clinging, though no greater than a husk of sesame,
Will always be the source of suffering and nothing more.

The natural flow of awareness, free of clinging, manifests as a vast and open immensity. It is the spontaneous flow of the nature of the mind. As the *Great Garuḍa Tantra* declares,

Nonmeditation's restful state,
Primordially unbounded,
Is the mind without contrivance in its true condition—
What need is there for alteration in this natural state?

Let us then be clearly decided, the root text says, that this is the state of the Great Perfection:

12. When objects of the senses,
Empty from their side,
Appear like moons reflected in the water;
When the mind is likewise empty

Of assumptions and of clinging,
The duality of apprehender-apprehended
Ceases, is no more.
No further link is there between
Sense objects and the mind.
This is the authentic state,
The Great Perfection free from all exertion.

When a state of mind arises that is free of all clinging toward anything, it may be called the spontaneous accomplishment of the Natural Great Perfection. As the *Great Garuḍa Tantra* says,

The uncontrived, pure, nondual state
Is indeed the Great Perfection.
What need is there for any alteration?

Yogis who realize the state of simultaneous purity and equality accomplish in a single stroke all the grounds and paths, and all their activities become the play of the dharmakāya.

13. All that happens then becomes your helping friend,
And great bliss unconfined is present of itself.
Knowing this, you have no need to travel on the grounds.
For you have gained enlightenment in the primordial ground.

Within awareness, all the grounds and paths are understood to be one and the same. And when awareness is realized as a vast, untrammeled openness, every activity undertaken perfectly embodies the two accumulations. And therefore, the phenomena of saṃsāra and nirvāṇa manifest as the display of a single maṇḍala. As one of the *Songs of Realization* says,

Grounds, paths, and buddhahood—
All is understood to be the same,

Primal wisdom uncontrived.
[To know that this is so]
The mind need only ask itself.

The *Guhyagarbha* also says,

For the yogi who has realized Great Perfection,
All that happens is experienced as one great maṇḍala.

And the *All-Creating King* also says,

Kyé! The center [of the maṇḍala] is the unerring actual
essence.
Its surround is but nirvāṇa and saṃsāra
All displayed as perfect bliss.
No ground, no root, and no duality
Is found in the enlightened mind's expanse.
And you should know this
As the maṇḍala of the all-creating king.

The stages of the path are now explained:

14. To stay within that state when this is understood
Is meditation that resembles an unmoving water moon.
Therefore, you who are so fortunate,
Habituate yourselves to seeing
All that manifests
As untrue, as elusive and intangible.

All sense objects, which are perceived even though they have no intrinsic being, are like the moon reflected in the water. When one reaches an understanding that this is so, one should leave one's mind in a state of meditative evenness, in a state of no-thought, free from any conceptual constructions of one and many. As the *Samādhirāja-sūtra* says,

At night the moon appears
Reflected in a pool of limpid water.
It is empty, hollow; it has no essential core.
Understand that all things are like this.

As for the way to meditate, the root text goes on to say,

15. As before, first practice the preliminaries
And pray to see all things
Like moons reflected in the water.
And then the main part is to think
That everything you actually perceive
Is exactly like the moon's reflection
And to place your mind in even meditation.

As previously, one should practice guru yoga, and with strong devotion pray to one's teacher that one might be able to realize that all things are as insubstantial as the moon's reflection—appearing without really existing. And as one ponders that everything is like this, one should, without thinking of anything else, settle in a state of meditative evenness. All things will thus manifest as mere appearances, empty and nonexistent. And in due course, even this will fade away and one will taste of a condition that is free of all mental focus. As it is said in the *Sūtrālaṃkāra*,

On the basis of a thing referred to,
The state that's free from reference arises.
First understand that there is nothing.
Later even this will be discarded.[101]

When one is one-pointedly and without distraction focused on a support for concentration (such as the reflection of the moon in water), if thoughts carry one away to some other thing, one should, with mindfulness, immediately steady one's attention and return to one's meditation on the water moon. As the *Sūtrālaṃkāra* says,

Concentrate your mind
On any object that is suitable.
And when you are distracted,
Note this quickly and repair it.

At that time, when the mind remains inwardly still and the body-mind is blissful and well tuned, defilements do not arise and thoughts do not spread out to the objects of the senses—even though sensorial appearances are not stopped. Thus one attains a kind of concentration endowed with a wisdom that perfectly discerns objects. Again, the *Sūtrālaṃkāra* tells us,

The mind, when still,
Brings forth a state of bliss.
Thus stilled, it is well tuned.
It has no thoughts, yet perfectly discerns.

The perfect discernment of objects is not incompatible with the nonproliferation of thought. Thought is the mind that moves [outward] toward an object, whereas thought-free wisdom understands an object inwardly and instantly. This state is associated with a self-illuminating concentration. The difference between these two states lies in an outward or an inward orientation and whether or not they are associated with nonconceptual concentration. This is a point of the highest importance.

Then, as the root text goes on to say,

16. In the nighttime, practice as before.
The only difference lies in your regarding
Dreams as water moons.
Stay within a state where there's no clinging,
Where everything is equal.

One should fall asleep while meditating that the central channel is filled with five-colored light. In this way, one will recognize one's dreams as being as insubstantial as the reflection of the moon in water, and one will be able to assume within the dream state various forms, transforming them at will. A meditative experience will occur in which all appearances will seem completely transparent, insubstantial, offering not the slightest resistance.

As for the result of this meditation, the root text says,

> **17. Swiftly you will gain the everlasting realm,**
> **The nature of the mind.**
> **Whatever you perceive,**
> **You will not grasp at it as real, as this or that.**
> **And luminosity will manifest**
> **As clear and limpid as the moon reflected on the water.**
> **O you who are endowed with perfect fortune,**
> **Meditate upon this well.**

In the immediate term, since clinging to the real existence of what appears has been undermined, all acceptance and rejection with regard to it fades naturally away. The appearances themselves are regarded as being [no more real than] a moon reflected in the water, and a limpid concentration free from conceptual activity manifests accordingly in all one's daily behavior. It is thus that the states of meditation and postmeditation blend together in the experience of luminosity. Seeing the infinitesimal particles of one's body, one gains the powers of vision and preternatural knowledge, and finally one accomplishes the dharmakāya. As we find in the *Ratnakūṭa*,

> The one who meditates that everything is unreal
> Will quickly come to unsurpassed enlightenment.

In conclusion,

All things are by their nature pure primordially,
Unreal and yet apparent like the moon reflected in the water.

Understanding this, and crossing thus
The sea of dualistic clinging,
May we reach the precious shore of perfect freedom.

Developing our strength through realization
Of the emptiness endowed with supreme qualities,
And shooting then the dart of wisdom
With the strong bow of our concentration,
May we utterly destroy
Our ignorance and our defilements
And bring to naught the onslaught of saṃsāra.

May the hare-marked moon, the qualities of perfect virtue,
Bathe with light the mind streams of all wandering beings.
May it dispel the gloom of ignorance,
The night of their existence,
And open the white jasmine flowers—
The dharmatā, the nature of phenomena.

This concludes the chapter that is like the moon reflected in the water, a commentary on the fifth vajra point of *Finding Rest in Illusion, a Teaching of the Great Perfection.*

The Sixth Vajra Point: Echo

Now that it has been established that phenomena are not nothing [for they nevertheless appear], we now go on to show that they are not permanent.

1. Listen now, and I will lucidly explain
The Victor's word that all is like an echo.

All phenomena resemble echoes. They have no intrinsic nature even in the very moment that they are perceived. They have no enduring permanence and are ineffable. Because they are not truly existent entities, they are like the resounding of an echo. As it is said in the *Middle-Length Prajñāpāramitā*, "O Subhūti, phenomena are by their nature without permanence. For that reason, they are like echoes." Once again, this topic will be explained in three sections according to ground, path, and result.

Let us first establish the ground:

2. Through human voice before a rocky cliff
An echo's sound arises in the form of what was said.
Likewise through conditions do phenomena arise.
They have no being of their own.
Be convinced that they are void of true existence.

When people speak or shout in front of a rocky outcrop, the echo of their cry resounds. But the sound resonates without being located anywhere, either outside or within. In just the same way, coemergent ignorance cocomitant with the empty and luminous character of the primordial ground (which lacks intrinsic being) acts as a cause—with the result that the ground's own radiance (namely, the appearances of the ground) manifests as different hallucinatory appearances. Since they appear even though they have no existence, whether in awareness or anywhere else, it is in the manner of an echo that saṃsāra arises. In truth, they are but the clear appearance of something nonexistent—and nothing else. As it is said in the *Samādhirāja-sūtra*,

> When people stand before a cliff,
> Their songs or speech, their laughter, lamentation
> Are circumstances for the sounding of an echo.
> Yet from their voice the sound does not reverberate.
> Understand that all things are like this.

The root text goes on to say that, while being perceived, phenomena transcend all ontological extremes because they are without intrinsic being:

> **3. If, when the echo sounds,**
> **You search for its resounding—**
> **Within you or outside, or somewhere in between—**
> **You do not find it.**
> **If likewise you now mentally investigate**
> **All things that are within you or outside—**
> **The mind and what appears to it—**
> **Nothing, gross or subtle, do you find.**
> **All things are empty; just like space**
> **They have no entity.**
> **If this you understand,**
> **You will not cling or hanker after things.**

The resounding of an echo cannot be located anywhere either in the people or the cliff or somewhere in between them. And yet it is perceived, existing as it were thanks to certain conditions. In the same way, if all outer phenomena, as well as the thoughts within the mind, are examined—the gross outer objects analyzed into their component parts, and the subtle [mental] phenomena examined for their shape, color, and so on—they are all found to be without the slightest degree of real existence. They are like space beyond the reach of conception and expression. It is as the *Two Truths* declares:

> If reasoning investigates appearing things,
> Not one of them is found.
> Their ultimate condition is precisely this nonfinding:
> Their final and primordial nature.

This empty condition of things transcends the ordinary mind.

> **4. "The relative appears;**
> **The ultimate is not observed."**
> **Yet even to conceive of these two aspects**
> **Is nothing but the mind's distinction.**
> **For in the moment they're perceived,**
> **Phenomena transcend the mind.**
> **The mind is but a fabric**
> **Of conceptual construction**
> **That the mind itself has posited.**
> **And as for things themselves,**
> **The mind does not affect them**
> **By enlarging or diminishing.**
> **They cannot be encompassed**
> **By the webs of thought—**
> **They cannot be identified.**
> **To know them to be so**
> **Is to transcend the mind's construction.**

Those who propound the objective reality of phenomena maintain that they have two aspects. They say that phenomena exist on the relative level but not on the ultimate level.[102] This, however, is untenable, for such phenomena have no existence even in the very moment that they are being experienced. It is only the mind that conceives of phenomena as having these two aspects, for it is obvious that the latter are not part and parcel of phenomena themselves. This is why [when the mind realizes that] nothing is established as really existent, phenomena are not themselves diminished. It is the mind that discerns these two aspects within phenomena. And although the mind may discern the emptiness of phenomena, the emptiness in question is a mere concept and is not actual emptiness in itself. By contrast, the Prāsaṅgika Mādhyamikas say that with regard to appearing phenomena, no assertion is to be made. This, it should be understood, is the hallmark of the genuine [prāsaṅgika] middle way. As master Nāgārjuna has said [referring to the experience of the āryas],

> Since things are as they appear to them,
> Analysis does not apply.

Saṃsāra is like an echo. It is just a kind of reverberation occurring through the play of dependent arising. And the root text goes on to describe how this happens:

> **5. The primordial nature of the mind resembles space**
> **Wherein are present of themselves,**
> **Like wish-fulfilling gems, the perfect qualities,**
> **The spotless attributes of buddhahood.**
> **Conditioned through conceptual ignorance,**
> **Saṃsāra's attributes appear without existing, echo-like,**
> **And thus one wanders through this world.**
> **The various perceptions of the six migrations**
> **Appear through beings' habitual tendencies**
> **And through the impure mind's engagement into action.**

When the primordial nature of the mind—a sky-like expanse, in which the jewel-like qualities of enlightenment are spontaneously present—is conditioned by coemergent and conceptual ignorance, the habitual tendency to the mistaken duality of apprehended object and apprehending subject takes form, and beings wander in saṃsāra, which is just like an echo. Owing to different habitual tendencies, there arise the appearances of the six classes of beings, who stray from one existential state to another. Owing to the fact that the mind is defiled, and thanks to positive actions leading to happiness, one rises to the higher realms. Because of negative actions one falls into the lower realms. As it is said in the *Ratnakūṭa*, "They are afflicted who, owing to their positive and negative actions, pass through the different states of existence, one after the other." And a text of one of the noble sthaviras says,

> The various worlds arise from actions,
> And actions come from various intentions.

The root text goes on to show that in the very moment that hallucinatory appearances arise, they are empty:

> **6. And so all false appearances and the minds of beings**
> **Are groundless, rootless, by their very nature.**
> ***Éma!*** **All such things, perceived yet nonexistent—**
> **How laughable, to take such figments for reality!**
> **In truth, all seeming things**
> **Are like the echo's sound.**
> **What does it serve to cling to them,**
> **Believing in their truth?**
> **Stay rather in a state**
> **Where all is equal and elusive,**
> **Where fleeting things sink back**
> **Into great nonreality.**
> **They are neither wide nor narrow,**
> **Neither high nor low—**
> **And how delectable that is!**

When it is realized that phenomena are groundless and rootless, they are viewed as a vast, fleeting, ungraspable display, impossible to qualify as either wide or narrow, high or low. Within the purview of ultimate reality, everything is perceived as being even or equal, and one is comfortable and at ease.

The way in which phenomena are equal is described as follows:

7. When all fixation falls away
Regarding things that may arise,
Affirmed or else negated,
They are like an echo's sound.
Since they subside
Within a state that's free of reference,
They are all equal,
Free from all one-sidedness.

When things appear and when one has neither hope nor fear in their regard, they are all similar to the resounding of an echo. Since everything subsides without being identified as this or that, all is leveled, being even, primordially pure , and without true existence.

It is then that all appearances and all experiences seem like one vast spectacle.

8. Ha! Now look! All these appearances—
They're just ridiculous!
There's nothing you can grasp at, nothing to define.
Things are loose, intangible,
Vague, uncertain, evanescent—
Not taken to be true, yet variously appearing.

When the root of the mind is cut, all clinging to an outer object naturally subsides. Then, once and for all, everything that appears is for the yogi just a dramatic spectacle. Since there is nothing to grasp and nothing to identify in all these appearances, there is no defining them. Since they are without any essential core, they are loose. Since they are unreal appearances, they are intangible. Since all fixation on them evaporates, they are uncertain. And since in phenomena there is no reference point, they are evanescent. The *Lion's Perfect Power Tantra* observes,

> When the Buddha's offspring see the truth of ultimate
> reality,
> They deeply understand and thus are always happy.

It is then that one's experience of phenomena in all their variety becomes different from the perceptions of ordinary people. And consequently,

> **9. For those unskilled who cling to them,**
> **Things are as true as true can be.**
> **For yogis who perceive their falsity,**
> **Things are all elusive and unreal.**
> **For those who think of fleeting things as permanent,**
> **All is fixed and everlasting.**
> **But when belief in permanence has naturally subsided,**
> **All things are empty forms—**
> **Neither wide nor narrow, neither big nor small.**
> **Is not this delectable?**

Sense objects that to ordinary people seem to be truly real appear to practitioners as elusive and false. People who assume that things exist permanently always perceive things as truly existent and truly permanent. For practitioners, on the other hand, such phenomena appear as the nonexistent but appearing radiance of emptiness, the ultimate nature of things that is seamlessly the same, unfragmented and unconfined. And what a delight this is! As we find in the *Six Expanses Tantra*,

> All appearing things are by their nature
> Pure and free of name and substance.

This is what is meant by "objectless, supportless view"
And is what I, Samantabhadra, teach.

Now with regard to the practice of the path, the root text says,

10. In order to grow used
To that which you have understood,
First practice the preliminaries as before
And pray that you may understand
That all is like an echo.
In the main practice, meditate
Reflecting then that everything
Is like an echo's resonance,
Which in the moment of its sounding
Is beyond your grasp.
Reflect like this in all that you experience.

As previously explained, one should practice guru yoga, praying to one's teacher, sincerely and from the bottom of one's heart, that one might succeed in seeing that everything is as unreal as an echo. Then in the main practice, one should meditate on the fact that everything that can be seen and heard is echo-like. It appears but is without any intrinsic being.

11. Especially all praise and blame,
All reputation, good and bad,
Resound but are an empty resonance
In which there's nothing to be grasped.
It's pointless to accept or to reject them.
Understand that all words are like echoes.

Praise or slander addressed to one by others is just like an echo. One should learn to take all such things and meditate on them as being of equal value. As it is said in the *Middle-Length Prājñapāramitā*, "O Subhūti, whether bodhisattvas who practice transcendent wisdom are slandered and decried by some, or whether they are praised and lauded by others, they should meditate that all remarks are devoid of intrinsic being. They are like echoes."

Unpleasant speech is the gateway to anger. One should therefore understand that this too lacks intrinsic being.

12. Wrath and other states of mind
Have no location, no direction.
They appear without existing;
When looked for, they are nowhere to be found.
Arising from conditions, they are empty
Like an echo's resonance.
And other people's words,
Likewise arising from conditions,
Are also like an echo.
When scrutinized, they're just reverberations,
Occurring yet without existence.
When closely analyzed, they are like space;
They have no solid entity.
They are neither good nor bad.
Excitement and dejection are not found in them.
So do not take these words as something real,
For they are empty, destitute of true existence.
Realize that, in every way, they are like echoes.

When one is the object of unpleasant speech, the words in question have no existence in either the inner or the outer sphere. There is no cause for unhappiness. And since the bad intention that provoked them has neither substance nor color and is incapable of inflicting any injury, there is no point in being upset. It should be understood that if one is unhappy, this has arisen from one's own mistaken thought that one is being criticized. In other words, the harm is self-inflicted. Words are empty; they cannot be pinpointed. There is nothing in them to be either gratified or depressed about. One should simply carry them on the path as being just empty sound that fades away all on its own, leaving no trace behind. As Śāntideva says,

> With things that in this way are empty,
> What is there to gain and what to lose?
>
> What is there to give me joy and pain?
>
> May beings like myself discern and grasp
> That all things have the character of space![103]

We should understand matters in the same way. The root text concludes with a reference to the result:

> **13. Through this are quenched**
> **The fires of hate and wrath**
> **And all the habits of beginningless saṃsāra.**
> **Through this, supreme acceptance is attained.**[104]
> **There is no further falling into evil destinies,**
> **And stage by stage is born the wealth of victory.**
> **At night, just as before, approach your dreams**
> **Like echoes, sounding and yet void of sound.**
> **Thus you will achieve acceptance**
> **With regard to all phenomena.**
> **Meditate therefore that all is like an echo.**

When one has become completely habituated to this kind of meditation during the daytime, one will also come to understand that even in one's dreams, all things are like an echo. One will be able to assume different identities in one's dreams and to transform the latter at will, just as was previously explained. It is then that one will, in the immediate term, have patience, that is to say, "acceptance,"[105] in respect of the words one hears, and thanks to this, all anger and irritation will subside. As we find in the *Ratnakūṭa*, "O Kāśyapa, those bodhisattvas who understand that phenomena are like an echo are patient with the words they hear. They are not made happy by my words; they are not angered by the words of others; and when they hear the teachings on emptiness, they are not alarmed. This is the first level of acceptance in respect of the words one hears."

In conclusion,

The state of peace that's utterly untroubled, unconditioned,
Is one great sea of excellence, a sea of sublime patience.
May all beings, leaving none aside,
Embark upon the mighty ship of concentration
And voyage on the path to liberation.

In the vast sky of their perfect aspiration,
May intelligence's lightning flash;
And from the massing clouds,
May the refreshing waters
Of the Doctrine's peaceful rain
Bring increase to the harvest
Of disciples blessed by fortune.

May compassion's tree
With boughs of benefit and bliss,
May concentration's flowers
And wisdom's perfect fruit,
May fragrance and cool shade—
Four ways whereby disciples are attracted—
Delight the flocks of birds, the minds of beings!

This concludes the chapter that is like an echo, a commentary on the sixth vajra point of *Finding Rest in Illusion, a Teaching of the Great Perfection.*

The Seventh Vajra Point: City of Gandharvas

Now that their impermanence has been demonstrated, it will be shown how phenomena, which appear even though they are without intrinsic being, cannot be differentiated.

> **1. And also the Victorious One**
> **Declared that everything is like a city of gandharvas.**
> **That you may meditate on this,**
> **Pay heed now to my explanation.**

In the very moment that things are perceived, they are completely without a supporting basis. They are like cities of the fairies, castles in the clouds! As it is said in the *Middle-Length Prajñāpāramitā*, "O Subhūti, since phenomena have no abiding place, no support, and since they are by their very nature unborn, they are like a city of gandharvas."[106] The meaning of this text is explained according to ground, path, and result. First we will explain the ground:

> **2. In the primordial expanse of luminosity**
> **Appears a city, fair and beautiful, of perfect qualities**
> **Spontaneously present.**
> **It dwells therein beginningless and without end.**
> **No center does it have, no limit.**

In the ultimate expanse of the primordial ground, in other words, empty awareness similar to space, the city of perfect, spontaneous qualities is said to be naturally present. This is to say that the kāyas and wisdoms, with which the ultimate expanse is primordially endowed, subsist there, beginninglessly and endlessly. As it is said,

> As it was before, so later it will be.
> It is unchanging suchness.[107]

And in the *Uttaratantra* we find,

> The buddha-element is void of what is adventitious,
> Which has the character of something separable.
> This element is not itself devoid of supreme qualities,
> Which have the character of what cannot be parted from it.[108]

As the root text goes on to say, the ground is the empty but luminous state of great spontaneous presence:

> **3. And from this luminous and empty state,**
> **Within the firmament of the unknowing mind,**
> **The six migrations—castles in the clouds—appear,**
> **Which take their origin in dualistic clinging**
> **To the apprehender and the apprehended.**
> **Devoid of ground and basis,**
> **They appear in different forms**
> **Deriving from deluded mind**
> **And its habitual tendencies.**

The state of awareness of the ultimate expanse is like space. But since its creative power is concomitant with coemergent ignorance, it strays into the duality of apprehender and apprehended, and because of this, the appearances of the ground [not being recognized for what they are] are mistakenly perceived as the different manifestations of the six classes of beings. These manifestations of beginningless habitual tendencies appear even though they are not really present, like cities of the gandharvas seen in the clouds. As it is said in the *Guhyagarbha Tantra*,

> *Emaho!* From the sugatagarbha
> Beings manifest through their thought's activity.

In whichever way phenomenal appearances manifest, they are devoid of inherent existence.

> **4. When this you see, there manifests**
> **The nature of the mind, the primal state.**
> **But when you fail to see it,**
> **There is just the mind of everyday confusion.**
> **And how are these appearances?**
> **They are ungraspable like castles in the clouds.**
> ***Kyé!* How else should we describe them?**

When appearances, vividly present to awareness, are not recognized for what they are, these same hallucinatory events seem true. But they are just like castles in the clouds. For within the state of awareness, they are simply the clear appearance of what does not exist. They are void of basis and intrinsic being, of ground and root. On the other hand, when they are recognized for what they are, they are simply seen as empty forms, for they have no substance. As the sūtra tells us, "All compounded things resemble castles in the clouds."

Since saṃsāra is primordially empty, one should come to the conclusion that it cannot be rejected.

> **5. Indeed they are all destitute of real existence;**
> **They are like the cities of the fairies seen**
> **Above a plain as sunlight sinks into the west.**
> **Supported and support**
> **Are simply the deluded mind,**

Which sees as it is wont to see.
When closely scrutinized, there's nothing really there.
Left to itself, the vision naturally fades.
So set aside your fear, for you have nothing hard to do.
Understand just how the world and beings
Are from the very outset pure and empty.

In the light of the westering sun, in the sky above a plain, one may see in the clouds a city of the gandharvas, filled with its townsfolk. But the fastness and its people have no existence whatsoever. In the same way, although beings appear to be inhabiting the universe, in the moment of their appearing, they are without inherent existence. They are but the hallucinatory perceptions of the mind and in fact do not exist at all. Therefore, since the ordinary mind subsides by itself—for it too is destitute of inherent being—and since hallucinatory appearances, which are empty by their very nature, do not for that reason need to be purposely rejected, one should simply and effortlessly settle in the state of great equality, leaving everything just as it is. As it is said in the *Ornament of the Light of Wisdom*, "O Mañjuśrī, castles appear in the clouds, and yet there is nothing there. Likewise all phenomena appear but they do not exist."

The root text now goes on to show that the duality of apprehender and apprehended is a state for which there is no objective correlate:

6. All appearing objects, empty of true being,
Are like castles in the clouds.
All mental states, by nature empty,
Are like castles in the clouds.
Both sense objects and mind are empty;
They're like castles in the clouds.
The slightest clinging or fixation—
Just leave it where it is!

Things that appear as if they were outside the mind are groundless and empty. And all thoughts and inner feelings, which naturally dissolve, are also empty. Thus affirmations and negations, clinging and fixation, with regard to all objects and mental states—which are empty by their nature—are delusive. One should simply keep, freely and evenly, to the flow of the natural state of the mind.

As it is said in one of the *Songs of Realization*,

> Whatever clinging you may have, just give it up!
> When realization comes, everything is that![109]

Once clinging and fixation have been revealed as the trap of saṃsāra, it is necessary to understand how they naturally subside.

> **7. How is this accomplished?**
> **Do not let your mind manipulate phenomena**
> **Appearing yet without existing.**
> **Simply leave them without grasping.**
> **Original delusion is itself the fruit**
> **Of all such grasping and fixation.**
> **And therefore you should know**
> **The state devoid of clinging.**

Phenomena appear even though they are without intrinsic being. To take them as truly existent is what constitutes delusion. The original delusion has itself arisen through the unfolding of this same clinging and fixation. It is therefore of the highest importance to train oneself so that they subside all on their own. Accordingly, even if unpleasant situations occur, if one can remain without clinging and fixating on them, no conflict or suffering will arise in relation to them.

Since everything is gathered in this essential point, the root text advises us to remain in a spacious state without clinging:

8. The sublime and spotless nature of phenomena,
Phenomena themselves,
And utter peace, the state beyond all sorrow,
Are not existent entities.
Understand that all phenomena,
Things and nonthings both,
All are empty, without true existence.
They resemble castles in the clouds;
They are like the vast abyss of space—
Primordially unborn, the state of utter peace.

Since the nature of phenomena is itself immaculate, phenomena are similar to nirvāṇa, the state beyond suffering. So it is that all the variety of functioning things and sense objects that appear are empty, just like castles in the clouds. And "nonexistent things," for their part, also come to rest within the space-like pure nature of the mind. As it is said, "All phenomena are like the Sugata." And as we find also in *The Way of the Bodhisattva*,

When something and its nonexistence
Both are absent from before the mind,
No other option does the latter have:
It comes to rest, from concepts free.[110]

As the root text says, such a state is beyond both good and bad, acceptance and rejection:

9. No desire is found therein.
Ignorance and anger, jealousy and pride
Are not observed. So therefore understand
That these and all thoughts
Are like castles in the clouds.
Defilements, void of real existence,
And enlightenment, the nature of the mind,
Are not two different things.

Know that they're like space;
They are both equal and immaculate.

If one analyzes the five defilements together with all thoughts (which, even though they are nonexistent, appear and are the cause of saṃsāra), everything is found to be devoid of intrinsic being—as also is the nature of the mind itself. These two absences of intrinsic being are not *two* [that is, distinct entities] within the sphere of emptiness, which itself is without inherent existence. This is why it is said that saṃsāra and nirvāṇa are not two different things. As it is said, "Ignorance is like space, and likewise phenomena are without defining characteristics." It is said in the *Root Stanzas of the Middle Way*,

The ultimate nature of nirvāṇa
Is the ultimate nature of saṃsāra;
And between these two the slightest difference,
Even the most subtle, is not found.[111]

Maitreya for his part also says that samsaric existence and the peace of nirvāṇa are equal, while Saraha declares that "saṃsāra is certainly nirvāṇa."

One can therefore settle with confidence in the equality of saṃsāra and nirvāṇa.

10. The nature of saṃsāra is nirvāṇa from the outset.
Deluded thoughts subside completely
Like the clouds that melt into the sky.
Know that they subside there whence they came.
Preserve this state of utter peace,
Primordial wisdom, empty, luminous.

The worlds that make up this universal system first take form in space. In the present moment, they subsist within it and, at the last, at the time of their destruction, they will dissolve back into space whence, in the beginning, they arose. In the same way, saṃsāra first manifests within the ultimate expanse. It is there that it now appears, and finally it will subside therein. When all mental elaborations fade naturally away, like clouds dissolving into space, and when one settles in meditative evenness in the state of empty luminosity, it is said that one "reaches the primordial expanse." As the *Samādhirāja-sūtra* says,

> These regions of the universe came into being,
> And having once arisen, they will be destroyed.
> They will become like space itself,
> And as before so later they will be.
> Understand that all things are like this.
>
> Within the cloudless sky
> There instantly appears the maṇḍala of clouds,
> Which having once appeared will melt away
> Into the state of cloudlessness.
> Examine whence it first arose
> And understand that all things are like this.

The crucial points of this teaching may be summarized as follows:

> **11. In the state of unborn nature,**
> **No thoughts, no sense objects are found,**
> **And yet, until the show of their arising**
> **Melts into the ultimate expanse,**
> **Cut through the root of your delusion—ordinary thought.**
> **Action and nonaction are not two;**
> **Not two are taking and rejecting.**
> **And yet, as long as in your mind**
> **You cling to self and real existence,**
> **I urge you to rely upon profound instructions,**

Antidotes for your defilements.
Not two are outer things and inner mental states—
Both sink into the nature of the mind.
Wise you are if this you understand.

Though all phenomena are unborn, until one's mind stream, inseparable from a limpid state of concentration, is free of thoughts, it is important to sever the root of delusion and to keep from straying into the ordinary state. As the sūtra tells us, "Saṃsāra comes from thought, not from the absence of thoughts."

Although, within the fundamental nature, there is nothing to adopt and nothing to reject, nevertheless, for as long as the mind clings to a notion of self, it is through the process of adopting and rejecting of virtue and nonvirtue that the principle of karmic cause and effect is unfailing. It is consequently imperative to strive in the accumulation of positive actions and in the purification of negativities. The *Prajñāpāramitā* says, "The right practice of Dharma is to understand that phenomena are like space and to be apprehensive with regard to one's actions and their fully ripened result." The *Samādhirāja-sūtra* also says,

If after death within this world
Beings did not migrate to other lives,
The gathering of their actions would be lost.

And Āryadeva says,

To see that all things are like space
And yet to be convinced of the full ripening of actions
Is a wonder yet more wonderful than wonderful,
A marvel yet more marvelous than marvelous.

The root text then goes on to mention the practice of the path itself:

12. Regarding how to meditate this point,
First perform, as previously, the preliminaries,
And in the main part of the practice
Know with a complete conviction:
All things are like castles in the clouds.

One should first practice guru yoga as previously explained, specifically praying to one's teacher that one might understand that all phenomena are like cities of gandharvas. And then one should meditate that phenomena, appearing in all their variety, are indeed like castles in the clouds.

How should one do this? The root text explains:

13. Form appears and yet is empty,
Like a castle in the clouds.
Sound, smell, taste, touch, mental objects—
All these six are castles in the clouds.
The mind, its affirmations and negations,
All arising thoughts, are castles in the clouds.
On all this meditate with clarity.
At all times, day and night, reflect just as before
That all appearing things are castles in the clouds.

During the daytime, one should accustom oneself to seeing that form and other objects of the senses—together with one's mind and its mental events—are empty of existence even though they appear. They are just like castles seen in the clouds. And at night, as one lies down in the lion posture, one should concentrate on the rainbow-like buddha fields within the white central channel. This will enable one to recognize that the visions of one's dreams are as insubstantial as castles in the clouds. One will behold strange and marvelous lands and things not seen before. And one will have the power to appear in different forms, transforming them according to one's wishes.

We now come to the result:

14. Having seen that all compounded things
Resemble castles in the clouds,
You should settle
In their absence of reality.
Your mind's proliferations all will cease,
And self-arisen, clear, and empty luminosity
Will manifest from deep within.
Even in your dreams
You will see everything
As cities of gandharvas in the clouds.
You will become proficient
In assuming different forms,
Transforming them as previously described.
And as belief in the reality of things subsides,
The dualistic chain of apprehender-apprehended breaks.
All bonds and all habitual tendencies subside
And freedom is achieved.
Meditate therefore upon these castles in the clouds!

Through training in this way day and night, the immediate effect will be that ego-clinging will subside and concentrations and other excellent qualities will be accomplished. And at last one will attain enlightenment. As the *Laṅkāvatāra-sūtra* tells us,

> The three worlds of existence are like cities of the fairies
> And like pools of water seen in mirages.
> Knowing them as false, you will not be engrossed therein.

In conclusion therefore,

Virtuous things resemble Indra's bow.[112]
Various they may seem, and yet they are not different—
All beyond conceptual extremes.
In the pure and luminous,
Limpid and immaculate expanse,

May all beings gain
Spontaneous accomplishment.

When the pollen of the lotus
With its petals spread is touched,
It turns into a wellspring of immortal nectar—
A basin of the gods, whence sweetly flows a cooling stream.
May beings come thereby to see
The marvelous place of joy made manifest.

This concludes the chapter that is like a city of gandharvas, a commentary on the seventh vajra point of *Finding Rest in Illusion, a Teaching of the Great Perfection.*

The Eighth Vajra Point: Emanated Apparition

It has been shown that phenomena are not different from each other in that they all resemble space. Now it will be shown that they are not identical—for sameness (or oneness) cannot be predicated of things that lack intrinsic being. It is consequently said that phenomena are not one and the same.

1. The Conqueror has said
That all things are the emanations of the mind.
Listen! I shall tell you what he meant by this.

Phenomena, which, like emanated apparitions, appear while not existing, are not one and the same. They appear differently on the conventional level, and investigation establishes that they are not the same. They are like reflected images. It is said in the *Middle-Length Prajñāpāramitā*, "O Subhūti, since phenomena are neither different nor the same, they are like emanations of the mind."

Again, this will be explained in three sections according to the ground, path, and result. The first explanation concerns the ground:

2. From within the state of primal luminosity,
Through ignorance, through clinging to the self,
There manifest saṃsāra's
Various hallucinatory appearances,
Which are like emanated apparitions.
They are perceived though they do not exist—
And thence come all experiences of joy and sorrow.

Within the space-like sphere of primordial luminosity, apprehending thoughts, which are like clouds ever liable to appear, abruptly occur; and the appearances of saṃsāra—nonexistent yet clearly perceived—manifest like emanated apparitions. It is said in the *Distillation of the Essence*,

> Within the core of primal luminosity
> There occurs concomitantly the core of ignorance.
> From this there spreads saṃsāra's dualistic scheme
> Of apprehender-apprehended.
> And here beings turn continually as on a waterwheel.

What then are these various phenomenal appearances of saṃsāra?

> **3. This is what appears to the minds of beings,**
> **The form of their habitual tendencies.**
> **When these are cleansed,**
> **There manifest spontaneously**
> **The triple kāya of the buddha-element,**
> **Together with the self-experience**
> **Of luminous primordial wisdom.**
> **It is as the *Māyājāla* says:**
> **There is the self-experience of the ordinary mind**
> **And then the self-experience of primordial wisdom.**

Whatever appears and manifests to samsaric beings is the subjective experience—the self-experience—of the ordinary mind. Whatever manifests for the buddhas (the kāyas and wisdoms, the pure fields, and so on) is the self-experience of primordial wisdom. As it is said in the *Longer Māyājāla*,

> All that appears respectively to beings and to buddhas
> Is the self-experience of the ordinary mind
> And of primordial wisdom.

Objects that appear outwardly to the mind—forms and so on—are simply the fructification of habitual tendencies accumulated from time without beginning. They do not exist either as the mind or as something else. They are like emanated apparitions. For if they were the mind, what kind of consciousness could they be? If they were the consciousness of the universal ground, it would be impossible for them to appear outwardly, for the consciousness of the universal ground is exclusively inward-turning. As it is said,

> "Mind" is the consciousness of the universal ground;
> Ego-clinging is, so to speak, the consciousness that is defiled.

Although the five sense consciousnesses—sight and so forth—do indeed look outward, they arise only in the moment of the apprehension of objects. This being so, since mind and material objects occur simultaneously, the five sense consciousnesses are not the appearing objects. Outer objects are neither the mental consciousness nor the defiled consciousness, for they appear to the limpid sense powers possessed of form. Neither are they subdivisions of the fifty-one mental factors. It should be understood that form and the other objects of the five senses are not the mind.

Consequently, as the root text goes on to say,

> **4. The primordial expanse is source of everything.**
> **When this is recognized and when,**
> **By such a means, defilements have been cleansed,**
> **The self-experience of primordial wisdom manifests.**
> **When this has not been recognized,**
> **Then through deluded clinging to a self,**
> **The mind's subjective vision of the world occurs.**
> **All joys and sorrows of the six migrations**
> **Appear like emanated apparitions.**

It is thanks to the recognition of the one ultimate expanse that the self-experience of primordial wisdom manifests. By contrast, when one fails to recognize it, the subjective perceptions of the deluded mind arise in the manner of emanated apparitions.

The comparison with emanated apparitions is supported by the root text as follows:

5. Just as an emanated apparition
Arises without any basis,
Likewise you should understand
That all hallucinatory appearances
Are pure and without any basis.
Just as those who have great power of mind control
Are able to produce an emanated apparition,
Likewise you should understand
That it is through the habits of the minds of beings
That various things appear.
Just as an emanated apparition
Appears according to the emanator's wish,
Likewise you should understand
That things arise from causes and conditions.
Just as an emanated apparition
Is an illusion that arises when there's nothing there,
Likewise you should understand
That things are just deluded mind's experience—
Its self-appearance, self-arising,
Wherein the mind is self-engrossed—
And things appear according to its habits.

An emanated apparition occurs without any basis, even in the absence of a material substance such as a stick or stone. Hallucinatory appearances occur in the same way, arising simply through the conditioning of the defiled mind, which is itself devoid of true existence. They are groundless and rootless. An emanated apparition occurs according to the wish of those who have power over their minds. In just the same way, hallucinatory appearances manifest through the power of beings' habitual tendencies and thus are equally unreal. Those who have gained complete control of their minds are able to display whatever emanated apparition they wish. Likewise, hallucinatory appearances manifest as the distinct results of causes and conditions, and they are thus devoid of true existence. As it is said in the *Prātimokṣa-sūtra*,

> Every thing arises from a cause.
> That cause the Tathāgata has explained.

Just as an emanated apparition manifests in the manner of a hallucinatory appearance, in the same way, phenomena are the empty forms of adventitious and subjective mental experience. As we find in the *Heart Sūtra*, "Form is emptiness; emptiness is form. Emptiness is not other than form and form is not other than emptiness. Likewise, feeling, perception, conditioning factors, and consciousness—all are empty." In brief, all that appears as phenomena manifests as the subjective experience of one's own mind. More specifically, all such hallucinatory appearances manifest because of different, ingrained habitual tendencies imprinted on the mind. They have no existence anywhere, whether within the mind or outside the mind. They are simply the clear appearance of what does not exist.

The root text now describes the kind of realization that may arise in relation to hallucinatory appearances:

> **6. If you do not indulge in any habits,**
> **If you leave things as they are,**
> **You will in no way be deluded.**
> **Abiding in the nature of the ground,**
> **You will remain within the mind's pristine expanse.**

Knowing that the hallucinatory appearances [of saṃsāra] arise through the protracted habits of mental activity, practitioners do not indulge in thought but remain in a nakedly pure and natural state. At that time, empty awareness remains within the ground without straying elsewhere. And just as when a vessel is broken, the space within it mingles inseparably with the space outside, when yogis realize the single timeless nature of the three times, they reach the primordial, pristine state in which [phenomena] are exhausted. They dwell in the inner ultimate expanse of great primordial purity, understood as "nondual primordial wisdom." They dwell within the dharmakāya endowed with the twofold purity and never stir from it. As it is said in the *Letter Entitled the Drop of Ambrosia*,

> Just as water into water poured,
> As oil that mingles into oil,
> When the knowledge object
> "Absence of conceptual constructs"
> Blends inseparably with primordial wisdom,
> This is called the dharmakāya of the buddhas.

And as the *Songs of Realization* tells us,

> Like salt dissolving into water,
> Ordinary mind dissolves into the nature of the mind.

As the root text goes on to say, whatever arises in the mind should be left in its own open and natural condition:

> **7. Now the three poisons, the five poisons—**
> **All derive from thought,**
> **But on examination they are nowhere found.**
> **Defilements are like emanated apparitions;**
> **They lack intrinsic being.**
> **Rest therefore in their unborn and empty nature.**

If the five poisonous mental states are closely examined, they cannot be pinpointed; they are not found anywhere, outside or in.

If they are left alone just as they are—like emanated apparitions—they subside; they are unable to endure on their own. This is the great secret of the mind. If one has no understanding of this, one may try to rid oneself of defilements, but they only increase and one gets trapped in the web of things to eliminate and the remedies for them. As it is said in *The Way of the Bodhisattva*,

> Defilements are not in the object,
> Nor within the faculties, nor somewhere in between.

And similarly,

> All those who fail to understand
> The secret of the mind, the greatest of all things,
> Although they wish for joy and sorrow's end,
> Will wander to no purpose, uselessly.[113]

The root text continues,

> **8. Phenomenal existence,**
> **The world and all the beings it contains,**
> **Their bodies and possessions,**
> **Their going, staying, joys, and sorrows all—**
> **Appearing while not really there—**
> **Are like the emanations of the mind,**
> **Without intrinsic being.**
> **They have no origin, they do not cease;**
> **They do not come, they do not go;**
> **They do not pass, they do not change—**
> **Yet variously they all appear.**
> **Understand this well therefore:**
> **They are indeed just emanated apparitions.**

Emanated apparitions derive from the miraculous ability of those who have a mastery of concentration. Although there is no change in their nature—which is the creative power of awareness—they seem to occur in various forms. Similarly, although there is no change in the partless particles of which phenomena are composed, these same phenomena seem to occur in various ways with regard to size and so forth. Although phenomena are not different from the wood and so on [of which they are made], they seem to occur differently according to the various ways in which they are fashioned. Likewise, although bodies and possessions are not substantially different from the elements of earth, water, fire, and wind, they seem different because of the way in which they are fashioned. But if all appearing things—which are not different from the infinitesimal particles that are their respective components—are examined, they are found to dwell in the unchanging fundamental nature and are without any existence whatsoever. For this reason, and given that phenomena manifest in various ways on account of causes and conditions, it should be understood that they are indeed mental emanations. It is said in the *Prajñāpāramitā in Eighteen Thousand Lines*, "O Devaputra, phenomena are without coming and going; they are consequently like emanations of the mind."

As the root text goes on to say, all that arises in the mind is merely a reflected image:

> **9. All deluded thoughts,**
> **All sorrows of the mind,**
> **Are just like emanated apparitions.**
> **They lack intrinsic being and yet appear without obstruction.**
> **Understand their emptiness of true existence.**
> **They are neither in the object nor within the mind itself.**

Moreover, whatever arises in the mind as something to be accepted or rejected is an appearance that is nevertheless devoid of intrinsic being. It is located neither in the object nor in the mind. Even though it seems to arise from both of them, there is neither something that arises nor indeed is there an act of arising. One must therefore simply recognize that what eventuates is simply the spontaneous radiance of the ground of manifestation.

And in a similar manner,

10. The universe composed of the five elements,
The beings that reside in the three worlds,
Whatever one affirms or else denies
Are all, without exception, emanations of the mind.
And the mind itself—though it appears—
Is also void of real existence.
Know that from the outset it is pure,
Just like an emanation, an illusion.

The world, the outer universal vessel, formed as it is of the five elements, and all the mental states of beings, the inner content of that same universe, are all emanated apparitions manifesting through the habitual tendencies imprinted upon the mind. And when analyzed, the mind itself is simply the way that the arising of the creative power of awareness appears. The mind cannot be identified in any way. It should therefore be understood to be like space. As we find in the *Ratnakūṭa*, "O Kāśyapa, the mind is not seen in the outer world; it is not seen in the inner world; and it is not seen in between these two. When you look for the mind, it is nowhere to be found; it cannot be observed."

As the root text goes on to say, everything that appears to the mind is devoid of inherent existence:

11. Ignorant and childish beings
Perceive and think mistakenly.
All concrete things endowed with features,
All objects that the mind has posited
Are but the outcome of habitual tendencies;
In truth, they have no real existence.
Do not indulge therefore in subject-object clinging,

Speaking of "these things."
Understand instead that all is free of ontological extremes,
Beyond the reach of words.

For common folk, who are like children and who have the common view of things, phenomena and thoughts have a hallucinatory quality. They are but the appearances of the ingrained habitual tendencies of the mind, which apprehends and clings to self. As it is said in the *Laṅkāvatāra-sūtra*,

Sense objects do not exist as such;
They are the mind stirred by habitual tendencies,
And this indeed *appears* as extramental things.

The minds of ordinary beings belong to the relative. And whatever is posited as the object of the ordinary mind or intellect is also just the relative, in the same way that whatever is drawn on wall or canvas is not separate from those same supports. As we find in *The Way of the Bodhisattva*,

The ultimate is not the object of the mind.
The mind is said to be the relative.[114]

Now the relative or "all-concealing" truth of childish people constitutes a blemish that hides the ultimate from view. As the *Introduction to the Middle Way* tells us,

The nature of phenomena, enshrouded by our ignorance, is
"all-concealed."
But what this ignorance contrives appears as true.
And so the Buddha spoke of "all-concealing truth."[115]

This is why everything that the mind reifies is but the fabric of thoughts, which consequently is something to be discarded. One should instead realize the space-like state that is free of all ontological extremes, a state that is beyond the ordinary mind with its assertions of "it is" and "it is not." It is said in the *Prajñāpāramitā, the Great Mother*, "Phenomena are just names, just words, just thoughts. And whatever is thought is not the ultimate. Suchness is devoid of thought."

Reaching the conclusion that phenomena are ineffable and beyond all concepts, the root text continues:

> **12. Although phenomena are labeled "this" or "that,"**
> **It's just as with the names for "space" or "rabbit's horns."**
> **Phenomena are not real things.**
> **They are just thoughts without existence**
> **In the fundamental nature.**
> **Understand that they are rootless,**
> **Empty from the outset.**

If phenomena are investigated, they are found to have no existence whatever. Even though they are indicated by words, they are not specifically characterized objects. Other than the mere apprehension and distinguishing of their names, one does not actually encounter them. And the names in question are just like the name "space," and the expression "rabbit's horns." As the *Ratnāvāli* says, "'Space' too is only a name." For this reason, it is important to understand that in the very moment that phenomena are perceived, they are mere appearances—the rootless forms of primordial emptiness.

Coming to the conclusion that whatever appears and is designated [as this or that] transcends the ordinary mind, the root text continues:

> **13. All that thought imputes is mind;**
> **It has no factual existence.**
> **All that seems to be an object of the senses**
> **Is just habitual tendency—appearing yet not real.**
> **And since there is no object,**

There's no apprehension of an object:
No duality of apprehender and the apprehended.
You cannot say, you cannot think,
You cannot indicate phenomena:
They are beyond the ontological extremes.
No one can identify them saying "this."
Know that they resemble emanated apparitions.
From the outset they are void of self.

Whatever is mentally imputed is nothing but the mind; everything that appears as a mental object is just the hallucinatory appearance, the outcome of habitual tendencies. It is necessary to understand that it is without true existence even though it is perceived; that it is empty and is thus beyond all ontological extremes—just like an emanated apparition.

It could be argued in that case that even the Buddha's nirmāṇakāya is a hallucinatory appearance. However, since, in his own perception, he does not exist in any way, he is not a hallucination as far as he is concerned. On the other hand, when he appears to beings, he is indeed a hallucination activated by the virtuous thoughts of those same beings. He is a positive hallucination, no more. The *Uttaratantra* tells us,

Just as in the spotless floor of beryl,
The image of the body of the lord of gods appears,
Likewise in the cleansed ground of the minds of beings,
There arises the reflection of the Powerful Sage's form.

It rises or it sets for each and every being
Utterly dependent on their cleansed or sullied minds.

Just as with the drumbeat of the gods,
The sound of which arises in dependence on their acts,
Just so, within the world, the teaching of the peaceful Sage
Arises in dependence upon beings' conduct.[116]

But how, it might be asked, can phenomena be shown to resemble emanated apparitions?

> **14. Just as apparitions emanated forth**
> **Are empty of existence in the moment they appear,**
> **So too are all phenomena**
> **Appearing and yet void of true existence.**
> **Emanated apparitions are beyond extremes**
> **Of being and nonbeing.**
> **Just so are all phenomena**
> **Beyond conceptual thinking.**

In the same way that an emanated apparition is empty in the moment of its being perceived, phenomena too are also empty. Just as an emanated apparition is found, when analyzed, to be beyond the extremes of existence and nonexistence, phenomena are also found to transcend all ontological extremes. This shows that they do indeed resemble emanated apparitions, appearing while being devoid of intrinsic being. It is as we find in the *Ornament of the Light of Wisdom*, "O Mañjuśrī, an emanation appears without existing. Likewise all phenomena appear even though they do not exist."

Phenomena simply appear just like emanated apparitions. And like emanated apparitions, they do not exist.

> **15. Although things may be variously described—**
> **"They appear," "they are empty," "they are true or false"—**
> **They have no reality at all.**
> **Do not apprehend them, then, as this or that;**
> **Just view them as a limitless expanse.**

However phenomena may be designated—whether as empty, true or false, and so on—they are in truth without existence. They transcend all the limits of the one-sided positions of philosophical systems and should be understood in terms of a vast immensity beyond the ontological extremes. As it is said in the *Root Stanzas of the Middle Way*,

> Do not say that they are empty.
> Do not say they are not empty.
> Empty or not empty—all the four alternatives:
> Where are they in the peaceful state?[117]

And,

> The buddhas said, "I am."
> They taught as well that self does not exist.[118]

It is now shown that if one does not hold to the extreme of existence, then [experientially] everything becomes vague and elusive:

> **16. If there is no clinging and fixation,**
> **Things are left just as they are.**
> **What purpose is there in negating or affirming**
> **What is simply words?**

If one does not hold to the extreme position of affirming the true existence of phenomena, however one may think of such phenomena, it goes no further than an understanding of the meaning of their names. For one has already established things as being empty and without true existence. It is pointless to quibble just on the level of words. Everything should be left just as it is. As the *Songs of Realization* say,

> When one comes to realization, everything is *that*.
> None will understand that it is something else.

On the other hand, if there *is* clinging or fixation to something, however high one's understanding may be, one has yet to realize the nature of phenomena.

17. If you have fixation, saying "this,"
It is not in any way the fundamental nature.
For what can webs of mind's analysis reveal?
Imputed by the mind, your thoughts might indicate
The final truth of emptiness, and yet
This is to cling to an extreme.
How therefore can it be the fundamental nature?

When one has a fixed idea such as "This is emptiness," it is simply a figment of the discursive mind. It is not actual emptiness in itself, for one is fixating on a concept. Moreover, the discursive mind is saṃsāra. For thoughts go ever on and on, in succession, driving one into the different realms of existence. On the other hand, when one is free of the discursive mind, one passes beyond suffering. As we find in the *Praises of Mañjuśrī*,

Other than discursive thinking,
There is nothing we might call "saṃsāra."
When you freed yourself from thought,
You passed beyond all pain forever.

It is wrong to think that, because they indicate emptiness, there is no harm in thoughts like "It is empty."

18. "And yet," you may object,
"Because they give an indication,
Will words not lead us to an understanding?"
But emptiness exceeds both words and definitions,
So what is there that words could indicate?
This objection therefore has no meaning.
The nature of the mind cannot be seen
Through concepts and fixated clinging.
Investigations of discursive intellect
Lead only to approximations.

The intellectual evaluation of emptiness will by no means lead to the realization of emptiness, the nature of the mind—the ultimate truth that is the fundamental nature of all things. This nature utterly transcends all names and definitions. It is beyond all conception. Intellectual evaluation, by contrast, leads only to broad, rough estimates of objects hitherto unknown. It is like a blind person who comes to an idea of various objects only by means of a good explanation.

By what means then, it may be asked, can emptiness be realized?

19. But when the blessings of a teacher
Penetrate your heart,
It's like the sun that rises in a cloudless sky.
Through the powerful conjunction
Of dependent factors,
The sublime will manifest.

The empty, fundamental nature, which cannot be realized by mere intelligence and is not just an approximate idea, is the ineffable and inconceivable nature of awareness. It manifests in the mind thanks to the presence of merit and the teacher's blessings. At the time of an empowerment or the introduction to the nature of one's mind, through symbolic indication and auspicious causal links, one may have the recognition of bare and simple awareness, empty and luminous. As the *Two-Part Hevajra Tantra* declares,

Know that it arises through your merit
And the teacher's timely skillful means.

And the *Songs of Realization* says,

The entry of the teacher's words into one's heart
Is like looking at a treasure placed in one's own hand.

How then, it may be asked, is the truth of phenomena seen?

20. All things then are equal.
There's no discerning them as this or that.
They are a naked state of voidness
Free from ontological extremes, like space itself:
A vast expanse, appearing yet empty,
Like emanated apparitions.
Thus all things come naturally to be realized.

When the fundamental nature is realized, all phenomena are seamlessly equal and yet vividly distinct, just like emanated apparitions. And a state of bare awareness that is pure and traceless arises as a perception in which there is no separation between outside and in—a state in which all discerning falls away. It manifests as a condition of evenness, spaciousness, and all-pervading immensity. As Saraha has said,

In front, behind, in all the ten directions,
Where'er I look, there, there it is . . .
Today I, like the Buddha, have cut through delusion.
I have no questions now for anyone.

When saṃsāra and nirvāṇa subside in awareness, a blissful state of mind spontaneously appears.

21. Saṃsāra in itself is just deluded thought.
And when the nature of the mind is seen,
It is nirvāṇa—there from the beginning.
It is primal wisdom, free of all fixation,
That, in self-knowing, knows its object.
Nothing that appears is real;
There is no apprehending it as this or that.
The mind finds comfort in a state
Where mind and what appears
Are seen as emanated apparitions.

Saṃsāra consists of discursive thoughts. When it is understood that these have no existence even though they appear—in other words, when their empty nature is realized—nirvāṇa, the state beyond sorrow, automatically manifests. So it is that thoughts and appearances sink back into emptiness without leaving any trace. This is referred to as "the stirring-up of the experience of nondual primordial wisdom." It is said in the *Great Garuḍa Tantra*,

> Within the space of mind, thoughts stir.
> Such movement is illusory
> For all is all-pervading primal wisdom.

When the state of awareness, bare and empty, is realized, it is as the root text goes on to explain:

> **22. When this is realized, you become**
> **A noble being who beholds the truth.**
> **This is the truth itself;**
> **There's nothing else to indicate.**
> **Everything, spontaneously arising,**
> **Sets in its own place, its very nature.**

The realization of empty, bare awareness is the vision of the ultimate truth—the expanse of emptiness. When this occurs, meditative experiences will arise on the basis of one's familiarization with this state, but as for the realization itself, there is no further progress to be made. For indeed, this is the vision of the state in which all phenomena are exhausted. It is as described in the *Prajñāpāramitā*, "The vision of the actual ultimate can neither intensify nor diminish. For it is like space itself."

Even if one were to set forth this realization, which derives from the power of blessing, to people who lack the requisite karmic fortune, they will only understand it in the most general way. It will not arise in the manner of a personal realization.

23. Such realization manifests
To none but those whose hearts
Are touched by blessings
Of a master of a thousand skillful means.
A visible thing, a blazing lamp
Is seen by those with eyes.
How can beings blind from birth
Perceive it even though it's shown to them?

A blazing lamp is visible to those who can see, but not to the blind however much it is pointed out to them. In just the same way, even if the realization of the fortunate is demonstrated—by every sign and method—to those of lesser fortune, they will be able to have no more than an intellectual estimate of it. They will not have the same realization. For the latter is born from supreme devotion to a teacher. As we find in the *Uttaratantra*,

> The ultimate condition of the self-arisen [buddhas]
> Is something to be understood through faith itself.
> The light that blazes from the sun
> Cannot be seen by those who have no eyes.[119]

Those without learning and also those who are learned but who rely on the discursive intellect are unable to gain realization in this present life.

24. Those who have no knowledge of the teaching,
Those who have no understanding of its meaning
Cannot see the sunlight of this excellence.
Others, yet more foolish and pretentious,
Are like reciting parrots.
Caught in the nets of their discursive thoughts,
They will never find the quintessential truth.
Suchness they will never know,

Like beings blind from birth in front of solid objects.
They will never come to realization,
For they take as true the findings of their intellects.
Alas for their pretentious lies,
Alas for their unhappy fortune!
They have no hope of reaching
Quintessential truth.

Those who in their past lives were destitute of the riches of the perfect teachings and whose intelligence in their present existence is greatly handicapped, and those who are like parrots and take the tangle of their thoughts as true, do not have the fortune to behold the luminosity of the mind's own nature. The former, in their stupid meditation, take their own ideas as the truth, while the latter cling to mental analysis as an end in itself. As the great master Garab Dorje has said,

A view wherein one clings to ratiocination—
What an affliction that must be!
A meditation based on such a view—
What misfortune that must be!
The hope to gain some fruit from it—
How deluded that must be!

The root text then goes on to praise the realization of the ultimate state, together with its cause, as described in our own school:

25. For us, it is the master
Who reveals the nature of the mind,
Sublime primordial wisdom.
Authentic, self-cognizing, primal wisdom
Arises when the mind is left
Unspoiled by tampering and alteration.
When there's neither hope nor doubt,
No clinging, no assumptions—it appears.

More clearly does it manifest
Within the state of emptiness and luminosity
Devoid of center and of boundary.
Thus to be accepted by a holy teacher,
The holder of the blessings of the lineage,
Is indeed of highest moment.

Even though primordial wisdom self-cognizing dwells at all times in oneself, it remains unrecognized. But in the very moment when the teacher points it out and it is seen directly, certainty is gained. Subsequently, this primal wisdom will manifest when the mind is left just as it is, without any alteration. At that time, even though the objects of the senses and one's own mental states are perceived, there is no clinging or fixation in relation to them. It is in that state that primordial wisdom is truly present. And when awareness, empty, luminous, and all-pervading, arises naturally, it is even clearer than before—a fact that is due to the kindness of one's sublime teacher. It is important that such experiences be traced to the lineage and to one's most excellent instructor. As Saraha tells us,

> Know that it's arisen through the fivefold blessing of the lineage.
> These blessings have arisen through the reverend teacher's power.

And the *All-Creating King* says,

> A teacher free of "self" and "other"
> Is indeed a precious treasure.
> With unwavering devotion keep to him;
> He is the king of all physicians.

And we find in the *Abridged Prajñāpāramitā*,

Constantly rely on learned teachers. And why?
From them derive all qualities of learning.

How then are we to meditate on this path?

26. For undistracted meditation on the fundamental nature,
As before, first practice the preliminaries,
And in the guru yoga pray that you succeed
In seeing all phenomena as emanated apparitions.
Then in the main practice, firmly take your stand
Upon the understanding that the mind
Is, by its nature, like an emanated apparition
And that everything appearing to the mind—
This too is, by its nature, like an emanated apparition.
Everything is unborn like an emanation.
With this understanding
Leave the mind at rest,
Devoid of mental agitation.

When one practices guru yoga, one should pray to one's teacher for success in seeing everything as an emanation. Then, in the knowledge that both the mind and everything appearing to the mind are like emanated apparitions, one should remain in a state in which memories, thoughts, and mental activity have no place.

27. As you rest then in a clear and empty state,
Devoid of mind's elaboration,
There comes a clear and limpid luminosity
Resembling an emanated apparition,
Motionless and free from the duality
Of apprehender-apprehended.
Sense objects appear and are perceived unceasingly,
And yet there is no grasping them as this or that.
There is no fabrication and no alteration.

> **It is a vivid, limpid, undistracted state of natural bliss,**
> **A state of mind that's bright, devoid of thoughts,**
> **And similar to space itself.**
> **Thus you see the nature of the mind**
> **Devoid of thought's construction.**
> **It's then that mental states**
> **Regarding things that are like apparitions**
> **Subside, themselves like apparitions also.**
> **Craving and aversion, hopes and fears,**
> **All clinging to a self—are all like emanated apparitions.**
> **The ground, the path, the fruit**
> **Are all the state of openness and freedom.**

All movements of thought, which are themselves like emanated apparitions, subside. They are not even regarded as emanated apparitions. This is the state of primordial wisdom free of all movement, divested of the duality of apprehended and apprehender. Even though appearing objects are perceived, no mental discernment occurs whereby such objects may be taken as something real. For this is a state free of apprehended and apprehender, designated in terms of object and subject. In limpid awareness, appearances are perceived, without any conceptual fixation, as luminous and empty, just like emanated apparitions. As one remains in the state of recognizing lucid awareness in the manner of self-illumination,[120] the body and the mind are in a state of bliss. Space-like luminosity is beheld beyond all conceptual extremes. At that time, since all things arise in the manner of emanated apparitions, one is automatically freed from the apprehension of them as truly existing phenomena, and the five poisons and every hope and fear cease to exist. So it is that even the apprehension of the phenomena of ground, path, and result—as antidotes to [the belief in] truly existing things—comes naturally to a halt. Consequently, regarding the outer apprehended object and the inner apprehending subject, when the self of the person (as something apprehended) subsides, there is, in that very moment, no further clinging to the antidote as something to be implemented on the path; and thus the nonexistence of the phenomenal self is automatically realized. Those who accomplish this are called "bodhisattvas who have realized the absence of the two kinds of self."

Practitioners who have such a realization are free of every fetter, of every kind of grasping and deviation. Their minds are in a state of unbounded openness.

28. Then however you may meditate, it will not fetter you.
Though you meditate on things as if they were existent,
You will be free from the extreme of permanence.
Though you meditate on things as nonexistent,
You will be unstained by nihilism.
Though you meditate in dualistic ways,
You will remain within the state of nonduality.
Though you meditate on self-identity,
You will be not be bound by clinging to a self.
Though you meditate on other things,
You will nonetheless be free of hope and fear.
Though you implement the generation stage,
You will naturally accomplish the perfection stage.
Though you practice the perfection stage,
The stage of generating an appearance is likewise done.

When one has looked upon awareness, uncontrived and bare, then even though one meditates with the thought that actions, their fully ripened karmic effects, and so on are all true and certain, one will not fall into the extreme of permanence. For groundless awareness is seen. Though one meditates on the understanding that everything in phenomenal existence is rootless, one does not fall into the extreme of nihilism, for one sees the luminosity of awareness. Although one may meditate in a dualistic manner on phenomena and the mind as being a measureless palace, deities and so forth, one will not fall into dualistic clinging because, at that very moment, one sees the nondual nature of self-cognizing awareness.

Although one meditates on emptiness endowed with supreme qualities—namely, the sugatagarbha, or the primordially present, spontaneous, and unconditioned identity of one's "self" (in other words, sublime luminosity)—one does not fall into clinging to self in the manner of the ātman of the non-Buddhist extremists. And this is so because one sees the nature of self-cognizing awareness as "great, spontaneous presence" that is empty yet luminous. And although one meditates on other things, such as the hallucinatory appearances of saṃsāra—the veils that are to be purified—one falls into neither hope nor fear because one sees that the nature of awareness is primordially unstained. As the *Abhisamayālaṃkāra* says,

> Therein is nothing to remove
> And thereto not the slightest thing to add.
> The perfect truth viewed perfectly
> And perfectly beheld is liberation.[121]

Even though, in the practice of the generation stage, one meditates on a deity with a face, arms, and so forth, one does not, when one is meditating, fall into conceptual fixation because one is actually seeing awareness, empty and luminous, devoid of characteristics.[122] And although one meditates on the subtle yogas of the perfection stage, whether these are endowed with visible form or, like space, are not so endowed, one does not fall into the extreme of emptiness. For one sees that all such forms are spontaneously present in the state of awareness that is never divested of its self-illuminating, bare nature. For a practitioner, these are points of the highest importance.

The root text goes on to describe the experience of the practitioner once this realization has been gained:

> **29. Arising and subsiding all occur at once,**
> **And thus from all defilements you are free.**
> **Within the natural state devoid of apprehending thought,**
> **You rest within the wheel of ultimate reality:**

The no-time of the triple time.
Meditation and postmeditation—
For you, there is no difference.
You experience them like emanated apparitions.

Although yogis on this level appear in the form of embodied beings, they dwell, nevertheless, in traceless emptiness. Others may think that such practitioners have bodies, but these are [for the latter] just a state of bare emptiness, no longer material bodies at all. And since such practitioners have stripped their minds to a state of naked, all-penetrating openness, thoughts vanish in the moment of their arising. They subside spontaneously in a state beyond all reference. Self-illuminating and all-penetrating awareness, in which there is no difference between past and future, continuously manifests; and whether such yogis are in meditation or have arisen from meditation, it is all the same to them. Such practitioners are said to have realized the equality of the three times. As is mentioned in the *Mañjuśrīnāmasaṃgīti*, "He is the one who understood the timeless nature of the triple time."

30. It's then that yogis seem to be
Like aimless lunatics,
Free of clinging, free of care.
They're totally bereft of hope and fear—
They do not alter anything that manifests.
All for them is equal and elusive.
They realize without effort
Wisdom mind, the all-embracing space.

For the minds of such yogis, free as they are of all fixation, the continuity of ordered conduct is abandoned and they react to whatever occurs with complete spontaneity. They are like lunatics, totally unpredictable in the way they act. This is the moment when the vast and space-like wisdom mind is actualized.

With respect to the result, the root text goes on to say that elusive appearances are not taken for real:

> **31. And then, both night and day,**
> **The yogi sees all things as emanated apparitions.**
> **In the cakra of great bliss,**
> **There is but a single space of bliss.**
> **In the cakra of enjoyment,**
> **All qualities are savored.**
> **In the cakra of the dharmatā,**
> **The ultimate is ever present.**
> **In the cakra of manifestation,**
> **Appearances are boundless.**
> **In the bliss-preserving cakra,**
> **Bliss is kept both day and night.**
> **So it is that, without any training,**
> **The wind-mind penetrates the crucial place.**
> **The ground of cleansing, factors to be cleansed,**
> **The cleansing agent, channels main and radial,**
> **Together with the winds, are all primordial wisdom.**
> **The fruit of cleansing—the single taste of all—**
> **Is thus made manifest.**

When the deluded body and mind are brought to an end, the auspicious link is created for the manifestation of excellent qualities. Those whose main practice is the generation stage (where effort is demanded) take the gross channels and winds as their path. In the case of the perfection stage (where no effort is called for), certain practitioners take as their path the subtle yoga by means of which the thought-free state is engendered. This path does in fact require a little effort in the training. On the other hand, those of highest capacity, that is, the practitioners of the Great Perfection who have realized awareness and have mastery of it, use as their path the absence of all effort and deliberate action. By this means, through the effortless preservation of the state of awareness, the channels and winds are mastered, and all their excellent qualities are rendered manifest. The first approach is similar to the path of the bodhisattvas, where all excellent qualities are actualized through the two accumulations, by means of which the channels and winds are rendered serviceable. The second approach is that of the common way of causing excellent qualities to manifest through the kind of training that brings the winds into the crucial place.[123] The third approach is that of the Natural Great Perfection, where the qualities of the channels and winds arise without any effort or the implementation of deliberate action.

With respect to this, the channels and winds (the support and the supported) are refined by means of physical postures and so forth. The wind is like a vehicle for the mind, and the essential constituents are like one's wealth, the bringer of enjoyment. Those who practice by means of effort purify and exercise the wind, which is like a horse, thereby mastering their minds, which are like riders. According to the image used (that of riders wishing to travel from one place to another), practitioners employ the technique of yogic exercises and strenuously concentrate on mastery of the four cakras and the three main channels, as if they were riders gaining control over their steeds.

The third approach, by contrast, is like that of a powerful man who, without moving from his seat, naturally accomplishes all his objectives. In the same way, if awareness does not stray from its natural condition, the result will be that the winds in the channels and the practitioner's mind separate from each other and all thought processes easily subside. Then, as the practitioner does not move from the natural state of ultimate reality, the qualities of the refined channels and winds are spontaneously perfected without this being consciously sought. It is thus that the practitioners of all the common vehicles are like ministers and subjects, who gain their objectives with effort, whereas the practitioners of the extraordinary vehicle of the Great Perfection are like kings who spontaneously and effortlessly achieve their purposes.

When awareness does not stir from its natural condition, both the mind and the winds, which are, so to speak, its steed, are mastered and their qualities become manifest. This happens in the following way:

When the wind-mind of the cakra of great bliss at the crown of the head is refined, thoughts of desire and attachment, which are the factors to be purified, dissolve into awareness, the ground of purification. It is then that the practitioner dwells in the expanse of bliss, in the greatly blissful, spontaneous samādhi that has the nature of uninterrupted ultimate reality—the result of purification.

When the wind-mind of the cakra of enjoyment at the throat is refined, thoughts of anger and aggression, the factors to be purified, dissolve into awareness, the ground of purification. Then, as the result of purification, the riches of concentration are spontaneously perfected.

When the wind-mind of the cakra of ultimate reality at the level of the heart is refined, the factor to be purified, namely, ignorance, dissolves into awareness, the ground of purification, and the result of purification, inconceivable luminosity, is spontaneously achieved.

When the wind-mind of the cakra of manifestation at the navel is refined, thoughts of pride, jealousy, and so forth, which are the factors to be purified, dissolve into awareness, the ground of purification, and the result of purification—the accomplishment of miraculous abilities, the power of emanation, and the four kinds of enlightened activity—occurs.

Through one's growing used to the view that is unspoiled by clinging—in other words, through recognition of the mind's nature, which is the agent of purification—the factors to be purified, namely, the various stains and defilements, dissolve into awareness itself, the ground of purification of all these factors. The result of this purification, the permanent state of awareness, is gained, and all qualities—in both the immediate and the ultimate term—become completely manifest. As it is said in the tantra the *Wish-Fulfilling Wheel of Bliss*,

The position of the Natural Great Perfection
Lies in leaving things alone within their natural state.
This means to leave the mind unaltered, as it is,
In its primordial state of openness and freedom.
The state of wisdom lies beyond the ordinary mind.
Therein is found the exhaustion of extremes
Of emptiness and true existence.
All things in their multiplicity are there exhausted;
Discursive thinking is no more.
All attributes subside in their own place.
And all spontaneous qualities,
Without the need for training,
Come naturally to perfection.

Then, as the root text goes on to say,

32. You will be able in your dreams
To take on different forms that you can change
And then behold the various buddha fields.
Later these deluded dreams will cease,
And day and night you will remain in luminosity.
Remaining in the concentrations
On bliss, on luminosity, and no-thought,
You will gain the powers
Of vision, preternatural cognition,
Miracles, and other qualities.
Your realization and experience
Will be unbounded, and thus you will achieve
Your own good and the good of other beings.
Therefore, you who are endowed with fortune,
Meditate unceasingly that all things
Have the nature of an emanated apparition.

At night, as one lies down in the posture of the lion, one visualizes the central channel with the four cakras—in which are contained the stable vessel of the universe together with its moving contents, as well as all the buddha fields. In the main, however, one should go to sleep thinking that all the phenomena of saṃsāra and nirvāṇa, which are like emanated apparitions, are found in the cakra of the throat. And when one recognizes one's dreams to be dreams, one should in those same dreams assume different forms for oneself, transforming them at will, and so on. Thereby one will accomplish powers of vision, preternatural knowledge, concentration, and the ability to work miracles. Remaining constantly in the state of luminosity, one will progress upon the grounds and paths, and finally one will reach the state of the supreme enlightenment of Samantabhadra. As it is said in the tantra the *Wish-Fulfilling Wheel of Bliss*,

> Thus the yogi graced with fortune,
> With no thoughts, with no intentions,
> Accomplishes the supreme maṇḍala,
> The highest ground of nature perfect in itself.

In conclusion,

Within the state of changeless great equality,
May we behold the enlightened mind,
Unmoving, free of mental fabrication—
Primordial wisdom, nonconceptual, self-arisen.
May we thus achieve the nonabiding pristine state.

Luminosity, the chief of perfect qualities of stainless peace,
Arises like the sun within the sky's expanse.
Let it drive away the dark of ignorance
Of both ourselves and others,
And may this only eye of beings reveal the land of liberation.

This concludes the chapter that is like an emanated apparition, a commentary on the eighth vajra point of *Finding Rest in Illusion, a Teaching of the Great Perfection.*

The Conclusion of the Treatise

The message of this text may be understood as follows:

1. To show that in the eight examples of illusion
Is gathered all the Dharma
That the Buddha has expounded,
Here has been distilled the quintessential sap
Of tantras, commentaries, and pith instructions,
Illumined by the dawning Rays of Spotless Light.[124]

In all the many sections of the teachings set forth by the Bhagavan Buddha, whether in sūtras or tantras, there is nothing greater than the eight examples of illusion as means to illustrate the nature of self-cognizing awareness and of the phenomena that appear within awareness. As it is said in the *Prajñāpāramitā*,

> O Subhūti, phenomena are like dreams, like magical illusions. Even nirvāṇa is like a dream, like a magical illusion. And if there were anything greater than nirvāṇa, that too would be like a dream, like a magical illusion.

And as we find in the *Root Stanzas of the Middle Way*,

> Like a dream and like a mirage,
> Like a city of gandharvas,
> So arising and abiding
> And cessation have been taught.[125]

The sense of these quotations is that self-cognizing awareness together with the phenomena that appear in that awareness are typified on the relative level in the eight examples of illusion. These texts teach that in the very moment that phenomena are perceived, their ultimately real status is beyond arising and ceasing. And within the state of awareness—that is, the ultimate truth, which is similar to space—the phenomena of both saṃsāra and nirvāṇa, all summarized within the eight examples of illusion, appear in the manner of clouds and rainbows. This is the relative truth. Such phenomena are established as dependently arising, as neither born nor ceasing and so forth—in other words, as not existing in any of the eight ways, as the great and noble master Nāgārjuna, the matchless sheltering protection of our world, has declared at the very beginning of his *Root Stanzas of the Middle Way*:

> To him who taught that things arise dependently,
> Not ceasing, not arising,
> Not annihilated nor yet permanent,
> Not coming, not departing,
> Not different, not the same:
> The stilling of all thought, and perfect peace—
> To him, the best of teachers, perfect Buddha,
> I bow down.

Because I have trained for unnumbered ages in this way of understanding awareness and the phenomena that appear in it in terms of the two truths (and this according to the vehicle of the Dharma unsurpassed), the sun of my intelligence in this present life shines out with countless rays of light in the immaculate sky of my discipline to dissipate the darkness of ignorance for fortunate beings who might be trained—and thus to cause the lotus garden of the sublime Dharma to appear and bloom.

As part of the dedication of the merit [of this composition] to enlightenment, the first step is to make the dedication so that, thanks to their implementation of the sublime teachings, beings may themselves be liberated.

> **2. By this merit, may all beings, leaving none aside,**
> **See phenomena as unborn, just like magical illusions.**
> **May they, progressing in their practice of the Dharma,**
> **Be graced with riches of the triple kāya of the Conquerors.**

Borne up by excellent virtue, which perfectly opens the door of the unsurpassed Dharma, may beings as infinite as space is vast pursue the sublime path of liberation. Perceiving all phenomena according to the eight examples of illusoriness, may they complete the accumulation of conceptual merit. By meditating on awareness similar to space, may they bring to completion the accumulation of nonconceptual wisdom. And by bringing to perfection the qualities of the grounds and paths, may they come at last to the state of full enlightenment. As it is said in the *Yuktiśaṣtika*,

> By this virtue, may all beings
> Complete the gatherings of wisdom and of merit.
> May they gain the twofold excellence[126]
> Arising from this merit and this wisdom.

Merit is then dedicated to the elimination of obstacles on the path:

> **3. Like dreams, illusions, mirages, reflections,**
> **Echoes, emanated apparitions—just so are all phenomena.**
> **Through giving up attachment to their true existence,**
> **May beings come to the primordial state endowed**
> **With all the qualities of primal wisdom.**

In consideration of the hindrances provoked upon the path, it is through the failure to recognize the fundamental nature that beings regard ordinary misfortunes, and also their slight experiences in meditation, to be truly existent things. Because of this, they are exposed to the activity of evil forces and obstacles. Therefore, may they realize that nothing exists truly and thereby come to achieve the ultimate result, the kāyas and wisdoms of enlightenment. As Śāntideva says,

> Whenever I desire to gaze on him
> Or put to him the slightest question,
> May I behold with unobstructed sight
> My own protector Mañjughoṣa.[127]

The expression "to gaze" here refers to the state of meditative concentration; "to put the question" refers to the wisdom of deep insight. Thus it is through the path of calm abiding and deep insight that the state of Mañjuśrī is attained, in other words, the ultimate result of buddhahood. And Śāntideva makes this aspiration in order to remove any hindrances and obstructions to his attainment.

It is in this connection that the *Prajñāpāramitā* says, "For some bodhisattvas there are evil forces. For other bodhisattvas there are no evil forces." The meaning of this text is explained in the *Ratnakūṭa*:

> For those who have the highest wisdom and endeavor there are no evil forces. Evil forces find no chance to harm them. The reason for this is that because such people see that all phenomena are by their very nature spacelike and unborn, they do not find anything that such evil forces could attack. Those, on the other hand, who have endeavor but little wisdom are exposed to the hindrances of evil. For while practicing with endeavor, they take phenomena as true. Finally, those who have no endeavor are not exposed to the workings of the evil ones. For the lack of endeavor is itself the work of evil forces.

Merit is then dedicated for the removal of distraction and busy occupations:

> **4. May they turn away from towns**
> **Where childish people dwell**
> **Amid their many occupations—**
> **Thick jungles of saṃsāra teeming with defilement.**
> **May they go away to pleasant forest wilds**
> **And there become a jewel that would adorn**
> **The crowns of hundreds, countless, gods.**

In villages and towns and in city-like monasteries are found childish people difficult to guide, immersed in riches and possessions that are the cause of conflict and the circumstances of many defilements. This is why those who wish for freedom should withdraw into the noble and complete solitude of pleasant forests and embrace the practice of meditative concentration, thereby gaining the qualities of the grounds and paths. And since on occasion such yogis bestow teachings even on assemblies of the gods, may they [through this merit] be taken by the latter as the jewels in their crowns.

As we find in *The Way of the Bodhisattva*,

> For if I act like childish beings,
> Sure it is that I shall fall to evil destinies.
> So why do I keep company with infants,
> Who lead me to a state so far from virtue?
>
> One moment friends,
> The next, they're bitter enemies.
> Even pleasant things arouse their discontent:
> Ordinary people—it is hard to please them!
>
> A beneficial word and they resent it,
> Turning me instead from what is good.

And when I close my ears to what they say,
Their anger makes them fall to lower states.

Jealous of superiors, they vie with equals.
Proud to those below, they strut when praised.
Say something untoward, they seethe with rage.
What good was ever had from childish folk?[128]

Merit is then dedicated to the goal of truly remaining in solitude:

5. May our minds grow weary of distraction
And take delight in peaceful forest solitudes,
Alone to meditate on profound suchness
And to attain the pure eyes of a noble mind.

On the whole, people who are deluded and who take for true what are just deceptive appearances similar to magical illusions, and who especially are deceived by the illusions of the eight worldly concerns, tell us that there is no point in our striving for liberation. Therefore let us get away from all those around us who are so difficult to guide—as well as all the distressing signs and circumstances of this evil age. Let us stay in solitude. May we gain sublime, primordial wisdom. As Śāntideva says,

For I am one who strives for freedom.
I must not be caught by wealth and honors.[129]

Merit is dedicated to taking pleasure in the excellence of forest solitudes:

6. The forest filled with foliage and flowers,
With fruits and water that is pure,
Is hallowed by the glory of austerity.
In such a place, with life's essential wealth
Of freedoms and advantages,

Assisted by a treasury of beneficial teaching,
May we journey on the path to liberation.

The forests are the haunts of utter solitude, adorned with flowers and waterfalls. There one finds caves lit by the bright water-crystal of the moon, pleasant places for meditation, enclosed with fences of reeds, climbing plants, and bamboo. In such localities, and throughout our days completely free, may we practice calm abiding and deep insight. Climbing thus the stairway of the grounds and paths, may we reach, while in this very life, the fastness of great liberation! As *The Way of the Bodhisattva* says,

In woodlands, haunt of stag and bird,
Among the trees where no dissension jars,
It's there I would keep pleasant company!
When might I be off to make my dwelling there?[130]

Finally, merit is dedicated to the welfare of others:

7. So that now our lives should bring forth fruit,
May we in this existence practice virtuous Dharma.
When we have achieved the many qualities
Of this, the path to peace,
May we deliver endless beings from saṃsāra.

Since in our present situation we are unable to bring benefit to beings, let us stay alone in solitude and implement with one-pointed concentration the peace-bestowing Dharma. May we thus give meaning to our human lives! And gaining buddhahood, may we then bring benefit to beings as infinite in number as space itself is vast! As we are told in the *Exhortation to Remain in Solitude*,

With no clear understanding of the meaning of such words,
To say "I shall bring benefit to others"
Is nothing but the babbling of madness.

Therefore I shall stay in solitude
And at length bring benefit and happiness to others.

As advice for future generations, the root text goes on to say,

8. This text is the essential heart
Of Dharma so profound,
A path where final teachings
Are distilled into their vital point.
You who wish for freedom
Should strive in it sincerely.
Not resting day or night,
Practice it with diligence!

All the sūtras and tantras of the definitive meaning are condensed in this text. Let those with faith implement it and without laziness practice it diligently.

The root text then encourages its readers to assiduous effort:

9. O you, the fortunate of future times endowed with faith,
Implement this text with constancy and diligence.
Sure it is that you and others
Will sail across this ocean of existence
And naturally attain the twofold aim of beings.

Fortunate beings should cherish this text of eight points set forth with vajra words. These last two stanzas are a general and then more specific instruction in both their words and meaning.

The root text then concludes with an indication of its author and the place of its composition:

10. This quintessential meaning
Of the sūtras, tantras, pith instructions
Was well set down upon the slopes of Gangri Thökar
By a yogi who, adorned with spotless rays of light,

Had eyes to see the truth profound
Of all without exception.

This text was composed by one who, through the radiating light of his intelligence, understood all the outer and inner tantras and all the pith instructions of the Secret Mantrayāna. It was set down in writing on the slopes of Gangri Thökar, king of mountains, a holy place, the perfect excellence of which should be celebrated with the melody of praise.

The merit of composition is again dedicated to the propagation of the teachings in the ten directions:

11. May this teaching of the Dharma,
The sun graced with a thousand stainless beams,
The light of primal wisdom,
Drive away the gloom of ignorance.
May it completely dry the ocean of saṃsāra.
May the brilliance of the isle of liberation
Spread and shine in all the ten directions.

May this teaching of the Dharma, which is like the brilliant network of rays of light of the suns at the end of the kalpa,[131] blaze forth and dissipate the darkness of beings' ignorance. May it dry up the ocean of saṃsāra together with its underlying habitual tendencies. May this extraordinary teaching, this shining light that reveals the island of liberation, radiate outward in all directions. This is intended as an elegant and poetic expression of good wishes! And with these lines I bring my text to an end.

Just as one might deck with jewels
A fine and handsome person,
For a wondrous root text deep in meaning
I devised a commentary
With various words profound in sense.

By such merit may the ocean of the teachings
Linger for a long time in this world of beings.
May the life of sublime masters know no limit,
And may the booming of the Dharma's drum
Adorn this world of ours.

May lands on all sides constantly enjoy
Prosperity and every happiness.
May beings practice virtue
And thereby enter on the path of liberation.
May their immediate and final wishes be fulfilled,
And may they gain the endless riches
Of the twofold lordly benefit.

May the sun of the three worlds,
This precious teaching,
Increase the joy and welfare
Of all beings, leaving none aside.
May it be, till time draws to its end,
The eye of all the universe
And spread on all sides everywhere within the world.

This text, *The Chariot of Excellence*, a commentary on *Finding Rest in Illusion, a Teaching of the Great Perfection*, was composed by one who was rich in the knowledge of all the subjects of the Sugata's teaching—one moreover who, having accomplished a meditative concentration immaculate as space itself, mastered all the topics of the teaching of the supreme vehicle. It was composed at the sacred place of Orgyen Dzong on the slopes of Gangri Thökar by the yogi Natsok Rangdröl, who had been accepted into the care of the great master Padmasambhava

Virtue! Virtue! Virtue!

Notes

Abbreviations

GP	Longchen Rabjam, *An Ocean of Elegant Explanations, a General Presentation,* in *ngal gso skor gsum.*
TPQ, Book 1	Jigme Lingpa and Longchen Yeshe Dorje, Kangyur Rinpoche, *Treasury of Precious Qualities,* translated by Padmakara Translation Group (Boston: Shambhala Publications, 2010).
TPQ, Book 2	Jigme Lingpa and Longchen Yeshe Dorje, Kangyur Rinpoche, *Treasury of Precious Qualities, Book 2,* translated by Padmakara Translation Group (Boston: Shambhala Publications, 2013).
WB	Shantideva, *The Way of the Bodhisattva: A Translation of the Bodhicharyāvatāra,* Translated by the Padmakara Translation Group. Rev. ed. (Boston: Shambhala Publications, 2006).

---

1. For a detailed explanation of the teachings of the Great Perfection, see particularly chapters 11–13 of TPQ, Book 2.
2. This was an oral teaching originally given in the three-year retreat center of Rinchen Ling in Dordogne, France. See Nyoshul Khenpo Jamyang Dorje, *The Fearless Lion's Roar,* p. 117.
3. See Longchenpa, *Finding Rest in the Nature of the Mind,* p. 127, v. 3.
4. Ibid., p. 128, v. 4.
5. Ibid., p. 134, vv. 27–28.
6. See Longchenpa's conclusion p. 250.

7. See *Root Stanzas of the Middle Way*, p. 2.
8. *grub mtha' rin po che'i mdzod.*
9. *yid bzhin rin po che'i mdzod.*
10. *theg mchog rin po che'i mdzod.*
11. The texts in question are *An Introduction to Suchness: A Summary of the Teaching of the Three Svātantrikas from the East* (*Rang rgyud shar gsum gyi don bsdus de kho na nyid la 'jug pa*) and *A Summary Explanation of the State of Complete Nonabiding: An Elucidation of the Principles of Prāsaṅgika Madhyamaka (dBu ma thal 'gyur gyi gnas gsal ba rab tu mi gnas pa'i don bsdus).* See Pettit, *Mipham's Beacon of Certainty*, p. 93.
12. *spros bral.*
13. See Shantarakshita and Mipham, *Adornment of the Middle Way*, p. 118.
14. Respectively *lung gi gter mdzod* and *chos dbying mdzod.*
15. See *chos dbyings rin po che'i mdzod kyi 'grel pa lung gi gter mdzod. A 'dzom chos sgar* edition, folio 76/b, lines 1–3.
16. *Madhyamakāvatara*, 11:54. See Chandrakirti and Mipham, *Introduction to the Middle Way*, p. 112.
17. Respectively, *rang stong* and *gzhan stong.*
18. See p. 70.
19. See in the eighth vajra point, p. 217.
20. See p. 72.
21. *ngal gso skor gsum gyi spyi don legs bshad rgya mtsho.*
22. See *An Ocean of Elegant Explanations*, pp. 98–99.
23. See Jamgön Mipham, *The Wisdom Chapter*, p. 276.
24. Ibid, p. 276.
25. See pp. 232–235.
26. See Jamgön Mipham, *The Wisdom Chapter*, p. 276.
27. See Longchenpa, *Finding Rest in the Nature of the Mind*, pp. xxii-xxiii.
28. See Nyoshul Khenpo Jamyang Dorje, *The Fearless Lion's Roar*, p. 126.
29. "Rays of Spotless Light" is a literal translation of Longchenpa's name, Drimé Özer.
30. This is a reference to ultimate bodhichitta, the nature of the mind or sugatagarbha.
31. *log rtog sgyu ma.*
32. *yang dag sgyu ma.*
33. The eight points presented in this treatise follow the eight negations set down in the prologue to Nāgārjuna's *Root Stanzas of the Middle Way*: not arising and not ceasing; not annihilated and not permanent; not coming and not going; not different and not the same.

34. This is a reference to one of the five great madhyamaka arguments used to negate the true existence of phenomena. See TPQ, Book 1, p. 427.
35. For an explanation of *nature* (*ngo bo*), *character* (*rang bzhin*), and *cognitive potency* (*thugs rje*) as these terms are used in the Great Perfection, see TPQ, Book 2, p. 237.
36. *yang dag dbyings kyi sgyu ma.*
37. *gzhi snang.* For a discussion of the appearance of the ground in the Great Perfection teachings, see TPQ, Book 2, pp. 237–38.
38. For a discussion of coemergent and conceptual ignorance as these are referred to in the teachings of the Great Perfection, see TPQ, Book 2, p. 244.
39. See pp. 181–82 of *Finding Rest in the Nature of the Mind.* The Great Chariot is Longchenpa's autocommentary to this.
40. I.e., the skandhas, dhātus, and āyatanas, respectively. The twelve sense fields (āyatanas) are the six senses and their six objects. The eighteen constituents (dhātus) are the twelve sense fields together with the six sense consciousnesses.
41. 1:55–57.
42. I.e., the "appearing object" (*snang yul*), which here corresponds to the "object to be dealt with or to be apprehended" (*gzung yul*).
43. For a discussion of appearing object, apprehended object, and apprehending subject, see TPQ, Book 2, p. 249, as well as *Finding Rest in the Nature of the Mind*, p. 263.
44. For an explanation of the dependent nature, see *Finding Rest in the Nature of the Mind*, p. 182.
45. *gzhan dbang* (dependent nature) means literally "other-power" or "other-dependence."
46. Respectively, the defiled mind, the five sense consciousnesses, and thoughts.
47. The three levels referred to here are the three pure grounds or *bhumis* (the eighth, ninth, and tenth) of the path of meditation. Their names are respectively *Immovable, Perfect Intellect*, and *Cloud of Dharma.*
48. For the different kinds of preternatural knowledge, see TPQ, Book 1, p. 387.
49. This refers to "warmth," the first of the four stages of the path of joining. The mention at the end of the citation to the sixteenfold increase of merit refers to "peak," the second stage of the path of joining.
50. For the qualities of realization, see TPQ, Book 1, pp. 387–90. For the qualities of elimination, see pp. 126–27 of the present text.

51. For the thirty-seven factors leading to enlightenment, see TPQ, Book 1, pp. 391–95. See also pp. 113–24 of the present text.
52. 2:53–56.
53. *sgyu ma.* In this context, the word *illusion* always carries with it the connotation of "magical illusion"—that is, an illusion conjured up by a magician. It does not refer simply to a mistaken perception, as when one takes a rope for a snake.
54. For a presentation of the winds, see TPQ, Book 2, pp. 160–63.
55. *mi ldan rnam bcad.*
56. This seems to be a reference to the *zhentong* (*gzhan stong*) view of the Jonangpa school founded by Longchenpa's contemporary, Dolpopa (1292–1361).
57. See *Root Stanzas of the Middle Way*, 24:14.
58. *'khrul gzhi'i rig pa.* This refers to the appearances of the ground (*gzhi snang*). See TPQ, Book 2, p. 434n443.
59. *rang bzhin sgyu ma.*
60. Longchenpa inserts the following scriptural citation by way of illustration: "As we find in the *Questions of Bhadra the Magician*,

    Illusions that appear through karma
    Are all the beings who live in the six realms.
    Illusions manifesting through conditions
    Are like the things reflected in a looking glass.
    Illusions that through Dharma manifest
    Are all the monks surrounding me.
    And I the truly perfect Buddha
    Am the illusion bodied forth by primal wisdom."

    Although, in the Tibetan text, this passage is located on the preceding page, its position seems more natural here.
61. 1:27.
62. 1:47.
63. See Shantideva, *Way of the Bodhisattva*, 6:25.
64. The reference here is to two of the four noble truths, which in the present context are to be understood not as general principles but as classes of phenomena. One therefore speaks not of the truth of suffering but rather of true sufferings, true origins, and so on, referring thereby to the phenomenal world.
65. For a more detailed presentation, see TPQ, Book 1, pp. 391–95.

66. The *Sūtra of Dṛdhramati*, the *Questions of Matisambhava*, and the *Questions of Kumāraprabha*, cited in this discussion, though not included in the Kangyur, are also cited in Niguma's autocommentary to her *Stages in the Path of Illusion (sgyu ma lam gyi rim pa'i 'grel pa)*. See Sarah Harding, *Niguma, Lady of Illusion*, pp. 98–130.
67. These are the three doors of perfect liberation. See TPQ, Book 1, p. 437.
68. The sūtra speaks of concentration based on conduct (*spyod pa*). On the other hand, commentators such as Yontan Gyamtso (in his commentary on the *Treasury of Precious Qualities*) speak, in the same context, of concentration based on analysis (*dpyod*).
69. See Shantideva, *Way of the Bodhisattva*, 8:4.
70. v.107.
71. The buddha-element (*khams*) is the buddha nature in its veiled aspect at the time of ordinary beings.
72. This is a technical expression referring to the attainment of the path of seeing. For a detailed presentation, see TPQ, Book 1, pp. 215–22.
73. I.e., the path of joining.
74. This system of four paths of elimination of defilements is not to be confused with the five paths of progression to buddhahood (accumulation, joining, seeing etc.).
75. The ten transcendent perfections or pāramitās are the six well-known perfections of generosity, discipline, patience, diligence, concentration, and wisdom with the addition of skillful means, strength, aspiration, and primordial wisdom. The last four are considered to be aspects of the sixth perfection of wisdom. The correlation between the ten perfections and the ten grounds of realization figures prominently in Candrakīrti's *Madhyamakāvātara*.
76. *skad cig yud tsam thang cig*. According to Mipham Rinpoche in his *Gateway to Knowledge (mkhas 'jug)*, a single instant (*skad cig*) corresponds to 1.6 seconds, one *thang cig* lasts 96 seconds, while a *yud tsam* lasts 2,880 seconds or 48 minutes. In the order given in the present citation, the longest moment follows the shortest one.
77. The term *measureless* is defined in the Abhidharma as 10^{58}.
78. For different kinds of Akaniṣṭha, see TPQ, Book 2, p. 461n538.
79. *mngon byang lnga*. See TPQ, Book 2, p. 104–5.
80. *gtsang ma'i rigs* or *gtsang ma'i gnas*. Above the three levels of the fourth samādhi are five pure levels on which superior beings are said to dwell. The highest of these is the realm of Akaniṣṭha the Fair. It is the dimension in which bodhisattvas spend their last life before achieving buddhahood.

81. The Tibetan of the text used for this translation reads *khrag chen gyi sangs rgyas bcu gcig* ("the eleven buddhas of great blood," that is, "desire"). In the autocommentary to Niguma's *Stages in the Path of Illusion* (*sgyu ma lam gyi rim pa'i 'grel pa*), this passage reads instead *grags chen gyi sangs rgyas sa bcu gcig pa* ("the renowned buddhas on the eleventh ground"). See Harding, *Niguma, Lady of Illusion*, p. 131. Although we have translated the text as we have found it, Dakpo Tulku, whom we consulted, considered the alternative reading given in Niguma's autocommentary to be more plausible.
82. Longchenpa classifies the inner tantras as father, mother, and nondual, corresponding respectively to Mahāyoga, Anuyoga, and Atiyoga.
83. The Tibetan word for *universe* (*'jig rten*) literally means "the support or basis for destruction."
84. The Tibetan here reads *gnyis ka 'jig rten du rdzogs pa*. According to Khenpo Tendzin Norgyé, this is probably a scribal error for *gnyis ka 'jig rten du brjod pa*.
85. *byang chub sgyu ma*.
86. *sna tshogs sgyu ma*.
87. *gshis kyi sgyu ma*.
88. This citation is not found in present versions of the *Sūtrālaṃkāra*.
89. Approach (*bsnyen*) and accomplishment (*sgrub*) are two phases in the generation stage practice (*bskyed rim*) of the Secret Mantra.
90. See Shantideva, *Way of the Bodhisattva*, 9:151, 152, and 154.
91. *lha sku rab tu mi gnas pa gsum*.
92. This refers to the twelfth ground, called Lotus Free of All Desire, corresponding to the level of the saṃbhogakāya.
93. *mig yor*. Longchenpa explains that this is a visual form of a nonexistent thing provoked by certain circumstances in imitation of something else. For example, when one presses one's eyes and looks at the moon, a second moon appears. This example is easy to understand; the example of a shadow is more obscure unless the point is that the shape of the shadow resembles the shape of the body that projects it. Longchenpa's example of the darkness and gloom that may be experienced in relation to a state of intense suffering or defilement is even more difficult to understand given that no physical form is involved. In general, however, the message is clear. The point at issue is the phenomenon of false appearances: the hallucinatory vision or experience of nonexistent objects.
94. See Shantideva, *Way of the Bodhisattva*, 6:93.

95. The indication that one is drawing near to the goal.
96. These are the signs that the winds have entered the central channel.
97. The use of the term *dhāraṇī* becomes more easily intelligible when one remembers that the word derives from a Sanskrit root meaning "to hold."
98. *rjes su ma chad pa.* See p. 250. This term was translated as "annihilated" in the *Root Stanzas of the Middle Way.*
99. The point here is contained in the first two lines of the quotation. These are, of course, the famous words spoken by the Buddha in the first moments after his enlightenment.
100. Shantideva, *Way of the Bodhisattva,* 9:2.
101. This and the following two citations are not found in present editions of the *Sūtrālaṃkāra.*
102. Longchenpa is here referring to (and rejecting) the position of the Svātantrika Mādhyamikas and their characteristic way of referring to the manner in which the two truths coincide within phenomena: as twin aspects in a single substance (*ngo bo gcig la ldog pa tha dad*). Moreover, when in order to explain the two truths, the Svātantrikas distinguish them—speaking of the ultimate and relative truths as if they were equal counterparts coinciding in phenomena—such an explanation occurs within the confines, so to speak, of the discursive intellect. The ultimate in question is therefore no more than a concept, a mental image that approximates to, but falls short of, the experience of the actual ultimate. It is consequently referred to as the "figurative ultimate" (*rnams grangs pa'i don dam*) or the "approximate ultimate" (*mthun pa'i don dam*). As such, it is intended as a pedagogical device, a stepping- stone, whereby the disciple may be led slowly but surely to the direct, liberative experience of the ultimate in itself. By contrast, the prāsaṅgika method, appropriate to disciples of superior capacity, is to place the mind directly in the realization of the union of the two truths, without dividing them—and into the immediate experience of the non-figurative ultimate (*rnam grangs ma yin pa'i don dam*). The Prāsaṅgikas therefore do not need to make a provisional division between the truths, and for that reason they make no assertions about the phenomena occurring on the relative level. They conduct their refutation of true existence exclusively by means of consequentialist arguments.
103. See Shantideva, *Way of the Bodhisattva.* These are excerpts from 9:151, 152, and 154.
104. Acceptance is the name of the third stage of the path of joining. When this is attained, it is no long possible to fall in the lower realms.

105. *bzod pa*. Patience or acceptance refers in general to the ability of understanding emptiness.
106. In Indian mythology, the gandharvas are semidivine creatures somewhat similar to fairies, the "fair folk," of Western legend. In company with gods and humankind, they were present at the exposition of the Prajñāpāramitā. Associated with music and art, they are often said to be of great beauty. Traditionally, strange and suggestive formations in the clouds seen at certain times and under certain climatic conditions are said to be "cities of gandharvas": beautiful, ephemeral, unattainable. Here, the image is used as an illustration of something that appears but has no real existence. We have occasionally used the common English expression "castles in the clouds" to express the same idea.
107. This citation is found in many texts, notably the *Uttaratantra* 1.51.
108. 1,158.
109. I.e., awareness.
110. See Shantideva, *Way of the Bodhisattva*, 9:34.
111. See *Root Stanzas of the Middle Way*, 25:20.
112. I.e., a rainbow.
113. See Shantideva, *Way of the Bodhisattva*, 4:47 and 5:17.
114. See ibid., 6:2.
115. See Chandrakīrti, *Introduction to the Middle Way*, 6:28.
116. 4:29; 4:30; 4:34.
117. This quotation seems to be an adaptation of the *Root Stanzas of the Middle Way*, 22:11 and 12.
118. Ibid., 18:6.
119. 1:156.
120. I.e., in a nondual manner.
121. This famous quotation occurs in many important Mahāyāna scriptures—for example, the *Uttaratantra*, 4:154.
122. It should be noted that this refers to the practice of the generation and perfection stages that, in the Nyingma tradition, are performed from within the view of the Great Perfection.
123. In other words, the central channel.
124. See note 29.
125. 7:34.
126. I.e., the dharmakāya and the rūpakāya.
127. See Shantideva, *Way of the Bodhisattva*, 10:53.
128. Ibid., 8:9–12.

129. Ibid., 6:100.
130. Ibid., 8:25.
131. According to ancient Indian tradition, the end of a great kalpa, or cosmic aeon, is marked by the rising of seven suns, which bring about the destruction of the universal system.

Texts Cited in *The Chariot of Excellence*

Abhidharmakośa: *Chos mngon pa mdzod* (*Treasury of Abhidharma*). By Vasubandhu.

Abhisamayālaṃkāra: *mNgon rtogs rgyan* (*Ornament of True Realization*). By Maitreya-Asaṅga.

Abridged Prajñāpāramitā-sūtra: *Prajñāpāramitāsaṃcayagāthā-sūtra, Sher phyin sdud pa tshigs su bcad pa.*

All-Creating King Tantra: *Kun byed rgyal po'i rgyud.*

Arrangement of Samayas Tantra: *Dam tshig bkod pa.*

Aspiration of Samantabhadra, in *rdzogs pa chen po kun bzang dgongs pa zang thal du bstan pa'i rgyud (Dzogchen tantra: The All-penetrating Wisdom of Samantabhadra),* a treasure text of Rigdzin Gödem.

Avataṃsaka-sūtra: *Phal po che* (*Ornaments of the Buddha*).

Bodhicittavivaraṇa: *Byang chub sems 'grel* (*Commentary on Bodhichitta*). Ascribed to Nāgārjuna.

Brāhmānanda-sūtra: *Tshangs pa kun dga'i mdo.*

Candrapradīpa-sūtra: *Zla ba sgron me'i mdo* (*Lamp of the Moon Sūtra*).

Distillation of the Essence: *Thig le 'dus pa.*

Distinguishing the Middle from Extremes: *Madhyāntavibhāga, dBus mtha' rnam 'byed.* By Maitreya-Asaṅga.

Exhortation to Remain in Solitude: *dBen pa la bskul ba'i gtam.*

Fifty Classes of Tantra: *rGyud sde lnga bcu pa.*

Gathering of Great Meaning Tantra: *'Dus pa don yod pa'i rgyud.*

Great Chariot: *Shing rta chen po* (autocommentary to *Finding Rest in the Nature of the Mind*). By Longchenpa.

Great Garuḍa Tantra: *Khyung chen gyi rgyud.*

Great Māyājāla in One Hundred Thousand Lines: *sGyu 'phrul drva ba chen po stong phrag brgya pa.*

Great Māyājāla Tantra: *Māyājāla Tantra. sGyu 'phrul drva ba chen po'i rgyud* (*Great Net of Illusory Manifestations*).

Guhyagarbha Tantra: *rGyud gsang ba snying po* (*The Secret Essence Tantra*).

Heart Sūtra: *Prajñāpāramitāhṛdaya-sūtra, Shes rab snying po'i mdo.*

Introduction to the Middle Way: *Madhyamakāvatāra, dBu ma la 'jug pa.* By Candrakīrti.

Irreversible Wheel Sūtra: *Phyir mi ldog pa'i 'khor lo'i mdo.*

Lalitavistara: *rGya cher rol pa* (*Vast Display*).

Lamp of the Three Jewels Sūtra: *dKon mchog sgron ma'i mdo.*

Laṅkāvatāra-sūtra: *Lang kar gshegs pa'i mdo.*

Later Tantra of Secret Primal Wisdom: *Ye shes gsang ba'i rgyud phyi ma.*

Letter Entitled the Drop of Ambrosia: *sPring yig bdud rtsi thigs pa.*

Letter to a Friend: *Suhṛllekha, bShes spring.* By Nāgārjuna.

Lion's Perfect Power Tantra: *Seng ge rtsal rdzogs kyi rgyud.*

Longer Māyājāla: *sGyu 'phrul rgyas pa* (*Longer Net of Illusory Manifestations*).

Longer Tantra of the True Arising of Primordial Wisdom: *Ye shes mngon par 'byung ba'i rgyud rgyas pa.*

Lotus Crown Tantra: *Pad ma cod pan gyi rgyud.*

Mañjuśrīnāmasaṃgīti: *'Jam dpal mtshan brjod* (*Litany of the Names of Mañjuśrī*).

Māyājāla Tantra: *sGyu 'phrul drva ba'i rgyud* (*Net of Illusory Manifestations*).

Middle-Length Prajñāpāramitā-sūtra: *Shes rab kyi pha rol tu phin pa stong phrag nyi shu lnga pa* (*Yum bar ma*).

Mirror of Vajrasattva's Heart Tantra: *rDo rje sems dpa' snying gi me long gi rgyud.*

Ornament of the Light of Wisdom Sūtra: *Jñānalokalaṃkāra-sūtra, Ye shes snang ba rgyan gyi mdo.*

Perfect Accomplishment of Susitikara Tantra: *Su si ti ka ra legs par grub pa'i rgyud.*

Praise of the Dharmadhātu: *Dharmadhātustotra, Chos dbyings la bstod pa.* By Nāgārjuna.

Praise to the Mother by Rāhula: *sGra gcan 'dzin gyis yum la bstod pa.*

Praises of Mañjuśrī: *'Jam dpal la bstod pa.*

Prajñāpāramitā in Eight Thousand Lines: *Astasāhasrikāprajñāpāramitā, Shes rab kyi pha rol tu phyin pa brgyad stong pa.*

Prajñāpāramitā in Eighteen Thousand Lines: *Shes rab kyi pha rol tu phyin pa khri brgyad stong pa.*

Prajñāpāramitā-sūtra: The Great Mother: *Yum chen mo shes rab kyi pha rol tu phyin pa.*

Pramāṇavārttika: *Tshad ma rnam 'grel* (*Commentary on Valid Cognition*). By Dharmakīrti.

Prātimokṣa-sūtra: *So sor thar pa'i mdo* (*Sūtra of Individual Liberation*).

Questions of Bhadra the Magician Sūtra: *sGyu mkhan rab tu bzang pos zhus pa'i mdo.*

Questions of Kumarāprabha Sūtra: *Khye'u rab snang gis zhus pa'i mdo.*

Questions of Matisambhava Sūtra: *bLo gros 'byung gnas kyis zhus pa'i mdo.*

Questions of Rāṣṭrapāla Sūtra: *Rāṣtrapālaparipṛcchā-sūtra, Yul 'khor skyong gis zhus pa'i mdo.*

Questions of Subāhu Tantra: *Subāhuparipṛcchā-tantra, dPung bzangs gyis zhus pa'i rgyud.*

Ratnakūṭa: *dKon mchog brtsegs pa* (*Jewel Mound Sūtra*).

Ratnāvalī: *Rin chen phreng ba* (*Precious Garland*). By Nāgārjuna.

Ratnolka-sūtra: *dKon mchog ta la'i mdo.*

Root Stanzas of the Middle Way: *Mūlamadhyamaka-kārikā, dBu ma rtsa ba'i shes rab.* By Nāgārjuna.

Samādhirāja-sūtra: *Ting nge 'dzin rgyal po'i mdo* (*King of Concentrations* Sūtra).

Saṃvarodaya: *sDom 'byung* (*Tantra of the Emergence of Cakrasamvara*).

Scripture of Summarized Wisdom: *Phyi mdo dgongs pa 'dus pa.*

Secret Essence of the Moon Tantra: *Zla gsang thig le'i rgyud.*

Six Expanses Tantra: *kLong drug gi rgyud.*

Songs of Realization: *Dohā, Do ha.*

Stages of Light. *'Od rim.*

Stages of Understanding: *Go rim.*

Sum of Precious Noble Qualities Sūtra: *Gunaratnasamchayagatha-sūtra. 'Phags pa yon tan rin po che sdud pa'i mdo.*

Supreme and Wish-Fulfilling Bliss Tantra: *Yid bzhin bde ba mchog gi rgyud.*

Supreme Essence: *sNying po mchog.*

Supreme Nonabiding Tantra: *Rab tu mi gnas pai rgyud.*

Sūtra Like a Magical Illusion: *sGyu ma lta bu'i mdo.*

Sūtra of Dṛdhramati: *bLo gros rab brtan gyi mdo.*

Sūtra of the Meeting of the Father and the Son: *Pitāputrasamāgama-sūtra, Yab sras mjal ba'i mdo.*

Sūtra of the Teaching of the Inconceivable: *bSam gyis mi khyab pa bstan pa'i mdo.*

Sūtra of the Wise and the Foolish: *mDzangs blun gyi mdo.*

Sūtrālaṃkāra: *mDo sde rgyan* (*Ornament of Mahāyāna Sūtras*). By Maitreya-Asaṅga.

Tantra of Self-Arisen Awareness: *Rig pa rang shar ba'i rgyud.*
Terrifying Lightning of Wisdom Tantra: *Ye shes rngam glog gi rgyud.*
Treasury of Precious Nonorigination: *sKye med rin po che'i mdzod.*
Two-Part Hevajra Tantra: *brTag gnyis.*
Two Truths: *Satyadvayavibhanga, bDen gnyis.* By Jñānagarbha.
Uttaratantra-śāstra: *rGyud bla ma'i bstan bcos* (*Sublime Continuum Treatise*). By Maitreya-Asaṅga.
Vajra Garland Tantra: *Vajramālā-tantra, rDo rje 'phreng ba'i rgyud.*
Vajra Peak Tantra: *Vajraśekhara-tantra, rDo rje rtse mo'i rgyud.*
Vajra Tent Tantra: *Vajrapañjarā-tantra, rDo rje gur gyi rgyud.*
Way of the Bodhisattva: *Bodhicāryāvatāra, sPyod 'jug.* By Śāntideva.
White Lotus Sūtra: *Puṇḍarīka-sūtra, mDo sde pad ma dkar po.*
Wisdom Unsurpassed Tantra: *Ye shes bla na med pa'i rgyud.*
Wish-Fulfilling Wheel of Bliss Tantra: *Yid bzhin bde ba 'khor lo'i rgyud.*
Yuktiśaṣtika: *Rigs pa drug cu pa* (*Sixty Reasonings*). By Nāgārjuna.

Bibliography

Sources in Tibetan

Khenpo Yontan Gyatso (mKhan po Yon tan rgya mtsho). 1984. *Yon tan rin po che'i mdzod kyi 'grel pa*. 2 vols. Kalimpong.

Longchen Rabjam (kLong chen rab 'byams). 1975? *bSam gtan ngal gso* and *Shing rta rnam dag*. Root text and autocommentary. Gangtok: Dodrupchen.

———. 1975? *Grub mtha' mdzod*. Gangtok: Dodrupchen.

———. 1975? *Ngal gso skor gsum gyi phyi don legs bshad rgya mtsho*.

———. 1975? *Sems nyid ngal gso* and *Shing rta chen po*. Root text and autocommentary. Gangtok: Dodrupchen.

———. 1975? *sGyu ma ngal gso* and *Shing rta bzang po*. Root text and autocommentary. Gangtok: Dodrupchen.

———. 1975? *Theg mchog mdzod*. Gangtok: Dodrupchen.

———. 1975? *Yid bzhin mdzod*. Gangtok: Dodrupchen.

Mipham Namgyal, Jamgön Ju. (Mi pham rnam rgyal 'jam mgon 'ju). 2009. *mKhas pa'i tshul la 'jug pa'i sgo*. Varanasi: Vajra Vidya Institute Library.

Secondary Sources

Asaṅga. 1982. *On Knowing Reality*. Translated by Janice Dean Willis. Delhi: Motilal Banarsidass.

Chandrakirti and Jamgön Mipham. 2002, 2004. *Introduction to the Middle Way*. Translated by the Padmakara Translation Group. Boston: Shambhala Publications.

Harding, Sarah. 2010. *Niguma, Lady of Illusion*. Ithaca, NY: Snow Lion Publications.

Jackson, David P. "Madhyamaka Studies among the Early Sa-skya-pas." *The Tibet Journal* 10.2 (1985): 20–34.

Jamgön Mipham. 2017. *The Wisdom Chapter.* Translated by the Padmakara Translation Group. Boulder: Shambhala Publications.

Jigme Lingpa and Kangyur Rinpoche. 2010. *Treasury of Precious Qualities, Book 1.* Translated by the Padmakara Translation Group. Boston: Shambhala Publications.

———. 2013. *Treasury of Precious Qualities, Book 2.* Translated by the Padmakara Translation Group. Boston: Shambhala Publications.

Longchenpa. 2017. *Finding Rest in the Nature of the Mind.* Translated by the Padmakara Translation Group. Boulder: Shambhala Publications.

Nagarjuna, 2005. *Letter to a Friend.* Translated by the Padmakara Translation Group. Ithaca and Boulder: Snow Lion Publications.

Nagarjuna. 2016. *The Root Stanzas of the Middle Way.* Translated by the Padmakara Translation Group. Boulder: Shambhala Publications.

Nyoshul Khenpo Jamyang Dorje. 2015. *The Fearless Lion's Roar.* Translated by David Christensen. Boston: Snow Lion Publications.

Pettit, John Whitney. 1999. *Mipham's Beacon of Certainty.* Boston: Wisdom Publications.

Shantarakshita and Jamgön Mipham. 2005, 2010. *The Adornment of the Middle Way.* Translated by the Padmakara Translation Group. Boston: Shambhala Publications.

Shantideva. 1997, 2006, 2008. *The Way of the Bodhisattva.* Translated by the Padmakara Translation Group. Boston: Shambhala Publications.

Vose, Kevin A. 2009. *Resurrecting Candrakīrti: Disputes in the Tibetan Creation of Prāsaṅgika.* Boston: Wisdom Publications.

The Padmakara Translation Group Translations into English

The Adornment of the Middle Way. Shantarakshita and Mipham Rinpoche. Boston: Shambhala Publications, 2005, 2010.

Counsels from My Heart. Dudjom Rinpoche. Boston: Shambhala Publications, 2001, 2003.

Enlightened Courage. Dilgo Khyentse Rinpoche. Dordogne: Editions Padmakara, 1992; Ithaca, NY: Snow Lion Publications, 1994, 2006.

The Excellent Path of Enlightenment. Dilgo Khyentse. Dordogne: Editions Padmakara, 1987; Ithaca, NY: Snow Lion Publications, 1996.

A Feast of the Nectar of the Supreme Vehicle. Maitreya and Jamgön Mipham. Boulder: Shambhala Publications, 2018.

Finding Rest in Meditation. Longchenpa. Boulder: Shambhala Publications, 2018.

Finding Rest in the Nature of the Mind. Longchenpa. Boulder: Shambhala Publications, 2017.

A Flash of Lightning in the Dark of Night. The Dalai Lama. Shambhala Publications, 1993. Republished as *For the Benefit of All Beings.* Boston: Shambhala Publications, 2009.

Food of Bodhisattvas. Shabkar Tsogdruk Rangdrol. Boston: Shambhala Publications, 2004.

A Garland of Views: A Guide to View, Meditation, and Result in the Nine Vehicles. Padmasambhava and Mipham Rinpoche. Boston: Shambhala Publications, 2015.

A Guide to the Words of My Perfect Teacher. Khenpo Ngawang Pelzang. Translated with Dipamkara. Boston: Shambhala Publications, 2004.

The Heart of Compassion. Dilgo Khyentse. Boston: Shambhala Publications, 2007.

The Heart Treasure of the Enlightened Ones. Dilgo Khyentse and Patrul Rinpoche. Boston: Shambhala Publications, 1992.

The Hundred Verses of Advice. Dilgo Khyentse and Padampa Sangye. Boston: Shambhala Publications, 2005.

Introduction to the Middle Way. Chandrakirti and Mipham Rinpoche. Boston: Shambhala Publications, 2002, 2004.

Journey to Enlightenment. Matthieu Ricard. New York: Aperture Foundation, 1996.

Lady of the Lotus-Born. Gyalwa Changchub and Namkhai Nyingpo. Boston: Shambhala Publications, 1999, 2002.

The Life of Shabkar: The Autobiography of a Tibetan Yogin. Albany, NY: SUNY Press, 1994. Ithaca, NY: Snow Lion Publications, 2001.

Nagarjuna's Letter to a Friend. Longchen Yeshe Dorje, Kangyur Rinpoche. Ithaca, NY: Snow Lion Publications, 2005.

The Nectar of Manjushri's Speech. Kunzang Pelden. Boston: Shambhala Publications, 2007, 2010.

Practicing the Great Perfection. Shechen Gyaltsap Gyurmé Pema Namgyal. Boulder: Shambhala Publications, 2020.

The Root Stanzas of the Middle Way. Nāgārjuna. Dordogne: Editions Padmakara, 2008. Boston: Shambhala Publications, 2016.

A Torch Lighting the Way to Freedom. Dudjom Rinpoche, Jigdrel Yeshe Dorje. Boston: Shambhala Publications, 2011.

Treasury of Precious Qualities, Book One. Jigme Lingpa and Kangyur Rinpoche. Boston: Shambhala Publications, 2001. Revised version with root text by Jigme Lingpa, 2010.

Treasury of Precious Qualities, Book Two. Jigme Lingpa and Kangyur Rinpoche. Boston: Shambhala Publications, 2013.

The Way of the Bodhisattva (Bodhicharyavatara). Shantideva. Boston: Shambhala Publications, 1997, 2006, 2008.

White Lotus. Jamgön Mipham. Boston: Shambhala Publications, 2007.

The Wisdom Chapter: Jamgön Mipham's Commentary on the Ninth Chapter of The Way of the Bodhisattva. Jamgön Mipham. Boulder: Shambhala Publications, 2017.

Wisdom: Two Buddhist Commentaries. Khenchen Kunzang Pelden and Minyak Kunzang Sonam. Dordogne: Editions Padmakara, 1993, 1999.

The Wish-Fulfilling Jewel. Dilgo Khyentse. Boston: Shambhala Publications, 1988.

The Words of My Perfect Teacher. Patrul Rinpoche. Sacred Literature Series of the International Sacred Literature Trust. New York: HarperCollins, 1994; 2nd ed. Lanham, MD: AltaMira Press, 1998; Boston: Shambhala Publications, 1998; New Haven, CT: Yale University Press, 2010.

Zurchungpa's Testament. Zurchungpa and Dilgo Khyentse. Ithaca, NY: Snow Lion Publications, 2006.

Index